William Shakespeare
The Problem Plays

Twayne's English Authors Series

Arthur F. Kinney, Editor

University of Massachusetts, Amherst

TEAS 499

Alan Scarfe as the Duke in *Measure for Measure*, directed by Michael Bogdanov, Stratford Shakespearean Festival of Canada, Stratford, Ontario, 1985
Courtesy of the Stratford Festival Archives
Photographer: David Cooper

William Shakespeare
The Problem Plays

Richard Hillman

York University

Twayne Publishers • New York
Maxwell Macmillan Canada • Toronto
Maxwell Macmillan International • New York   Oxford   Singapore   Sydney

William Shakespeare: The Problem Plays
Richard Hillman

Twayne Publishers   Maxwell Macmillan Canada, Inc.
Macmillan Publishing Company   1200 Eglinton Avenue East
866 Third Avenue   Suite 200
New York, New York 10022   Don Mills, Ontario M3C 3N1

Library of Congress Cataloging-in-Publication Data

Hillman, Richard, 1949–
    William Shakespeare : the problem plays / Richard Hillman.
       p.   cm. —(Twayne's English authors series ; TEAS 499)
    Includes bibliographical references and index.
    ISBN 0-8057-7035-6 (hc : alk. paper)
    1. Shakespeare, William, 1564–1616—Tragicomedies.
    2. Shakespeare, William, 1564–1616. All's well that ends well.
    3. Shakespeare, William, 1564–1616. Troilus and Cressida.
    4. Shakespeare, William, 1564–1616. Measure for measure.
    5. Troilus (Legendary character) in literature. 6. Trojan War in
literature. 7. Tragicomedy. I. Title. II. Series.
    PR2981.5.H55   1993
    822.3'3—dc20   92-30216
                                      CIP

10 9 8 7 6 5 4 3 2 1 (hc)

Printed in the United States of America

Contents

Editor's Note

At every turn, Richard Hillman's fresh new study of Shakespeare's problem plays is original, bold, and steadily illuminating. "The plays," he writes, "remain provocative today, even threatening, in ways that the Histories have long ceased to be." Combining the latest theoretical work in intertextuality, characterization, and subject construction with detailed critical readings of the texts, he shows how *Troilus and Cressida*, *All's Well That Ends Well*, and *Measure for Measure* share with each other and with their shadow Problem Tragedy *Hamlet* the contingency of genre and character that registers a period of major social and cultural transition. Hillman begins his study by redefining the genre of "problem play" itself, drawing on the work of Stephen Greenblatt and Michael Riffaterre, among others, seeing the genre as itself radically unstable in its attempts to fuse the content of traditional romance with a realistic style, comedic overlays with the mechanics of power. Rereading the three plays often line by line from the margins, by concentrating on Lucio as well as the Duke, Isabella, or Angelo, for instance, in *Measure for Measure*, Hillman shows with dazzling insights and virtuosity how uncertain persons, caught up in their own tentativeness and artificiality, manage to construct their lives. The immediate result is powerful new readings of each of the plays that give to each new force and significance, but this study moves beyond that task to formulating a new critical method by which to handle the inconsistencies that have of late been more and more observed throughout Shakespeare's work. The final consequence is a new way of reading and a new method for seeking meaning. "Whatever particular directions literary criticism in general may take," Hillman concludes, "precedent suggests that the Problem Plays will readily adapt themselves, or even serve as a leading indicator. For their problematic nature ultimately consists in their capacity to demonstrate, both as objects of interpretation and within themselves, the chameleon-like nature of meaning—literary and otherwise." Easily accessible to the reader first approaching these plays and forcefully original for those who know the plays well, this is a book that should change the way these Shakespearean plays are read and debated.

Arthur F. Kinney

Preface

To produce a book on Shakespeare's Problem Plays for a series such as this, in which genres are covered by separate volumes, entails a special set of challenges and opportunities stemming from the nature of the subject. On the one hand, there are only three works that fall into the Problem Play category, according to contemporary scholarly consensus, although others have often been discussed in relation to them (especially *Hamlet*, for reasons I will be exploring, but including plays as far afield, chronologically, as *Cymbeline*). The author of the present book, therefore, has the privilege of going into far greater depth than can most of his colleagues when it comes to textual analysis: the core of the volume comprises three substantial chapters, each focusing on a single play. On the other hand, the relation between these texts and the category itself—hence, their relation to one another—is part of what is *problematic* about them. As my introduction will stress, the "consensus" regarding categorization is a fragile one, arrived at largely by default and by no means universally recognized as critically useful. I begin by accepting the premise that the very notion of the Problem Plays is artificial and anachronistic.

I am nonetheless enthusiastic about discussing these plays as a group—apart from the fact that each of them is an exceptionally provocative text on its own. In fact, I consider the question of genre especially fertile precisely because it is indeterminate, yet insistently present—to the extent, I will argue, of figuring as a quasi-thematic issue within each of the texts. Far from aspiring to erase such indeterminacies, therefore, I am happy to make them the foundation of the case for common ground, or of diversity against a common *back*ground, that I have undertaken to present.

There are naturally many things that this book will *not* attempt to do, and this is the place to set out a few of them. First, in order to make the most of the critical freedom afforded by the narrow focus of the work, I will not be duplicating basic information easily accessible elsewhere, except insofar as such information has a direct bearing on my analysis. Because the subject is, after all, Shakespeare (if not, historically, Shakespeare at his most popular, for either audiences or critics), there exist numerous works of reference, or combined reference and analysis, dealing with such matters as the sources and stage histories of the plays; my notes and bibliography indicate some of the most useful resources of this kind. The latter also includes what is necessarily, given the enormous body of material, a highly selective sample of the interpretative criticism, chosen largely to illustrate the varied approaches to these texts that have emerged, and inevitably formed into "schools," with the evolution and proliferation of Shakespeare criticism in this century. The problematic status of the plays is naturally reflected in the range of these approaches, and it has seemed important to include representatives of critical outlooks with which my own is thoroughly incompatible, as well as to identify some recent works that, whether or not they will rate as significant for future generations of critics, have helped to focus my own thinking, through either agreement or disagreement.

This brings me to my next disclaimer. While my introduction and conclusion will be concerned largely with critical trends, I will not be attempting a comprehensive survey of the existing criticism or incorporating it systematically within my discussions of individual plays. The work of other critics will be referred to as it is engaged by my argument or offers a useful perspective on it—or, of course, where I am conscious of an idea as deriving, or provocatively diverging, from a particular source. However, for reasons of space alone, no critic of Shakespeare today, even one concentrating on only three plays, could hope to be exhaustive in documenting the published commentary. Although my discussions are not, I trust, wholly lacking in originality, many specific points inevitably will have been made in one form or another by previous critics. By the same token, there is little to be gained from stating disagreement for its own sake, especially where views are obviously remote from each other.

As this implies, I cannot hope to cover all of the aspects of all three plays that have been raised by previous critics, or even to examine the texts from all the angles that might attract my own interest in other circumstances—or have done so in the past (hence the occasional references to previous work of my own). This imperfect coverage is a matter partly of practicality but also of the specific nature of this volume. Again, the challenge that I perceive involves approaching the plays in terms of a discrete subgenre, or quasi-generic collocation, and such a perspective leads me to focus on those particular elements in each text by which it defines itself in relation to the others. The result is to bypass certain familiar critical routes, however well worth following in themselves, for the sake of opening up others.

Thus, for instance, I do not deal with the relation between *All's Well* and Shakespeare's Sonnets—a subject intriguing in itself and of importance to many critics who have approached the play through the nature of Shakespearean love, beginning with G. Wilson Knight in *The Sovereign Flower* (1958). This considered omission on my part follows from my view that the idea of love, especially in the context of the three plays taken together, is less a subject for serious scrutiny than a red herring. Similarly, my inclusive approach to the ironic mechanisms of dramatic, personal, and political power within the plays renders tangential both the Old and the New Historical treatments of *Troilus* and *Measure for Measure* (Achilles as Essex, Vincentio as James I)—not to mention (and I scarcely do) the allegories of a theological stripe that have been invoked to smooth out the anomalies of *Measure for Measure* and *All's Well*. Then, my broad perspective makes it impossible to deal in detail with the plays' language, except where linguistic questions directly bear (as of course they often do) on points of interpretation. Finally, while my discussions will pervasively reflect, and occasionally cite, the important work of several schools of feminist criticism over the past twenty years or so, I am far from presuming to exhaust the particularly rich possibilities for analysis in terms of gender.

Let me conclude, after all this exclusionary talk, by briefly declaring my own critical bias and methodological preference, which in fact underlie my affinity for the Problem Plays as a group. My interest in genre is already apparent, but I wish it to be clear that this interest is not particularly traditional—that is, concerned with the measuring and classifying of established forms. Rather, I engage issues of formal definition as part of the internal dynamics of the texts themselves—more particularly, as an index of the instability and conflict that are inextricable from their self-referential theatricality. For this latter element—in my view, perhaps the single most important factor linking the plays—I employ the term "metadrama," which (with "metatheater") quickly made itself at home in Shakespearean criticism following the publication of Lionel Abel's *Metatheatre: A New View of Dramatic Form* (New York: Hill and Wang, 1963). Through this approach, questions of genre, one might say, define the genre in question. Last—and this has an equal bearing on my attitude towards sources and on my method of comparing texts, including the three central ones—I owe a debt to the theoretical concept of intertextuality, as developed by certain French poststructuralist critics, most notably Julia Kristeva and Michael Riffaterre.

Even to speak of intertextuality as *the* theoretical concept is misleading, given the diversity of definitions available, some of which actually

preclude the exploration of specific textual relations. I have recently
attempted (in my book *Intertextuality and Romance in Renaissance Drama*)
to extrapolate and implement a definition of my own, and there is no
point in reentering this theoretical arena under the very different circumstances of the present volume. Suffice it to say that, in comparing
given texts, including a play and its putative source(s), I am concerned
not with issues of influence or indebtedness but rather with the way in
which the works may become actively *present* within one another, regardless of chronological priority, for a reader (or theatergoer) who has them
simultaneously in mind, or who inhabits what Jonathan Culler calls the
same "discursive space."[1] And it seems particularly appropriate, in the
case of plays known for their *problems*, that such intertextual presence
should be signalled, according to those versions of the theory that I
consider to be of greatest practical use, by *intra*textual anomaly—what
Riffaterre terms "ungrammaticality." For with regard to the established
language of the theater of their day—and of our own—this trio of plays
stands out for playing with, rather than by, the grammatical rules.

Chronology

1600–1601   Probable date of *Hamlet*, divergent Quarto editions of which appeared in 1603 and 1604.

1601–1602   Probable date of *Troilus and Cressida*.

1602–1603   Probable date of *All's Well That Ends Well*, although it has been argued that the play, perhaps in an earlier form, is identical with the otherwise unexplained *Love's Labor's Won* mentioned as Shakespeare's by Francis Meres in 1598.

1603   *Troilus and Cressida* first entered in Stationers' Register (7 February), where it is described as having been acted by the King's Men. Publication did not ensue.

1603   Death of Queen Elizabeth I; accession of King James I.

1603–1604   Plague causes closing of London theaters from mid-1603 until April 1604.

1604   Probable date of *Measure for Measure*. The only recorded early performance of a Problem Play is the presentation of *Measure for Measure* before King James on 26 December.

1609   Reentry of *Troilus and Cressida* in the Stationers' Register (28 January) and printing of two versions of a "good" Quarto text with a puzzling variation: the first version describes the play as having been "acted by the Kings Maiesties seruants at the Globe"; the second corrected version omits this statement and includes a notice assuring the reader that the work, praised as a "Commedie" (both versions of the title use the term "Historie"), is "a new play, neuer stal'd with the Stage, neuer clapper-clawd with the palmes of the vulger."

1616   Death of Shakespeare, 23 April (born 1564).

1623   Publication of the First Folio of Shakespeare, prepared with the assistance of two of his former fellow actors and containing almost all of the plays now considered canonical, including the three Problem Plays. *All's Well* and

Measure for Measure appear here for the first time, and all subsequent editions of them derive from the First Folio versions. The volume's text of *Troilus and Cressida* diverges in approximately 500 points from the Quarto version, possibly as a result of some form of revision. (Most modern editors use the latter as a copy-text, while adopting a number of Folio readings.) It has sometimes been considered significant (but is probably accidental) that *Troilus and Cressida* was evidently moved to a location between the histories and the tragedies in the course of printing and that it does not appear in the table of contents, which is arranged according to genre. In the Folio, the play is entitled *The Tragedie of Troylus and Cressida.*

Chapter One
Introduction
Problems, Problems: Terms and Concepts

One point, with two superficially contradictory aspects, needs to be established at the outset: first, it is the premise of responsible criticism nowadays that Shakespeare's personal intentions and attitudes regarding his work are quite irrecoverable; secondly, whatever he may have had in mind when he wrote the Problem Plays, he certainly did not think of himself as doing *that*. As with Shakespeare's four late "Romances," the term "Problem Play" came into general critical use well after Shakespeare's time because it conveniently signals an anomalous position vis-à-vis modern concepts of genre. These plays are most basically defined, then, by their resistance to formalist analysis; in particular, they represent the less academically digestible remnants of the great feast of comedies provided by Shakespeare over the first half of his roughly 20-year career as a playwright. Yet they are also, paradoxically, widely held to have come into their own, to have struck a chord with audiences and critics, in the twentieth century. Certainly, for much of the period between Shakespeare's era and our own their perceived moral, if not formal, indigestibility kept them, to a large degree, unread and off the stage.

The anomalous generic status of the Problem Plays was not necessarily perceived by Shakespeare's contemporaries, who (with the exception of such fastidious neoclassicists as Sir Philip Sidney and Ben Jonson) were generally unconcerned with fine distinctions, much less "rules," of literary genre, at least when it came to the dramatic experience. The three "Romances" included in the First Folio of 1623 (the first collected edition of Shakespeare's works, from which *Pericles* was omitted) were classified as two comedies (*The Tempest, The Winter's Tale*) and one tragedy (*Cymbeline*). Two of the three Problem Plays, *All's Well That Ends Well* and *Measure for Measure*, are ranked with the comedies, while *Troilus and Cressida*—a mystery in several textual and theatrical respects[1]— though it had been praised as a comedy in the preface to the

Quarto edition of 1609, is included in the Folio with the tragedies. This grouping combines with formally tragic features of the play—most basically, the fact that characters are killed—to keep many (though by no means all) critics from using the description "problem comedies," and to keep some from admitting *Troilus* into the same generic company as the other plays. Finally, still others have recourse to the label "dark comedies," thereby, it seems, taking a kind of refuge from the problem of defining "problem" in the subjective realms of tone and attitude (and originally in the fictional construction of a melancholic Shakespeare). Yet I continue to prefer the standard term, on the grounds that however "equivocally" it may signify for different interpreters (to echo E. M. W. Tillyard's discussion of his decision to use it[2]), at least it cannot be accused (except in the ultimate sense in which Macbeth so accuses life itself) of "signifying nothing."[3]

Apart from the question of its validity, the grouping together of the Problem Plays has doubtful critical utility, or at least appears played out in its ability to inspire, judging from the relative paucity of recent scholarly commentary that actually approaches this group of plays in terms of genre (or indeed as any sort of ensemble). The term itself carries an old-fashioned air in an intellectual climate where the problematic has become the norm, if not the universal condition. Previously received ideas and texts are now routinely subjected to skeptical scrutiny that exposes previously unsuspected self-contradiction and ideological bias. When Shakespeare's seemingly most straightforward works are thereby deprived of their "innocence"—witness, for instance, Louis Montrose's influential reading of *A Midsummer Night's Dream* as reinforcing repressive Elizabethan patriarchal social structures[4]—not only do the Problem Plays blend more smoothly into the canon, but setting them apart as such threatens to appear merely naïve, since this is to imply that some works are problem-free. Part of the challenge I set for myself is to demonstrate that, even in a poststructuralist critical milieu, there remains a problematic quality sufficiently distinctive, in kind as well as in degree, to justify setting these plays apart for at least some critical purposes.

More specifically, however, the shopworn quality of the term "Problem Play" is due to its origins in early twentieth-century literary thinking.[5] Indeed, the first critics to use this label borrowed it from the late nineteenth-century theatrical movement, prominently including Henrik Ibsen and George Bernard Shaw, that sought to direct dramatic writing away from idealized conventions and towards "real life," understood as the confused intersection between social conditions and individual psychological imperatives. This conflictual space was typically dramatized in the dilemmas of individual characters (Nora in *A Doll's House*, Vivie Warren in *Mrs. Warren's Profession*). Thus William Witherle Lawrence, a highly influential critic of the Problem Plays ever since his book's first edition in 1931, framed his definition as follows: "The essential characteristic of a problem play, I take it, is that a perplexing and distressing complication in human life is presented in a spirit of high seriousness."[6] This notion of "high seriousness" in comedy—for Lawrence's title endorses the generic category—is reminiscent of Shaw's praise of Mozart as his model for treating serious things lightly,[7] and it is not surprising that Lawrence invokes Shaw's own projection of a kindred revolutionary sensibility (and consequent unpopularity) upon the plays. Shaw liked to think that Shakespeare was prevented only by the perverse interference of chronology by following in his footsteps, and he saw his predecessor as taking, in the three "unpopular" plays, a tough-minded approach to moral issues that showed him "ready and willing to start at the twentieth century if the seventeenth would only let him."[8]

However, even in the first adaptations of the modern term to Shakespeare's work, the problems of characters shaded into those of critics (speaking on behalf of readers and audiences). For Frederick S. Boas, who seems to have applied the label first (in 1896), and who also established the tradition of including *Hamlet* in the group, the presentation of characters under such stress ("abnormal conditions of brain and of emotion") and faced with "intricate cases of conscience" in turn conducts the audience "along dim untrodden paths," confronting us with "enigmas" that leave us "excited, fascinated, perplexed."[9] Increasingly, with the waning of morally oriented (and indeed character-oriented) commentary, critics taking up the term have allowed concerns with ethical impasse to be subsumed within, or wholly eclipsed by, the broader difficulties that the texts present.[10] Certainly, from a late twentieth-century perspective, the Problem Plays appear to stand at an enormous cultural and aesthetic distance from the modern dramatic model to which they owe their definition—a perception that carries an implicit caution, incidentally, against now finding them remarkably *post*modern. At the least, a critic who perpetuates the tradition of calling these works Problem Plays incurs the obligation of renewing that term's vitality. To accept it uncritically is to remain constricted by its history, and to risk falling into the sort of nondefinition provided by Shakespeare's Antony for the drunken Lepidus, who is curious about the crocodile: "It is shap'd, sir, like itself, and it is as broad as it hath breadth."[11]

Texts

The distinctive problematic quality to which I alluded several paragraphs above ultimately derives, in my view, from an audience's sense of the power granted to key characters of controlling not merely their lives within the texts but aspects of those texts themselves. This necessarily entails the characters' participation in forming the generic identities of the works—precisely the sphere that, historically, has marked these plays as difficult and anomalous, rife with mixed messages. Obviously, such control is as much a fiction as is the text as a whole: we take it for granted (or should do) that in the actual compositional process the playwright—understood as including any actor-collaborators—retained both the upper hand and the last word; at the least, he could always consign his production to the fire. Moreover, I am far from invoking the postromantic model of the genius helpless in the grip of runaway imagination. On the contrary, it is the depersonalizing of the processes of literary production, the effective liberation of texts from authors, as promoted by poststructuralist schools of criticism, that theoretically empowers such metadramatic fictions. For an artistic work does not, from this perspective, figure as a composition at all, in the sense of a formal structure of elements with fixed identities, positioned so as to convey a coherent "meaning"; rather, it becomes a dynamic site of struggle among multifarious intra- and intertextual forces, which are themselves fluid, subject to shaping and reshaping influences. This view, one might add, however subversively it may bear on the traditional attitude towards literary artifacts, closely corresponds to the nature of the theatrical experience. And, on the basis that dramatic gestures, in art as in life, express engagement in such a struggle, as Stephen Greenblatt's influential notion of "self-fashioning" would suggest,[12] there is a particular affinity between textuality so understood and concepts of self-conscious theatricality, plays within plays, manipulation as textual production—in short, metadrama of all kinds.

Important as it is, this realization again broadens, rather than narrows, the critical focus; such a problematizing function applies to texts at large, while I am in search of the conditions that specifically connect those at hand. A useful restarting point may be the fact that the problem-generating mechanism shared by these three plays goes well beyond the influential presence of a metadramatic manipulator. (I will be making my case shortly that Troilus is such a personage, as surely as Helena in *All's Well* and Duke Vincentio in *Measure for Measure* have often been so identified.) After all, as Anne Barton was the first to demonstrate, internal creators of quasi-theatrical scenarios—amongst whom she includes Vincentio[13]—appear in Shakespeare's work from the beginning to the end of his career, from Petruchio (in *The Taming of the Shrew*) to Prospero (in *The Tempest*); as that consummate actor-director Richard III illustrates with stark clarity, this is a natural development of presenting characters intent on getting their own way. But while the operations of such figures tend to create problems, for others and sometimes for themselves, they also tend to produce resolutions, if only at the cost (as in Richard's case) of scripting a spectacular exit for the manipulators in question. Closure entails, broadly speaking, a satisfying denouement of whatever complications have been generated—as is conspicuously not the case in the Problem Plays.

Let me go out on a limb by risking a large generalization: arguably, the key to the sense of resolution associated with Shakespeare's analogous internal dramatists is a sense of these characters' transcendent status, their position, virtually by definition, on a different plane from the text's representatives of ordinary humanity. In Richard III, as in several other Machiavellian villains (Aaron in *Titus Andronicus*, Iago in *Othello*, Edmund in *King Lear*), this distinction comes in a negative form: Richard is widely recognized as deriving a magnetic energy from his roots in the immoral and irreligious villainy that in the earlier English drama explicitly carried the (titillating) menace of the diabolical. At the other end of the moral scale (at least superficially) stand Henry V, whose heroic qualities lend him a supernatural aura, and Prospero, raised above his fellow mortals by his magic, which reflects his virtuous wisdom. The "purest" internal dramatist of them all (in that this is his only function)—Puck in *A Midsummer Night's Dream*—comes closest to embodying pure magic. Indeed, to set him side by side with Henry and Prospero is to come closer to the Problem Plays. For the latter two heroes are human after all, and—thanks to occasions when their idealized power is framed "realistically" (Henry's dispute with the common soldiers, Prospero's lapses into anger and despair)—not unproblematically so.

In the Problem Plays, the potential thus adumbrated for friction between a manipulator's implicit claim to transcendent authority and elements that ironically qualify—or outright resist—that claim is carried further, even to the point of impasse. On the one hand, the manipulators themselves are implicated much more thoroughly in the worlds they manipulate, their "specialness" considerably curtailed; on the other hand, the play worlds themselves, together with their inhabitants, are dominated by the realistic mode that remains in *Henry V* and *The Tempest* isolated and contained. It would be preferable in this discussion to avoid speaking of "realism," but for reasons of practical convenience, the term, however problematic in itself, is inescapable, and few critics of the Problem Plays have managed wholly to dispense with it: no other so effectively conveys the grittily down-to-earth quality—in representational style, subject matter, and the sense of the way things actually work in the world—that characterizes the ambience of these texts. We do need, however, to play down the implications of honest confrontation with the moral "facts of life" that accompany the term's usage in the nineteenth century and so inevitably infiltrate the original concept of the Problem Plays. Moreover, as far as Shakespearean drama is concerned, there is no necessary implication of verisimilitude: to take an obvious instance, nobody would call the bawd Pompey in *Measure for Measure* a "realistic" character; with his subversive wordplay and exuberant immorality, he is recognizably a stylized low-comic Clown, the descendant of the Vice figures of Medieval drama. Yet he functions, no less than Angelo or Isabella, with their vastly superior quotient of psychological plausibility,[14] to define a fictional universe that ultimately fails to defer on the stylistic level—in contrast with the level of plot—to the transcendental imperatives embodied in its exemplary ruler. Those imperatives belong—as, confusingly, do aspects of Angelo and Isabella themselves—to another literary mode, which may be summarized without undue distortion as that of "romance."

At least from the time of Lawrence's important book, the Problem Plays have been seen in terms of romantic material subjected to realistic treatment (to put the argument in reductive form). Allowing for the slippery nature of "romance" as well as "realism" as literary designations, such a view has a strong claim to historical accuracy. The stories dramatized in all three of the Problem Plays have Medieval (and to some extent folktale) origins and appear to have come to Shakespeare in versions that preserved qualities typical of romance: fairy-tale simplicity in the depiction of good and evil; convoluted plots involving journeys and fantastic coincidences; idealization of chivalric values, with the consummation of love figuring as ultimate felicity; above all (as all of this implies), a pervasive flavor of escapism and wish fulfilment. Significant refinement of this picture is in order—especially when it comes to

Chaucer's *Troilus and Criseyde*—and each of my three subsequent chapters will provide some of this. However, they will do so on the widely accepted basis that Shakespeare was making more or less radically different uses of familiar and old-fashioned fables, translating their black-and-white and primary colors into various shades of gray.

The Problem Plays particularly contrast, in this regard, with Shakespeare's own earlier comedies, most of which qualify as "romantic" in terms of theme, structure, and plot conventions. (Not, of course, that these plays necessarily make straightforward use of their own romantic elements.) None of the Problem Plays employs the two-world principle (court vs. natural or "green" world), as found in comedies ranging from *The Two Gentlemen of Verona* to *As You Like It*, although intriguing vestiges exist in all three of them. There is no alternative setting in which the rules of reality are suspended and true lovers are more or less magically united. But then lovers of the romantic breed, as defined in the previous plays, are not much in evidence here. The identification of sexual consummation with marriage—an absolute rule in the previous comedies—is disrupted in all three works. Indeed, in *Measure for Measure*, the young lovers who should by convention be the "romantic leads," and whose names (Claudio and Juliet) recall the passionate innocents of Shakespeare's romantic tragedy, begin the play guilty of fornication, with Juliet conspicuously pregnant. In general, chaste love gives way to sexual pursuit, with "supporting players"—including the Clowns, always practitioners of double entendre—modulating into active and dubious promoters of sexual liaisons. The marriage bed to which happy couples normally retire at the conclusion is displaced forward in the texts and associated with marriage, if at all, in backhanded ways. In *All's Well* and *Measure for Measure*, the disquieting device of the bed trick displaces the less intimate deceptions of the earlier plays. As for marriage itself, conventionally the emblem of romance fulfillment, although it technically figures as a closural motif in the same two plays, it is invested with connotations of emptiness, futility, and even punishment.

These problematizing shifts have significant consequences, as feminist commentators have stressed, for the portrayal of gender and gender relations in the plays. Yet these consequences remain elusive, given that, at least superficially, the Problem Plays differ sharply amongst themselves in this regard. On the one hand, one of the most distinctive products of Shakespeare's romantic-comic technique, the arguably (though arguably *not*) protofeminist "witty heroine"—Portia in *The Merchant of Venice*, Viola in *Twelfth Night*, above all Rosalind in *As You*

Like It—goes by the boards. For the first time in Shakespearean comedy, we are confronted by near-caricatures of disempowered femininity: the fickle, sexually lax Cressida; the self-righteous, sexually repressed Isabella. On the other hand, *All's Well* assigns the role of chief manipulator to a sympathetic and virtuous heroine, even if she lacks her precursors' brilliance, and even if the object of her amorous pursuit exceeds even the usual Shakespearean standard of male unworthiness. From this point of view, her story virtually epitomizes the Problem Play pattern of romance brought, indeed bringing itself, down to earth, but it does so in a way that has often attracted critical approval: Helena is widely taken to possess the power, if not of reformulating the patriarchal order, at least of making it come to terms with its inevitable imperfections. This is, perhaps oddly, to return to something like the late Victorian moral sense of "realism."

As the history of criticism subsequent to Lawrence abundantly shows, the observation that the Problem Plays subject romantic elements to a fundamentally disjunctive, sometimes jarring, realistic treatment is adaptable to many perspectives. My own contribution consists in approaching this fundamental incongruity, not in terms of static juxtaposition, as the product of an intractable inconsistency that (according to critical taste) the playwright either valued or would have erased if he had been able, but as part of a metadramatic dynamism, at once the origin and object of play. The mixture of modes is a way of throwing control over the script up for grabs. In particular, I would argue that the promotion and construction of romantic conditions to match inherited romance premises inform the hegemonic drives of the plays' dominant internal dramatists—whether male or female. For although the social and cultural givens of these play worlds, realistic as those worlds are, pointedly circumscribe the possibilities for action open to female characters, the love project of Helena may be seen as having its roots in the same sort of "ambition" (her own word) that underlies the sociopolitical project of *Measure for Measure*'s Duke. The power that all three central figures exercise—Troilus no less than the others, if more obliquely— involves nostalgically reviving absolutist ideals by rewriting them in terms that will "stick" in the relativism of a power-broking decadent present. Such a procedure needs not only to manipulate characters but to re-create them, to cultivate and appropriate their very subjectivity. They must be made first to develop beyond the usual scope of figures who execute the imperatives of comic plots, then to withdraw to passive positions in the new dramatic order. And as a far-reaching corollary, essence and meaning—being itself—are called into question. This is to extend, and to apply as a fundamental critical principle, the fascinating remark of Rossiter that "[a]ll the Problem Plays are profoundly concerned with seeming and being" (Rossiter, 127). It is also implicitly to confirm that *Hamlet*, perennially the Problem Tragedy, is insistently present, intertextually, in the margins of the picture.

Contexts

These few pages are hardly the place to attempt a survey of the society, culture, and politics of Early Modern England, or even of that period of four years or so following the turn of the sixteenth century that furnishes our texts with their immediate contexts. Such investigation has been the business of much historical writing and of much historically oriented literary criticism, some of which will be cited below as occasion arises. Nevertheless, I would like to conclude this introduction by relating my approach, as I have just sketched it, to several features of the late Elizabethan and early Jacobean scene, necessarily delineated in equally broad strokes. These elements have often been brought to bear on the plays' generic anomalies and, especially, on their perceived "darkness" of tone and outlook.

To begin with and fundamentally, there is, as the terms "Elizabethan" and "Jacobean" themselves indicate, a transition (in 1603) between Elizabeth I and James I—monarchs with dramatically different (and differently dramatic) personal styles and approaches to government. The cliché holds that Elizabeth had enjoyed her subjects' warm affection and admiration. Elizabethan society, in this view, had been orderly and harmonious, respectful of hierarchy, in accordance with the vision (based, in fact, on a reductive mélange of decidedly prescriptive rather than descriptive texts) that Tillyard did much to institutionalize in the 1950s and 1960s under the comprehensive rubric of "The Elizabethan World Picture."[15] Such domestic unity, the story goes, provided solid support for a sense of national purpose that expressed itself in heroic military exploits—including, of course, the defeat of the Spanish Armada in 1588—and colonial expansionism. Above all, it was an era, according to the panegyrical peroration provided by A. L. Rowse for his history (1950), comprised of Great Men, with an honorary Great Man at the helm of the ship of state and, inevitably, Shakespeare himself as the cultural crowning glory. After praising the way in which the relentless insistence on authority and hierarchy actually proved "no bar, but a stimulus, to creative achievement," this scholar (sounding more like a cheerleader) moves on to the theme of "genius and greatness of spirit": "a society that had Elizabeth at its head, Burghley as its statesman, Philip Sidney as its pattern of chivalry, Drake for its sea captain; whose poet was Spenser, whose philosopher Bacon; that had Shakespeare for its dramatist, may well bear comparison, so far as civilisation is concerned, with any of the larger societies of our time."[16]

Now, although Rowse, as one keenly sensible of the need for the ruling classes to "[keep] order in the nursery"—that is, amongst the "idiot people" (Rowse, 265)—is never too hard on James (or on the nation he governed), even he characterizes the aftermath of this transcendent historical moment in terms that hint at the jaded mood of the Problem Plays: "our people passed, in a decade, to maturity and awakening, awoke to self-consciousness and self-questioning" (Rowse, 533). Indeed—and its literature naturally has much to do with this—Jacobean society is widely thought of, by contrast, as morally corrupt and politically fractious. Especially for the many admirers of the outstanding anti-Catholic heroes of Elizabeth's day, such as Sir Philip Sidney and Robert Devereux, Second Earl of Essex (whose rebellion in 1601, however, had led to his execution that year), the conciliatory foreign policies of its ruler meant making ignoble and dangerous accommodations, even alliances, with England's traditional religious enemies. James himself, distant and authoritarian, at once mean-minded and both intellectually and politically arrogant (to the point of pushing to new extremes the doctrine of the monarch's Divine Right), became a focus early on for contempt and alienation. The practice of selling knighthoods, instituted immediately on his accession, seemed to many at the time to epitomize the devaluation of Elizabethan ideals of honor and the breakdown of the traditional social hierarchy, both of which went hand in hand with a new spirit of sordid commercialism associated with the increasingly powerful (and Puritan-leaning) middle class. It is very much to the point, as my discussion of satire in the next chapter will make clear, that Ben Jonson, John Marston, and George Chapman were imprisoned (and menaced with mutilation) for ridiculing the new king's mercenary Scottish followers in their collaborative comedy, *Eastward Hoe!* (1605). A version of the changes in England particularly striking in its inclusiveness and metaphysical quality is offered by Lawrence, who is specifically concerned with the origin of the Problem Plays:

The temper of the English people was very different from what it had been at the time when Shakespeare began to write. Something was wrong with the world;

the effort of the day was to strip away glittering illusions and expose the ugliness of vice. To healthy honest frankness of speech succeeded brutal coarseness of language, and to robust joy in active life and to delight in the world of illusion, a passion to reveal, often for melodramatic effect, the baser forms of sin, and a feverish desire to expose the hidden mysteries of sex. (Lawrence, 202)

The traditional celebrations of Elizabethan England to the detriment of that of James leave out, as is the nature of mythologies, a great deal on both sides, most notably the perspective of the ordinary people, many of whom suffered appallingly over the course of Elizabeth's reign as a result of economic and social conditions. Such histories also tend to bypass the grievances to which some of the queen's more distinguished subjects would appear entitled; these make a long list when one includes the English recusants and the numerous courtiers whose personal lives she ruined through her tyrannical interference, not to mention her cousin Mary, Queen of Scots (a nonsubject). But of course historical scholarship has passed decisively beyond the panegyrical mode, as is evident from the current preference for the term "Early Modern" over the traditional "Renaissance." A very different picture, or rather—and this is equally important—set of pictures, has been provided in recent years, thanks to new information on economic, social, and demographic forces (especially the research of Lawrence Stone[17]), more hard-nosed sociopolitical analyses (for instance, by Mervyn James[18]), and revaluations of the myth-making mechanisms of the courts themselves (these range from examples of the sort of analysis practiced by Montrose to the work of Frances Yates on Elizabeth and that of Roy Strong on James's son, Prince Henry[19]). Not, however, that a much more positive view of Jacobean England has gained currency. On the contrary, the most prominent contemporary trends in criticism of the period's literature, which happen to be historically oriented (New Historicism, to which Montrose belongs, and Cultural Materialism[20]), tend broadly to endorse, and regularly surpass, earlier characterizations of James as a devious tyrant—though this is now taken to go with the royal territory—and of his realm as thoroughly rotten, hence ripe for the coming Puritan revolution.

One obvious defect of the now all but defunct myth of Elizabethan harmony has particular significance for study of the Problem Plays. Elizabeth was still the reigning monarch when two of the three, as well as *Hamlet*, were written, and the fact is that expressions of pessimism, social disaffection, and moral outrage were well established in a variety of literary and subliterary forms by the turn of the century. Most obviously in this category (because in no other) are the proliferating pamphlets of moralistic social criticism, including attacks on the theater (and on women). Within the theater (and apart from *Hamlet*) the stereotype of the malcontent is certainly to be found before Marston's play of that name in 1604—witness Shakespeare's Jacques in *As You Like It* (1599) and Malvolio in *Twelfth Night* (1601–2). Related to this is the vogue for bitter verse satire, which I will be taking up in connection with *Troilus*. This highly specific genre flourished towards the turn of the century and came to an end by official edict in 1599. As for the trend towards realism and disillusion, as opposed to illusionary romanticism, in comedy—the trend that reaches its height in such relentlessly satirical "Citizen Comedies" as Middleton's *A Chaste Maid in Cheapside* (1611)—this, too, has roots in the late 1590s, with Jonson, Marston, and Chapman. It is a movement to which Shakespeare himself made a mild-mannered contribution in *The Merry Wives of Windsor* (perhaps as early as 1597, though probably revised several years later). This work revolves around the bringing down to earth, as a pathetically ineffectual would-be lover, of Sir John Falstaff—a figure (from *Henry IV*, parts 1 and 2) usually thought of as the ultimate in comic resilience. Worth nothing are both the legend that Shakespeare wrote the play at the request of the queen herself and the fact that, even in his original setting, Falstaff—scrounger, drunkard, whoremaster, thief, coward, corrupt officer—necessarily carried a considerable burden of satirical commentary on the status of knighthood. Sir Philip Sidney was, after all, not merely an exception but a construction—the product both of his own "self-fashioning" and, especially after his heroic death in (anti-Catholic) battle in 1586, of the Elizabethan myth-making machine.

This leads to a point with considerable critical utility for the plays in question. The stereotypical differentiation of Elizabethan glory and stability, Jacobean decadence and dissolution, is not wholly a modern invention.[21] Rather, it formed an active strain of thought at the time—one that anticipated the transition as a "falling-off" (to use the expression of Old Hamlet's Ghost for his successor) well before that event took place. The last years of Elizabeth's reign appear to have been lived, at least for those close to the center of political and cultural life, within an atmosphere of decay and borrowed time: the queen's ill health and the uncertain succession of the realm combined with economic and social changes to produce a threatening sense of instability, if not of impending catastrophe. The physical aging of the queen began to conflict grotesquely with the elaborate fictions of courtly love, centered on Elizabeth as object of amorous worship, by which she had mediated political power and maintained authority over her courtiers. Many writers at the time were already looking backwards, if they were not (as in all of Shakespeare's romantic comedies) looking elsewhere, setting their work in the traditional never-never land of romance. When Thomas Dekker created his romantic-comic celebration of the citizenry of London, *The Shoemakers' Holiday* (1599), offering one of the most quintessentially "Elizabethan" visions of social harmony, he not only focused on a Medieval citizen-hero, Simon Eyre, but departed from strict historical accuracy (the reigning monarch would have been Henry VI) to evoke Shakespeare's contemporary emblem of past glory and common national purpose, Henry V.

In sum, it is difficult to escape, even in the survivals of romantic attitudes towards the turn of the century, an undermining element of nostalgia quite foreign to such "high" Elizabethan romance productions as Sidney's *Arcadia* and Edmund Spenser's *The Faerie Queene*. This nostalgia continues to assert itself in the drama of succeeding years, notably (but far from exclusively) in the "escapist" romantic plays associated (rather loosely, since most of them were not collaborations) with the partnership of Francis Beaumont and John Fletcher.[22] It is a romanticism that contains a countercurrent acknowledging its own futility, and the new element of realism may be seen as less its opposite than its corollary. Meanwhile, that realistic tendency, originally apparent in comedy, is channelled increasingly into tragedy, where it is often heightened so as to produce the bizarre and grotesque extremities usually thought of as specifically Jacobean. Inevitably, such a summary oversimplifies and distorts, imposing rigid patterns on what was an astoundingly lively and diverse theatrical scene. Yet the concept of a transitional period in the evolution of dramatic forms and styles is broadly sustainable and sheds significant light on the Problem Plays, which themselves occupy a transitional position in Shakespeare's career, intervening chronologically (as they mediate generically) between the earlier comedies and the sustained period of tragic writing that followed. This, too, is to speak broadly, but the major exception—*Hamlet*—serves to prove the rule.

It is telling that in drawing his comparison between the Problem Plays and the self-styled revolutionary drama of the turn of his own century (the nineteenth) Boas was implicitly responding to an analogous fin de siècle decadence in Shakespeare's time: "All these dramas introduce us into highly artificial societies, whose civilization is ripe unto rottenness" (Boas, 345). His blunt moral perspective convincingly connects, if not with the texts at large, which are actually sensitive to a wide range of moral shadings, at least with the self-appointed moralists within and outside them, including both earnest Puritan pamphleteers and witty posturing satirists. There does seem to have been a roughly similar *perception* of social institutions as hollow and of identity itself as subject to redefinition and reconstitution. This is arguably the most basic point made in Middleton and Dekker's *The Roaring Girl* (published in 1611), whose heroine dresses as a man—thus defying the statutes regulating public dress, which were imposed with an urgency suggestive of desperation in the last years of Elizabeth and under James—while she goes about exposing the mercenary and immoral practices of citizens and gentry alike.

Such a view of a culture already self-consciously in decline helps to account for the Problem Plays as being Jacobean before their time by portraying James, in effect, as a monarch whose time had come. It also opens a space between Shakespeare as practicing dramatist, responsive to both the intellectual currents of his day and the preoccupations of his broadly inclusive audience, and Shakespeare as prominent member of the theatrical company that, upon James's accession, was taken under the king's personal patronage and often performed before him. This space, I take it, also furnished an audience with sufficient interpretative flexibility to accommodate intractable ambiguities without enforcing their resolution. As it happens, the only recorded court performance of a Problem Play is of the last (and only unequivocally Jacobean) one, *Measure for Measure*, on December 26, 1604. An identification has often been perceived between the play's Duke and the King himself, and the readings of the first critics to propose this were positive enough to allow for the standard flattering relation between artist and patron.[23]

Now it is difficult for most late twentieth-century critics to think of this work as holiday fare in any case, but those of us who find the Duke's portrayal to be at least as negative as positive incur the responsibility of accounting for the seeming lack of violent royal indigestion, if we allow, as seems reasonable, that there is at least a basic structural resemblance between the roles of spectator-King and player-Duke. It will not do to assume that authority would enjoy watching itself in effective action, regardless of the moral implications. We need to explain how authority could stand seeing itself exposed as brutally manipulative, even as playing fast and loose with religion.[24] Rather than suppose James merely stupid (he was not), indifferent (he rarely was), or negligent (he *may* have been), I prefer to posit playwright and spectators as entering into tacit agreement to suspend certain forms of referentiality—an agreement that has the corollary effect of freely proliferating signification, and not necessarily in a single direction. Thus both James and the most skeptical critic can be accommodated: the Problem Play is allowed to retain its problematic; to adapt Jonson's famous encomium (in a dedicatory poem in Shakespeare's First Folio [*Riverside*, 65–66]), Shakespeare can be both "of an age" and "for all time."

Finally, it seems beyond question that the sense of social disintegration and personal insecurity evident in turn-of-the-century English culture is related to the ongoing, increasingly insistent fragmentation of religion—a process that had begun scarcely a hundred years before with internal and external challenges to that great Medieval monolith, the universal Roman Catholic Church. The religious conflicts that would soon tear apart every aspect of English national life—and close the theaters in 1642—had been intensifying for years. The tendency towards spiritual crisis amongst intellectuals, including the most fundamental sorts of doubt, is well documented, though still subject to underestimation: there was by law, after all, one established church in England, and attendance was compulsory. Yet very often, not far beneath the moralist's railing at corruption, lies a palpable sense of that corruption as innate in the human condition and beyond the reach, or even the interest, of any supernatural power—proof that it could be a short road indeed from Calvinism to a more-or-less atheistic despair. These are vaster topics even than those I have already touched on, and I will restrict myself to pointing out the existence of this shadowy dimension of the puzzles of self-definition that lie at the heart of the Problem Plays.

And for the last time in *this* chapter I will invoke *Hamlet* again, in particular its uniquely introspective hero's confrontation with the "question" of "being" itself. For Hamlet, feeling himself trapped, in effect, between a script imposed by the past, which casts him as a romance hero, and the sordid debilitating reality of the present translates his dilemma into universal terms involving a collision between two views of the human condition. The essentially Medieval "Elizabethan World Picture," with its assurance of an immortal soul in the divine image, fades before the stark image of mortal clay "crawling between earth and heaven"[25] and desperately seeking to create a sense of meaning—that is, an alternative "soul"—for itself: "What a piece of work is a man, how noble in reason, how infinite in faculties, in form and moving, how express and admirable in action, how like an angel in apprehension, how like a god! the beauty of the world; the paragon of animals; and yet to me what is this quintessence of dust?" (*Hamlet*, 2.2.303–8). Nor are our problems, as interpreters, coterminous with Hamlet's; for even at this apparent moment of starkest truth telling he is, to a certain extent that is notoriously hard to agree upon, putting on an act.

Chapter Two
Troilus and Cressida
Constructing Genre, Truth, and the Self

However little store is to be set by the First Folio's diffidence about classifying the play, the fact remains that, of the three Problem Plays, *Troilus* is the most openly problematic—and therefore the most productive—to consider in terms of genre. And since these are the terms essential to defining the group itself, *Troilus* is well suited, for more than chronological reasons, to initiate this sequence of chapter-by-chapter analyses. The generic complexity, in this case, is not primarily a question of friction between romantic plot elements and their realistic treatment, though this is at least intermittently an issue; here there is flagrant contradiction even with regard to the categories of the action itself. While the neutral term "Historie" is used in both Quarto versions of the title, the Epistle in the corrected version insists on invoking the model of the decidedly nonheroic, minimally romantic Roman comedy of intrigue, claiming the play's comparability to "the best Commedy in *Terence* or *Plautus*" (cited in *Riverside*, 492 [Textual Notes]). Yet heroic and romantic elements furnish Shakespeare's basic material. Moreover, at least the savage murder of Hector and the multiple unhappy ending, if nothing else in the play, violate the basic rules of comedy and would clearly apply a tragic stamp, in accordance with the Folio text's title, were it not that the protagonist's death is deferred. (It is deferred, however, only into one of the best known of tragic literary futures: the Fall of Troy.) Certainly, the late seventeenth-century poet, dramatist, and critic John Dryden, thinking along neoclassicial and heroic lines, had no hesitation in speaking of it as "the Tragedy which I have undertaken to correct."[1] (He assumed that it was an early effort on Shakespeare's part, hence especially in need of "correction.")

Into this inconclusive generic dialectic, moreover, a third term—satire—inserts itself. While all three of the texts in question (as well as *Hamlet*, the "honorary" Problem Play) contain elements reminiscent of the neo-Juvenalian poetic satire of the late 1590s—a genre, we should note, officially banned from publication in 1599[2]—only *Troilus* can be taken as a sustained stage version of the satirical mode. A number of critics do, in fact, apply this perspective, usually in tandem with the hypothesis that the play was originally designed as an entertainment for the Inns of Court, with which most of the satirists were connected. A reading in terms of satire should not be allowed to obscure the play's cross-connections with both tragedy and comedy, or otherwise to impose a reductive grid on this generally fluid and elusive text, which I believe amounts to far more than an "anatomy of folly."[3] Still, one cannot go far wrong by using the satirical dimension as a starting point for discussion. And there is further encouragement for this approach to be found even in the play's subject matter, given the intellectual fashions of the day. (The play's relation to its towering predecessor, *Troilus and Criseyde*, Chaucer's nobly tragic—if intermittently satiric—version of the story, is a separate question, which will be considered more fully below.)

Homeric themes became even more than usually current with the 1598 publication of George Chapman's translation of seven books of the *Iliad*, on which Shakespeare may have drawn.[4] There was also ample precedent for adapting such themes, as well as the non-Homeric love story itself, to satirical ends. Walker (xxvii–xxviii) has outlined a tradition of satirical and deflationary treatment of the Trojan War that dates back to Horace's *Epistles*. To this may be added the adaptation of elements of Chaucer's *Troilus* by Chapman himself in his satirical drama, *Sir Giles Goosecap, Knight* (1602), and Marston's choice of the story for the play-within-the-play in *Histrio-Mastix* (c. 1599). But a broader basis for such satire is the fact that, in the symbology of the age, London (founded, according to legend, by the Trojan Brutus) was also Troia Nova or Troynovant. Thus Thomas Middleton, in his *Micro-cynicon: Sixe Snarling Satyres* (1599), speaks ironically of "Troynovant, that all-admirèd town, / Where thousands still do travel up and down."[5] He is attacking, incidentally, that town's decadent sexual practices by recounting a sort of bed trick played on him by a transvestite prostitute, and he states a moral that Shakespeare's disillusioned Troilus ("Never did young man fancy / With so eternal and so fix'd a soul"[6]) might also have drawn from his experience, mutatis mutandis:

> Tie not affection to each wanton smile,
> Lest doting fancy truest love beguile;
> Trust not a painted puppet, as I've done,
> Who far more doted than Pygmalion:

The streets are full of juggling parasites
With the true shape of virgins' counterfeits.
(*Micro-cynicon*, 133)

Among the group of self-styled witty sophisticates who participated in the vogue for verse satire in the years preceding the Problem Plays, John Donne stands out for modern readers. Little of Donne's poetry was published during his lifetime; indeed, the twentieth century's enthusiastic "rediscovery" of his toughly intellectual poems in a variety of modes is a counterpart of the newfound predilection for Shakespeare's *Troilus*. Perhaps the most remarkable of Donne's five satires is the third, on religion, which, in expanding its scope beyond the genre's standard preoccupation with terrestrial follies, conveniently illustrates a point germane to the satire of the period—indeed, to satire in general:

on a huge hill,
Cragged, and steep, Truth stands, and hee that will
Reach her, about must, and about must goe;
And what the'hills suddennes resists,winne so.[7]

What is striking in this image from the perspective of genre is the centrality, stability, and implied attainability—by however indirect an approach—of a definitive Truth. That such an affirmation figures in a work concerned with religious belief is hardly surprising, but there is a useful lesson in its emergence from the Juvenalian satirist's conventional pose of bitter indignation and cynicism, as established in the poem's first lines: "Kinde pitty chokes my spleene; brave scorn forbids / Those tears to issue which swell my eye-lids, / I must not laugh, nor weepe sinnes, and be wise" ("Satyre III": 1–3). The bleak landscape of frustration, pessimism, and world-weariness on which the satiric fictions of Donne and his contemporaries are customarily played out is here relieved by a stable landmark, a means of taking moral and spiritual bearings. But the very fact that Donne's sacred subject prevents him from laying claim to Truth and forces him to locate it outside himself is a reminder that such a landmark normally exists implicitly—as the satirist's standpoint, from which he projects his privileged vision.

Certainly, a reader often finds an Elizabethan satirical persona implicated by intense melancholy or scurrility in the very viciousness it excoriates—the doting lecher of Middleton's attack is such a case—but the satirists consistently revert to assertions of unimpeachably detached selfhood, and Truth, in the moral if not the religious sense, is understood to supply both that self's foothold and its raison d'être. Thus Joseph Hall, claiming to be the first English satirist ("I First adventure"[8]), undertakes "[t]o tread the steps of perilous despight" with "Truth on my side" and "Truth my guide" (*Virgidemiarvm* 1, Prologue, lines 2, 5, 6), with whose aid his poetry may rise to the level of his Muse: "Let lowly Satyres rise aloft to thee: / Truth be thy speed, and Truth thy Patron bee" (*Virgidemiarvm* 1, Prologue, lines 23–24). Evarard Guilpin concludes his *Skialetheia; or, A Shadowe of Truth, in Certaine Epigrams and Satyres* by proclaiming transcendence of praise or censure on the grounds that "My lines are still themselues, and so am I,"[9] while his friend, the future playwright Marston, who actually dedicates *The Scourge of Villanie* "To his most esteemed, and best beloued Selfe,"[10] appropriates the power of "True iudgement" en route to affirming, "I am my selfe, so is my poesie" (*Scourge*, "To Detraction I present my Poesie," lines 17, 25).

I stress the prominent place of Truth—and of Truth's frequent identification with Self—within the dynamic of poetic satire in the years immediately preceding the Problem Plays in order to highlight the problematization and dislocation of Truth as an issue in *Troilus*. This is the case despite—or rather, in part, because of—the insistent identification of that quality with the play's hero, according to the common proverb, which the audience is never allowed to forget: "As true as Troilus." In the first place, although Truth is typically bound up with the satirist's voice, Shakespeare's Troilus is no satirist; on the contrary, he is—to some extent, at least—an object of satire. And this points to the more fundamental difficulty: the Truth he purports to represent is, as the following discussion aims to show, called into serious question.

On the other hand, to attempt to pin down the satirist's perspective in *Troilus*, to fix the site of an alternative Truth, is an equally dubious exercise—more so than in almost any other satiric drama of the period. Characters move in and out of the satiric spotlight; situations—from the parting of the lovers to the killing of Hector—fluctuate between absurdity and high seriousness. And the only openly satiric voice within the text is implicated in this fragmentation of Truth. For the play's self-appointed satirist-in-residence, the railing Thersites, is both deformed and deforming—an emblem (and so established in rhetorical tradition, independently of literary sources[11]) of the satiric persona's propensity to befoul himself with the mud he slings. This is not to say that his voice does not, by and large, ring true—even in mocking the Truth of Troilus, as he does, in effect, towards the end of the play. And throughout,

Thersites signals the possibility of viewing through a skeptical lens not only the towering figures of Homer but the very values that lay claim to Truth in Chaucer's precursor romance—namely, honorable heroism and courtly love. But for Thersites to steamroll the text's complex moral and emotional topography into a barren desert of "wars and lechery" (5.2.195) is to deny himself a height from which to speak.

This lack is confirmed by our final sight of him, swallowed in the turmoil of battle, deprived of the platform of the privileged fool and reduced to proclaiming himself "in every thing illegitimate" (5.7.18) in order to save his skin. Unlike the cowardly but irrepressible Falstaff, who is similarly cornered on Shrewsbury field in *Henry IV*, part 1, Thersites at this point possesses the capacity neither to question heroic pretenses—pretenses that, admittedly, are more obviously self-discrediting in this case—nor to die and come back to life. Instead, he threatens to become a mere insignificant casualty—the Homeric equivalent of the "food for powder"[12] conscripts that Falstaff leads to their deaths, displaying a particularly cynical version of the satirical propensity for gladly seeing fools suffer. The true satirist preserves himself, as he exempts himself from criticism, by offering substitute victims; Thersites must, in effect, renounce satire by unsaying himself.

Indeed, the limits on Thersites' potential to function as satirist-spokesman for the text at large relate less to his narrow and distorted vision than to his marginality vis-à-vis the action—a position formalized in his low social status. His deformity cannot, in this context, participate in the paradoxical power of marginality, as does that of Shakespeare's villain Richard III, who for a while triumphantly unites satire and manipulation. Even Caliban, the "salvage and deformed slave"[13] of *The Tempest* who, satiristlike, proclaims the hypocrisy of his master Prospero, attempts to act on his vision. By contrast, Thersites' incessant railing gains him nothing but repeated beatings—one of the more obvious links with the classical comedy cited in the Epistle. His impotence is all the more apparent because of the active operation within the text of not one but several more-or-less effective manipulators—to the point where the dramatic structure, like those of the other Problem Plays, invites consideration as a texture of play scripts in more or less direct competition for textual hegemony—that is, not only for control over the plot but also for control over the act of interpretation, the production of meaning. In this case, with the spheres of love and war contributing a premise of generic polarity and pointedly identified with the promoters of specific interests, such a view has particular significance for the question of genre, as well as for the affiliated issue that is inescapable in the Problem Plays—the dynamics of power relations between the sexes.

The (Problem) Plays within the Play

Again, *Troilus* offers an especially productive avenue to a characteristic feature of the Problem Plays in general, but in this instance precisely because the avenue is indirect. The absence of a dominant controller of the action from start to finish becomes conspicuous by comparison with the script-writing activities of Vincentio in *Measure for Measure* or Helena in *All's Well*. Here metadramatic meddling is an open issue only because of secondary figures—notably, the politically scheming Ulysses and the sexually scheming Pandarus. Yet, clearly, genre is at stake. With regard to Pandarus, insofar as his manipulations serve the interests of romantic love (and however travestied that sentiment may appear in his mediation of it), his affiliation is obviously with the processes of comedy. From a structural point of view, if not in detail, he promotes a version of the conventional comic resolution, which depends on the union of lovers; in ethical terms, he subverts the heroic values associated with the cult of manly honor: witness his "reading," for Cressida's benefit, of the procession of battle-scarred warriors in act 1, scene 2, where he adapts their public heroism to his private erotic purposes. Confirmation, if any were needed, is provided by his perfect sympathy in act 3, scene 1, with the self-indulgent sensuality of Paris and Helen—the "botchy core," one might say (following a hint from Thersites [2.1.6] and anticipating the "putrified core" [5.8.1] of Hector's final victim), of the entire heroic enterprise. Evidently, the moralistic opposition—a Renaissance commonplace—between honor and love, reason and passion, duty and pleasure, is hard at work.

Yet the conservative values conventionally privileged by this opposition are also undermined, not only by their frequent satirical presentation but also by equivocal aspects of their most eloquent spokesman and most active promoter, Ulysses, whose speech on "degree" (1.3.75ff.) has customarily been served up "straight" as testimony to the "Elizabethan World Picture." A Renaissance audience, familiar with Machiavelli at least by (distorted) reputation, would have had less difficulty than some modern scholars in recognizing that while the scaffolding of degree that keeps at bay "appetite, an universal wolf" (1.3.121) may be imitated from natural phenomena, it is not naturally present in human society; in the time-honored fashion of politicians—and in his case the cynical Renaissance meaning of this term coincides with more neutral modern usage—Ulysses' conservative rhetoric thinly overlies a commitment to power broking premised on the assumption that social structures, even individual identities, are not fixed and stable but subject to manipulation and construction. In terms of genre, Ulysses, in plotting to reenlist the lapsed power of Achilles on behalf of the Greek cause, is an advocate for tragedy, as would be recognized by a Renaissance audience, for whom the fall of Troy had archetypal tragic status. (Thus Hamlet seeks to penetrate to the very heart of the tragic experience when he asks the Player for a speech on the final agonies of Priam and Hecuba.) The fleeting suggestion of a potential for comic resolution on the political level is effectively raised and dismissed by way of the bloodless encounter of Hector and Ajax, who abandon their combat because they recognize their kinship—conceivably, a model for Trojans and Greeks at large. This teasing suspension of tragic destiny is Ulysses' doing—he has maneuvered Ajax into the false and temporary position of Greek champion—and it merely sets the scene for the far different meeting he seeks to engineer between Hector and Achilles; the death of Hector intertextually imports the full weight of the high tragic ending of the *Iliad*, although the heroic single combat of Homer is replaced by the mass onslaught of the Myrmidons, with the result that Achilles' boast of victory becomes grotesque. In this context, it is significant, as I will argue, that Troilus supplies the gloss on that event, and that he does so in heroic terms belying the sordid slaughter of Hector in Shakespeare's version.

The mingled elements of comedy and tragedy in the play as a whole reflect the fact that Ulysses and Pandarus each achieve a measure of success, though the outlook of the former appears to prevail, as is consistent with the traditional reading of his character—another Homeric derivative—as wise and cunning. In fact, however, both Ulysses and Pandarus are ultimately failures as manipulators. Neither actually has events under control, even at the point where his project comes to fruition. Having mocked Pandarus's inflationary comments on Troilus in the procession scene, Cressida ironically reveals, in soliloquy, that she is attracted to Troilus despite, not because of, her uncle's inept advocacy: "But more in Troilus thousandfold I see / Than in the glass of Pandar's praise may be" (1.2.284–85). She also shows herself aware of the hazards of yielding, given the rules of the seduction game as established by male prerogatives and attitudes:

> Yet hold I off. Women are angels, wooing:
> Things won are done, joy's soul lies in the doing.
> That she belov'd knows nought that knows not this:
> Men prize the thing ungain'd more than it is.
>
> (1.1.286–89)

That she *will* yield despite her better knowledge, as is clear enough from her speech, lends her a gift of tragic prophecy akin to Cassandra's but enhanced by a tragic self-consciousness unique in the play—a quality, intriguingly, that is submerged in the ostentatiously tragic ending. By that point, however, her own ability to "read" behavior and situations more astutely than her uncle has been superseded by the reading given her, not only by her former lover but by her uncle's successor as producer of the script:

> There's language in her eye, her cheek, her lip,
> Nay, her foot speaks; her wanton spirits look out
> At every joint and motive of her body.
> O, these encounterers, so glib of tongue,
> That give a coasting welcome ere it comes,
> And wide unclasp the tables of their thoughts
> To every ticklish reader! set them down
> For sluttish spoils of opportunity,
> And daughters of the game.
>
> (4.5.55–63)

Ulysses' reading here carries weight within the text but is subject to qualification from outside it: in terms of speech-act theory, one might term this portrait performative rather than constative. It helps to produce Cressida as she will become, but it is notably inadequate to account for Cressida as she has been, and to this extent the speaker's position of authority is undercut. At the least, his view, like that of Pandarus—with which it essentially agrees, as far as Cressida's character is concerned—is exposed as severely limited. Even in his main sphere of action, moreover, Ulysses' success resembles his amatory counterpart's in being fortuitous. Achilles is not brought onto the battlefield by the scheme to exalt Ajax. Indeed, love prevails over war in this case, too, for Achilles, Patroclus, and Ulysses all agree (3.3.193ff.) that it is the hero's liaison with Polyxena, Hector's sister, that is holding him back. The balance shifts with the death of Patroclus, not with Achilles' recognition that "my reputation is at stake, / My fame is shrowdly gor'd" (3.3.227–28): this merely engenders "a woman's longing, / . . . / To see great Hector in his weeds of peace" (3.3.237–39)—a longing that will be doubly fulfilled, ironically, when Achilles catches Hector "unarm'd" (5.8.9) on the battlefield. Achilles' present "unarm'd" (3.3.237) condition thus echoes that of Troilus in the first scene, who, when asked by Aeneas why he is not on the battlefield, replies with a "woman's answer" suitable because "womanish it is to be from thence" (1.1.106–7). The parallel will develop in a way that sets the scene for Troilus's final constitution of himself as the ferocious adversary and "wicked conscience" (5.10.28) of the "great-siz'd coward" (5.10.26)—in effect, as Achilles' intimate in enmity: "No space of earth shall sunder our two hates" (5.10.27).

Thersites typically exaggerates when he accuses Patroclus of being Achilles' "masculine whore" (5.1.17)—Patroclus, after all, in a private dialogue between them, accuses Achilles of being made an "effeminate man" (3.3.218) by his infatuation with Polyxena. Still, as is now commonly recognized, there are strong homoerotic overtones embodied in the warrior code:[14] these come closest to the surface, perhaps, when Achilles fulfills his "woman's longing" and makes Hector's body the object of his devouring gaze, examining him "limb by limb" (4.5.238) in a way that recalls a male *blazon* of female beauty (a conventional type of literary catalog), but for the purpose of deciding where he will inflict the fatal wound.[15] (Ironically, Hector instead becomes the recipient of his own counterthreat to "kill thee every where, yea, o'er and o'er" [4.5.256].) Certainly, such an erotic dimension is insistently present in Achilles' love for Patroclus, which is what finally succeeds in arousing his heroic fury, as it is in the aroused fury of Troilus, first against Diomedes, then against Achilles himself. And in the processes that effect Achilles' shift in orientation from love to war, from the sphere of women to that of men, the precise observations and confident *sententiae* of Ulysses function to no greater effect, despite the successful outcome from his point of view, than do the foolish saws of Pandarus, which cannot keep Troilus from making the same shift.

Thus a metadramatic reading of *Troilus* is at once encouraged—even imposed—and frustrated. The two overt manipulators introduce, in remarkably symmetrical fashion, the pattern of plays-within-the-play, of scripts competing for textual hegemony, in a manner that focuses the contradictions of tone and genre. Yet both are ultimately if not defeated at least superseded by the text's overarching trajectory. The obvious factor at work here is the preexisting shape of the story itself, well known as it was (though with significant variations of emphasis) to

Shakespeare's audience. Hence, too, there is a pervasive and inescapable allusiveness that appears to figure, as a sort of metaconsciousness of legendary (hence transtemporal) existence, even in characters' ways of conceiving themselves.[16] But such a perspective also returns us to a sense of the predominance of Troilus, the basis of whose self-image, from start to finish, is his proverbially sanctioned monopoly of eternal Truth—the point at which his textual and extratextual destinies unite.

Even to speak of a self-image is to invoke the principle of metadrama, at least on a small scale; to recognize such an image as congruent with, indeed promoted by, the text at large implies either a simple coincidence of perspectives or a large-scale internal reshaping. Traditional readings have tended to accept Troilus's estimation of himself at face value, together with his judgments of other characters. Once the presence of other possible perspectives is allowed, however—including the view that his high romanticism is satirical in a profound sense (and is not just an illustration of folly in love)—then the door is opened to recognizing Troilus as a manipulator in his own right, albeit one whose relentless emotionality carries no trace of the Machiavellian and so obscures, even more thoroughly than in the case of Helena in *All's Well*, questions of consciousness and motive. But then the sort of manipulation I discern in these plays is not—even, at the most basic level, in *Measure for Measure*'s Vincentio—the scheming Machiavellian sort. Rather, it is a process of improvisational self-construction through the construction of others, premised on the absence of essential identity—hence, even of a "motivated" self—and the primacy of perception over "reality." Manipulation is as manipulation does.

Such empowerment of Troilus is, of course, fundamentally paradoxical, given Troilus's status as victim par excellence. Traditionally, even criticism that finds fault with Troilus has accepted his powerlessness. Yet empowering Troilus arguably accommodates his thematic and structural centrality more fully than does the traditional approach, offering a more satisfactory explanation of why, at the "heart" of this text (to use a term significant within it), when approached from any direction, there should lie a conspicuous void in the form of an indistinct and largely passive protagonist. In particular, we thereby gain a foothold on the otherwise slippery issue of Troilus's successive identities as lover and warrior, as well as on his shifting relations with the two active promoters of the causes of love and war. And inevitably, such a perspective entails a fundamental revaluation, such as much recent feminist criticism has undertaken from a variety of angles (though never quite from this one), of the figure of Cressida: arguably, to view her, in the older disparaging critical style, as "cheap stuff" (Walker, xii) is the ultimate sign of the subtle but thorough efficacy of Troilus's assumption of control over the text, the more so if he himself is taken to figure as an exemplum of naïveté (Walker, xix–xx), akin to Middleton's victim of "doting fancy."

What emerges from a thoroughly metadramatic approach is a figure who corresponds more closely with Vincentio and Helena—who, indeed, combines elements of the two. The latter's domination of her script is similarly achieved from a position of initial helplessness and within the romantic sphere; the former initially entrusts his case, with some sense of the probable result, to a would-be scriptwriter who eventually writes himself out—and so out of the picture. So Troilus, in a sense, does with Pandarus, initially a sort of deputy, "Who"—to invoke the Duke's explanation for delegating authority to Angelo—"may, in th' ambush of my name, strike home, / And yet my nature never in the fight / To do in slander."[17]

Once Pandarus's script is exhausted, however, Troilus does not openly impose one of his own. Instead, he integrates himself into, or rather appropriates, the agenda of Ulysses, which provides for the denigration of love (and of Cressida in particular) and the exaltation of heroic valor, though as a means rather than an end. There is, I would argue, a paradoxical coincidence of interests between the two enemies, as well as a symbiotic fit between Ulysses' power-broking cynicism (a quality shared with Pandarus) and Troilus's ostentatiously naïve idealism. The two enemies make common cause in a way that highlights Ulysses' limitations. The Trojan's effective enlistment of the shrewd but unwitting Ulysses on his behalf is reflected in the unlikely outcome, in which the hitherto passive Troilus comes to dominate the play's ending and superficially to confirm tragedy (the generic cause of Ulysses) as the concluding note, while at the same time, I will argue, subversively exempting himself.

The domination of Troilus is impressive for its grounding in the dynamic of victimization and martyrdom, according to which Troilus, already the object of betrayal in love, is effectively doomed anew, this time in his capacity as the most heroic remaining champion of the lost Trojan cause. To come into his own, after Hector's ignoble end, as what Ulysses—and his role here is particularly suggestive—designates as Troy's "second hope" (4.5.109) is to become a study in double hopelessness. Yet such a destiny is also an indirect response to Ulysses' attempted incitement of Achilles with the image of Time's "alms for oblivion"

(3.3.146)—the reminder of Time's power to erase the memory of human exploits—as well as to the vision of social instability and unfixed identity underlying the Greek statesman's machinations. More directly, Troilus is fulfilling his own determination in the earlier council scene to consider Helen, not as worth fighting for in herself, but as

> a theme of honor and renown,
> A spur to valiant and magnanimous deeds,
> Whose present courage may beat down our foes,
> And fame in time to come canonize us.
>   (2.2.199–202)

Troilus's idealistic declaration amounts to a counterprophecy to Cassandra's echoing cries of doom, as well as a rebuttal of Hector, who seeks to measure Helen's value (or, rather, the lack thereof) in terms of the intrinsic and essential. Troilus, on the contrary, affirms both the need and the capacity to construct the heroic self by constructing others in its service: "What's aught but as 'tis valued?" (2.2.52). Especially given Troilus's first scene insertion of himself, in terms reminiscent of Hamlet's self-interrogations, into the conventional conflict between the claims of manly duty and those of love, the heroic idealism of the council scene does more than place on record—though the public record is indeed being established—a young man's impetuous fantasies; it presages a rejection of the sphere of love as surely as Hamlet's deliberations modulate into his repudiation of the claims of Ophelia in the "nunnery scene" immediately following his famous soliloquy:

> *Oph.*   My lord, I have remembrances of yours
>   That I have longed long to redeliver.
>   I pray you now receive them.
> *Ham.*   No, not I,
>   I never gave you aught.
>   (*Hamlet*, 3.1.92–95)

It makes a trenchant comment on the mechanisms of patriarchy that both these young men effectively seize the occasion to pronounce women false that has been engineered behind the scenes by a woman's deceitful—in the case of Calchas, literally traitorous—father.

The intertextual relation between *Troilus* and *Hamlet* has significant dimensions, and I will return to it later. For the moment, I will add only that Hamlet's father is also very much to the point. As the armed ghost of old Hamlet supplies an ironic informal prologue to the introduction of his son in a notably unheroic posture, in *Troilus* a similar polarity of values is first established by the juxtaposition of the "prologue arm'd" (Pro.23)[18] and Troilus's decision to "unarm" (1.1.1) on the grounds that only a Trojan who is "master of his heart" (1.1.4) can take the field. His first words proclaim a self divided: "Why should I war without the walls of Troy, / That finds such cruel battle here within?" (1.1.2–3). In the cause of producing the myth of an integrated self, of mastering his heart, Troilus will slide naturally from the defense and overvaluation of Helen to the devaluation and sacrifice of Cressida. Indeed, in acquiescing so readily in her expatriation from Troy to accommodate the Greeks, Troilus will effectively apply to Cressida the very dismissal of Helen by Hector—"she is not worth what she doth cost / The keeping" (2.2.51–52)—to which the young man so violently objects. It is, from this perspective, an old and banal story: beneath the chivalrous rhetoric by which warriors present themselves as women's champions lies a profound misogyny.[19]

The construction of Troilus's unitary self entails moving through triumph and betrayal in love—that is, beyond subservience to his emotions—to a realization in action of this staging of himself as honor's devotee. The text—and to some extent Troilus himself—measures this process in terms of the progressive self-division of Cressida. Her early participation in the discourse of witty sexual repartee initiated by her uncle has often been cited as evidence of her "natural" lasciviousness and propensity to deceive:

> *Pan.* You are such a woman, a man knows not at what ward you lie.
>
> *Cress.* Upon my back, to defend my belly, upon my wit, to defend my wiles, upon my secrecy, to defend mine honesty, my mask, to defend my beauty, and you, to defend all these.
>
> (1.2.258–63)

In fact, the sharply different lexis and tone of her soliloquy immediately following—"though my heart's content firm love doth bear, / Nothing of that shall from mine eyes appear" (1.2.294–95)—reveal her very adoption of that discourse as self-protective and suggest the fragility of her defenses. Her sexual double entendre here ("joy's soul lies in the *doing*," "the *thing* ungain'd") becomes a clear reflection of male cynicism.

Already, then, Cressida's passion produces a disjunction of self, which will become so acute as to surface at the very moment when Troilus, reintegrating the earlier discourse of his emissary, misreads as sexual provocation her defensive protest—"See, see, your silence, / Cunning in dumbness, from my weakness draws / My very soul of counsel! Stop my mouth" (3.2.131–33)—and seizes the occasion for his first kiss. Cressida's words here, "I have a kind of self resides with you; / But an unkind self, that itself will leave / To be another's fool" (3.2.148–50), add an edge to the tired love conceit of self-loss (the basis of Shakespeare's own Sonnets 44 and 45). More ominously, the exchange and accompanying action allude parodically—with a problematizing of gender roles—to the famous scene in Christopher Marlowe's drama of damnation, *Doctor Faustus*, in which the protagonist kisses a devil in the seductive form of Helen of Troy and exclaims, "Her lips suck forth my soul: see where it flies!"[20] Souls, in a less literal sense, but equally implicated in the question of mortality and immortality, are also the currency of this encounter:

> O that I thought it could be in a woman—
> As, if it can, I will presume in you—
> To feed for aye her lamp and flames of love,
> To keep her constancy in plight and youth,
> Outliving beauties outward, with a mind
> That doth renew swifter than blood decays!
>   (3.2.158–63)

Whose soul, we wonder, is more deeply at sake? All in all, Troilus's later "discovery" of Cressida's divided nature—"This is, and is not, Cressid" (5.2.146)—comes as more of a surprise to him than to us, and *not* because we have been prepared to expect her infidelity.

It is part of resisting the reduction of Cressida's self-fragmentation to mere duplicity to recognize that, in contrast with Troilus's fantasy in the first scene of a risky voyage to her bed over "the wild and wand'ring flood" (1.1.102), the uncertainty she displays in the next scene's corresponding soliloquy is grounded in her personal circumstances. The daughter of a Trojan traitor, whose only relation and protector is Pandarus, is hardly the equal of one of the most prominent and *hope*ful of King Priam's sons. (This makes a pointed change from Chaucer's version, where Criseyde is a widow with social status and other powerful friends.) Her situation adds weight to her comment that in relations between the sexes women have power only as long as they hold out: "Achievement is command; ungain'd, beseech" (1.2.293).

In light of the realities of sexual politics, as they apply here, Troilus's self-dramatizing and ineluctably materialistic comparison of himself to a venturing "merchant" (1.1.103) has a particular intertextual resonance. In Shakespeare's *The Merchant of Venice*, the romantic hero Bassanio, who has more than a touch of the mercenary about him, undertakes a voyage to win the hand of the rich heiress Portia. This he can do only by choosing what is outwardly the least valuable of three caskets, for which he must "give and hazard all he hath."[21] In *Troilus*, a glance at the relative stakes suffices to show that the true giving and the hazarding are on Cressida's side. If Troilus's "heart" is regained in the very process of giving it away, there is no recovery possible of the self that has deserted her "To be another's fool."

One can begin to grasp the anomalous position of Troilus as passive metadramatist by recognizing that his proverbial destiny entails two corollary contributions, not merely to legend but to language itself—the falseness of Cressida and the perpetuation of the name of Pandarus in the term for all go-betweens. Indeed, Troilus's parting curse on Pandarus, which sends that signification flying over the wall of the dramatic structure—"Ignominy, shame / Pursue thy life, and live aye with thy name!" (5.10.33–34)—merely puts into practice what Pandarus has already taken upon himself in theory in the scene (act 3, scene 2) where he brings the lovers together. In his final words before sending them off to a bed that will be punished for keeping silent ("because it shall not speak of your pretty encounters, press it to death" [3.2.208–9]), Pandarus ritualistically commits all three of them to a determinate future of signification: "Let all constant men be Troiluses, all false women Cressids, and all brokers-between Pandars! Say, amen" (3.2.202–4). Yet he began this speech by volunteering his own notoriety contingently—*in case* "ever you prove false one to another" (3.2.199); a mere three lines later, the possibility of Troilus's falsehood has been erased. This is implicitly to accept the Prince's constancy as the fixed term, the landmark by reference to which the others will have their measures taken. Troilus's Truth is not a function of proverbs but the producer of them, a transcendental signifier beyond the reach of language itself because it precedes language ("I am as true as truth's simplicity / And simpler than the infancy of truth" [3.2.169–70]) and has its roots in essence and origin: "after all comparisons of truth / (As truth's authentic author to be cited) / 'As true as Troilus' shall crown up the verse" (3.2.180–82).

Pandarus is also here accepting at the level of signification itself essentially the same role that he performs on behalf of Troilus throughout—not persuasion, as Cressida's soliloquy makes clear, but the preservation of the Prince's pure image, which depends on his being a romantic hero rather than a seducer, a passive sufferer rather than an active pursuer. The poet-Prince can confine himself to the translation of his amorous aims into the realm of the sublime, out of time and space—"Her bed is India, there she lies, a pearl" (1.1.100)—because his friend is in the furniture business: "Cupid grant all tongue-tied maidens here / Bed, chamber, Pandar to provide this gear!" (3.2.210–11). And despite Pandarus's assumption to the contrary, even that bed will, indeed, be made to speak to the ages—the suggestion of coercion is apt[22]—in the language of Troilus's triumph-betrayal.

The scene in which these identifications are established all but makes explicit the idea of competing scripts. And it is a competition that Troilus sets himself up to win by setting down the rules. He begins the sequence of affirmations by proclaiming himself unmatchable for constancy—a position, as has been pointed out, that virtually forbids Cressida's compliance with his pleas for her good faith. But more fundamentally, he establishes fidelity itself, not only as the measure of their love but as a site of struggle for supremacy. Once Cressida has been drawn into this perspective—"In that I'll war with you" (3.2.171)—she is automatically placed on the defensive, as is evident when she formulates her corresponding affirmation in negative terms, invoking a proverbial future not to be aspired to but to be shunned: "'As false as Cressid'" (3.2.196). The audience's sense of discursive destiny affords as little hope for her as there is of averting the doom that Cassandra's prophetic discourse ordains for Troy itself.

Amidst the painful farewells in act 4, scene 4, which follow the discovery that Cressida has been exchanged for Antenor, Troilus again insists on portraying love as a war of truths—that is, a contest for the possession of Truth—and on implicating Cressida. This time, however, she is not wholly contained within his script. His position, moreover, is newly problematized in the eyes of the audience, thanks to the contrast between his and Cressida's responses to the news. Hers has bordered on hysteria; in the face of this irresistible stroke of fate, her defiantly repeated "I will not" (4.2.94, 96, 109), has an authentic air of impotent desperation, supporting her claim that her entire self—metaphorically, her soul, asserting itself against the conditions of mortality that weigh so heavily on all characters in the play—has been wholly assimilated into her love of Troilus:

> Time, force, and death,
> Do to this body what extremes you can;
> But the strong base and building of my love
> Is at the very centre of the earth,
> Drawing all things to it.
>
> (4.2.101–5)

Also striking is her unprompted reiteration of the prayer that the gods may "Make Cressid's name the very crown of falsehood, / If ever she leave Troilus!" (4.2.100–1). More than the familiar irony is involved here: Cressida is equating with infidelity the mere idea of accepting their parting.

By now in this scene of schism and fragmentation—Troilus has already parted from Cressida once, received the news from Aeneas, then left Pandarus to inform her—his ready acceptance of their fate has already been recorded in a line that the most devoted champion of Troilus-as-lover would have difficulty stripping of solipsism, even without its suggestion of sexual fulfillment as material acquisition: "How my achievements mock me!" (4.2.69). The suggestion is nothing new, however—we recall the venturing merchant of the first scene—and the line itself resonates the more strongly because it picks up her soliloquy's comment on men, "Achievement is command; ungain'd, beseech" (1.2.293). That sentiment has newly been made current again by her complaint in the morning-after scene about Troilus's eagerness to be gone at the sound of the lark—a parody of Romeo and Juliet's more reciprocally romantic ornithological dispute ("It was the nightingale, and not the lark"[23]): "You men will never tarry. / O foolish Cressid! I might have still held off, / And then you would have tarried" (4.2.16–18). (Incidentally, in its context, and given Cressida's capacity for rueful worldly wisdom, her generalization by no means testifies to extensive personal experience.) Nor does Troilus's image benefit from the way in which Pandarus, as his agent, "fills" the emotional gap in the lover's response, even—a telling presage of things to come—laying all the blame for Troilus's suffering upon Cressida: "Would thou hadst ne'er been born! I knew thou wouldest be his death" (4.2.85–86).

Finally, it makes a vivid impression in performance—or at least should do—that (presumably in order to preserve the lady's honor) Troilus rushes off to meet the advancing party and is next seen entering with them in a new role—or rather roles. On the one hand, he is love's martyr, the object of sacrifice. On the other hand, he is the sacrificer who will "deliver" Cressida's hand to Diomedes as if he were "A priest there off'ring to it his own heart" (4.3.7, 9). This is, in effect, to become "master of his heart," like those Trojans who can take to the battlefield (1.1.4–5). If Cressida's status as his "heart" manifests his powerlessness, he regains power over that heart by giving her away. Formerly, he had "none" (1.1.5) because it was in her possession; but logically, and in a more profound sense, he has "none" now. This condition represents the ultimate fulfillment of the suggestion, present from the first scene, that the discourse of idealized passion and unattainability defining his Truth is also a discourse that presupposes, hence requires, her absence and loss.

The stage is now set for Cressida to respond less complacently than earlier when Troilus, at their final parting, again demands vows of fidelity from her, while reasserting his own possession of Truth as an unalterable condition of nature—his essence. His very terms carry ironic negative overtones: "Alas, it is my vice, my fault: / Whiles others fish with craft for great opinion, / I with great truth catch mere simplicity" (4.4.102–4). While the lexis of Truth is unchanged, it is clear by now that there is slippage between signifiers and signifieds: Troilus and Cressida are no longer speaking the same language. If the line of fidelity, in her view, is drawn precisely at their parting, beyond which there is not merely no more seeing each other but no seeing at all ("When shall we see again?" [4.4.57]), no existence, Troilus actively takes that parting as his premise, and—with conspicuously more realism than idealism, for a change—presses home its inevitability in the face of her impulse to defy the situation. Suggestively, he aligns his own essential quality with this reality in labelling it "A hateful truth" (4.4.31). And if she has, in her view, just given him the ultimate evidence of her own "truth," subordinating the differences within her "self" to his hegemonic desire, that commitment is simply discounted in his urgent doubts about her temptation by charming Greeks. In effect, by placing their relation on the level of seduction and conquest, he denies that there has been anything special about it.

Cressida registers these fundamental disjunctions of perception in bridling at Troilus's need for further vows—"I true? How now? what wicked deem is this?" (4.4.59)—until his obvious lack of faith in her, his infidelity, drives her to an exclamation that should be allowed, arguably, to resonate emphatically in production: "O heavens, you love me not" (4.4.82). This thought forms in the heat of the moment and is never returned to—a measure of its terrible potency. For a significant emotional gap is thereby defined—one that coincides with the conspicuous gap in her presentation as a character from this point forward in the play. Given Cressida's investment of being in Troilus's love, the outburst takes on the quality of a glimpse into the abyss and marks a turning point, not only in the scene but in her progression towards her inexorable proverbial destiny. It has been observed that Cressida recedes from the audience, appearing increasingly at a distance.[24] But however much character in this play is shown to be contingent on context, subject to deconstruction and reconstruction, the audience does not simply jettison the impression made by the intense dynamics of the previous scenes, and against that background such a receding conveys the radical diminution of her emotional engagement, not only with Troilus but with all others, including the lover she accepts in his place.

When she participates in the round of kissing initiated by the Greeks on her arrival in their camp—and thereby gives Ulysses the opportunity to classify her among the "daughters of the game" (4.5.63)—Cressida's hollow banter feebly recalls the determination of her as-yet-uncommitted self to rely "upon my wit, to defend my wiles" (1.2.260–61). That there is so clearly little left to defend renders all the more vivid the sense of her abandonment and vulnerability. The effect is even more striking in the crucial night scene—doubly glossed by Thersites and by Troilus, guided by Ulysses—wherein Diomedes, cynical seducer in the transparent guise of self-appointed champion, manipulates her into further concessions by threatening to leave her completely on her own. Diomedes' scornful, "I'll be your fool no more" (5.2.32), which Troilus echoes with an affirmation of his injury ("Thy better must" [5.2.33]), parodically recalls her moment of painful protest against "an unkind self, that itself will leave / To be another's fool" (3.2.149–50). Her only subsequent reference to the relation on which she had staked selfhood—"Troilus, farewell! one eye yet looks on thee, / But with my heart the other eye doth see" (5.2.107–8)—merely records her redivided self with eerie detachment, as if a change of heart were a mechanical matter. Indeed, that change of heart is self- trivialized, as she submerges her very individuality in the cliché of female fickleness in the face of superficial charm: "Ah, poor our sex! this fault in us I find, / The error of our eye directs our mind" (5.2.109–10).

Cressida's language has the effect of reminding us that the cliché is not typically Shakespearean: in comedies and tragedies alike (but especially in the early comedies, such as *A Midsummer Night's Dream*), erring eyes that (mis)direct the mind figure prominently as a male specialty. Indeed, it is a remarkable fact that Cressida is Shakespeare's only portrait of an unfaithful woman in the conventional sense; and the exception proves the rule, since he both inherited and problematized this feature of the story. In general, the stereotype of female inconstancy is articulated and promoted by men—in this case, significantly by Troilus himself, as when he expresses in the parting scene his fear of "[h]ow novelty may move, and parts with person" (4.4.79). Cressida, then, is observably enacting the part scripted for her by her lover in a way consistent with the rules of the "game" as he first established them; she proves, as he effectively foreordained, that she cannot match his "integrity and truth" (3.2.165), that, indeed, it cannot "be in a woman / . . . / To keep her constancy in plight and youth" (3.2.158–61). The mechanism by which this script imposes itself is, in part, the script's very banality.

Troilus's forcing of the point in the parting scene, where his unconditional love is all she has to cling to ("Be thou but true of heart" [4.4.58]; "be thou true" [4.4.66]; "[b]ut yet be true" [4.4.74]), directly assaults the faith she had allowed to cloud her initial cynicism about the usual pattern of male-female relations. But that faith was already fading in the face of Troilus's postcoital coolness (subtly introduced through his opening line: "Dear, trouble not yourself, the morn is cold" [4.2.1]). On the basis of what she has seen, or imagined, to exist in Troilus beneath the superficial attractions celebrated by Pandarus, she had entertained the hope, despite her better knowledge—her *kinder* self—that somehow this relationship, this man, would be a miraculous exception: she, after all, is the one who actually demonstrates, without fanfare, the willingness Troilus merely professes to "presume" a capacity for constancy in at least one member of the other sex. His unmistakable retraction at the moment of parting, all the more cutting because it is accompanied by hollow professions of confidence, threatens to expose her faith as mere self-delusion, the enabling condition of a commonplace seduction. One man *is* just like another, Diomedes no different from Troilus, and a woman who sleeps with one might as well sleep with them all.

These are not responses that Cressida articulates, as she grasps at the elusive straws of her love, her unravelling lifeline; rather, they are subtextually constructed, as part of the (re)construction of her character, by the operation of external textual forces, and those forces are conditioned less by circumstances of plot than by Troilus's mediation of those circumstances: the parting, however unforeseen and inevitable, becomes grist to his mill. In effect, Troilus ensures that she will identify, then identify with, his infidelity. In this way, the legendary destinies of the eponymous protagonists are established as no more stable in significance, no less a site of rivalry and struggle, than Troy itself, yet with an outcome no less predetermined. And this view at least allows Cressida, too, as seen by the audience, to participate in the tragedy otherwise monopolized by her lover, causing some part of his vow, offered in response to her accusation that he does not love her, to be ironically fulfilled at his expense: "Die I a villain then!" (4.4.83).

Yet part of Cressida's tragedy is a fundamental irony at her expense: when she effectively denies Troilus's sincerity, idealism, and even individuality by placing him in the category of cold-hearted seducer ("You men" [4.2.16]), she is obviously wrong, despite the fact that he thinks in terms of "achievement." Certainly, such a seducer may become obsessed with his object and invest his machinations with the trappings of spiritual elevation, as Troilus does—and can do the more freely because of the mediation of Pandarus. But such a figure, according to the model evoked by Cressida's generalizations, typically moves from one woman, one "achievement," to another. Troilus's failure to follow through, except in the most ironic sense (when he spies on her with Ulysses), on his promise to "corrupt the Grecian sentinels / To give thee nightly visitation" (4.4.72–73), might plausibly fit the pattern, from Cressida's perspective; so might his failure to answer her letter. (Even his promise, of course, is made contingent on the fidelity he so clearly refuses to grant her: "be thou true, / And I will see thee" [4.4.66–67].) However, the audience has the privilege, not accorded Cressida herself, of witnessing his continuing obsession with her, in particular with her truth or falsehood. Having seemed—certainly to her—ready to put the affair behind him, in her absence Troilus renews his commitment to the idea of Cressida, in effect returning to his earlier mode of fantasy. His obsession associates her absolutely with his experience of love and women and so feeds directly into his absolute rejection of such experience in favor of the masculine world of war.

From his first appearance, the claims of the world of war have been not merely in abeyance but in suspension within the emotional mixture that he presents. Moreover, they have been associated with an ever-present potential for disillusion—never more clearly so than at the very moment of his meeting with her:

> I am giddy; expectation whirls me round;
> Th' imaginary relish is so sweet
> That it enchants my sense; what will it be,
> When that the wat'ry palates taste indeed
> Love's thrice-repured nectar? Death, I fear me,

> Sounding destruction, or some joy too fine,
> Too subtile, potent, tun'd too sharp in sweetness
> For the capacity of my ruder powers.
> I fear it much, and I do fear besides
> That I shall lose distinction in my joys,
> As doth a battle, when they charge on heaps
> The enemy flying.
>
> (3.2.18–29)

The narcissism and ambivalence expressed (and concealed) in this extraordinary speech lend themselves to psychoanalytic readings, according to
which Troilus's alienation from Cressida, once he has actually had sex with
her, is inevitable because it is subconsciously desired:[25] thus when he assures
Cressida, "In all Cupid's pageant there is presented no monster" (3.2.74–
75), he is belying (and betraying) his own fear, as well as projecting it upon
her. But the lexis of war does more than furnish imagery for conveying a
neurotic attitude towards women; it reflects the prior claim of an alternative,
more profound, and primary mode of being. Much as the Trojan War
supplies the looming background to the love story, Troilus's sense of warrior
identity naturally emerges to measure—and menace—other possible selves.
And when he uses the battle simile, with its notion of submerging individual in collective triumph, he indirectly affirms the underlying opposition
between love and war in terms of the nature of heroic destiny.

In his immediately preceding speech to Pandarus, Troilus has envis-
aged the consummation of his passion in terms of paradise, developing
his early image of an exotic voyage. He is dead already, a wandering soul
with no heart, but the transcendent pleasure he achieves with Cressida
will bring him immortal life:

> Pandarus, I stalk about her door,
> Like to a strange soul upon the Stygian banks
> Staying for waftage. O, be thou my Charon,
> And give me swift transportance to these fields
> Where I may wallow in the lily-beds
> Propos'd for the deserver! O gentle Pandar,
> From Cupid's shoulder pluck his painted wings,
> And fly with me to Cressid!
>
> (3.2.8–15)

In effect, and with the implicit support of the Renaissance commonplace
figuration of orgasm as death, this vision propounds sensual ecstasy

as an alternative route to the immortality to be earned ("Propos'd for the deserver") through heroic death. When fear enters the picture midway through the following soliloquy, however, it carries an association with another sort of death, spiritual rather than physical, in which "distinction" (surely, at this level, with connotations of "reputation") is lost, in which the "joy" of joining in a slaughter of fleeing soldiers offers a momentary exultation but a hollow victory, with no overtones of eternal fame.

The ultimate that love has to offer, then, even as "expectation" giddily "whirls [him] round," exposes itself in Troilus's imagination as flawed and fraudulent—the equivalent of the sham heroism exemplified by Achilles in setting his Myrmidons on the unarmed Hector. But then the latter act is made possible by Hector's own descent from the heroic stage in the sordid pursuit of an attractive armor. The play's constant undercutting of the heroic ethic throws into relief the element of incongruous fantasy in Troilus's idealism. The speeches of anticipation show him recycling his earlier valuation of Helen as nothing in herself but infinitely valuable as "a theme of honor and renown"—that is, as a means to an end. And for Cressida to function in this way requires her to awaken his heroic fury, much as Hector imagines that his challenge will galvanize the "drowsy spirits" (2.2.210) of the Greeks. The intensity of Troilus's commitment to his amorous ideal must be transferred to a violent disillusion that can produce deeds of transcendent glory—the means to a conquest of time and death by way of his Truth-ful apotheosis.

The key speech chronicling this process is, significantly, Troilus's expostulation to Ulysses on the occasion of his "nightly visitation," after the exit of Cressida and Diomedes:

> Never did young man fancy
> With so eternal and so fix'd a soul.
> Hark, Greek: as much as I do Cressid love,
> So much by weight hate I her Diomed.
> ·
> Not the dreadful spout
> Which shipmen do the hurricano call,
> Constring'd in mass by the almighty sun,
> Shall dizzy with more clamor Neptune's ear,
> In his descent, than shall my prompted sword
> Falling on Diomed.
> (5.2.165–76)

Immediately striking here is Troilus's depersonalized distance on his own experience and feelings, which corresponds to his distance from Cressida, both physical and psychological, during the interchange between Diomedes and Cressida. The question of where the truth (hence "Truth") lies in this scene is complicated by the multiple demands for, and assertions of, certainty emanating from the characters surrounding the ambivalent, fragmented Cressida, who indeed "is, and is not," (5.2.146) herself in a sense that only the offstage audience has access to.[26] Diomedes' bullying insistence on disclosure and commitment, as manifested in the love token, is echoed in passive terms by Troilus. The latter's reading—contrary to his ostentatious profession of disbelief—makes no allowance for ambiguity: his perception of two alternative Cressidas, his own and "Diomed's" (5.2.137), confirms his commitment to the "rule in unity itself" (5.2.141); a choice between them is necessitated by the presumed existence of a "soul" in "beauty" (5.2.138). Thus Troilus's final affirmation of self-division ("O madness of discourse" [5.2.142ff.]) modulates into recovered wholeness. Meanwhile, the complex emotional dynamics of the scene are reduced to a pageant of lechery by the satirical perspective of Thersites, whose gloss on Cressida's confession of fickleness is typically uncompromising and simplistic: "'My mind is now turn'd whore'" (5.2.114).

It is nonetheless useful, as usual, to have Thersites' bluntness set side by side with other discourses, and here the contrast with Troilus's idealistic rhetoric, his insistent talk of souls, is particularly effective in calling attention to a contradictory subtext. However, the point of that subtext is not lechery but power. The Cressida reduced to blandly echoing the stereotype of female inconstancy, in words as in action, has in the truest sense lost (though not sold) her soul, the core of her being; trapped in the motions of a quasi-posthumous existence, a living death, she enacts Troilus's earlier hyperbolic portrait of his precoital self as "Like to a strange soul upon the Stygian banks / Staying for waftage" (3.2.9–10), but in lieu of a ticket to paradise there is merely Diomedes and infamy. Her loss is Troilus's gain, because it feeds the self-mythologizing that enables him to transfer his exclusive claim to Truth in love ("so eternal and so fix'd a soul" [5.2.166]), by way of an exactly equal quantity of anger ("So much by weight hate I her Diomed" [5.2.168]), to an image of himself as an elemental, and therefore disembodied, force ("hurricano" [5.2.172]). His strange use of the term "fancy" to describe his consuming passion, even as it confirms the distance imposed by his use of the third person and the past tense, ironically brings out the contradiction between such a perspective and the emotion's supposed status as "eternal."

Throughout this scene, Ulysses, hitherto the manipulator of scenarios, takes on the more passive role of Troilus's guide and, especially, sounding board. If, suddenly, *he* "cannot conjure" (5.2.125), Troilus abundantly can, on the basis of an ambiguous and elusive tableau that Ulysses need merely guarantee as "real." To the extent that he has become a sort of anti-Pandar, doing even dirtier work on Troilus's behalf than the functionary he replaces, Ulysses may be seen as one of the "Grecian sentinels" whom Troilus earlier promised to "corrupt." Part of the background here may be book 10 of the *Iliad*—one of the seven books published in Chapman's translation in 1598—in which, after consultations involving the troubled Agamemnon and Nestor, among others, Ulysses and Diomedes undertake a scouting expedition, "Exposed alone to all the feares that flow in gloomie night."[27] In fact, their association as cunning deceivers was cemented in later (but still pre-Shakespearean) literary history: they are joined within a single flame in Dante's *Inferno*.

In light of a second, and more widely known, epic analogue, it becomes especially significant that Aeneas, having already figured as the messenger who informs Troilus that he must part with Cressida, is named by Ulysses in act 4, scene 5, as the informant regarding the heroic future that awaits the young Trojan. The principal association of Aeneas for a Renaissance audience was not Homeric but Vergilian, and he was perhaps most famous for his painful and pain-causing repudiation of love for the sake of a transcendent heroic destiny. The protagonist of Vergil's *Aeneid*, in whose background lies the catastrophe of Troy (and whose grandson, according to legend, will be the founder of Britain), is recalled to that destiny by the gods from his dalliance with the Carthaginian queen, Dido, who subsequently commits suicide. Thus the necessity that Aeneas sacrifice love in order to realize his immortality—that he break one faith in order to keep another—has tragic implications for his lover, which she was allowed to experience, one might say, not only in Vergil but in subsequent readings of her story: witness Marlowe's tragedy, *Dido, Queen of Carthage*, as well as Chaucer's depiction of her in *The Legend of Good Women*. The latter poem, incidentally, is significantly placed in Renaissance editions of the works of Chaucer, being separated from *Troilus and Criseyde* only by the (unattributed) *The Testament of Cressid* (which was in fact written by the fifteenth-century Scottish poet Robert Henryson). Moreover, the *Legend* is introduced as the author's penance for, amongst other misdeeds charged by the God of Love, having told the story of Criseyde "as the lyste, / That maketh men to wommen lasse triste, / That ben as trewe as ever was any steel."[28] Dido, here, as in other versions from the *Aeneid* on, prominently laments the loss of her "name" (*Legend*, 1361)—precisely the terms in which Cressida's doom is sealed. These intertexts throw into relief Troilus's appropriation of the tragedy inherent in Cressida's situation, his effective denial of her subjectivity, as a result of his monopoly of Truth.

Ulysses' verbal portrait of Troilus as epic hero-to-be follows the turning of attention in the Greek camp away from the newly arrived Cressida and towards the Trojan warriors who now appear to witness the combat between Hector and Ajax. Ulysses has just finished reading the "language in her eye, her cheek, her lip" (4.5.55), and the shift of focus is announced by a trumpet blast, which serves, the more clearly because of the dislocating pun ("The Troyans' trumpet" [4.5.64]), as a sort of pivot between his two attitudes: suddenly, the worldly-wise cynic becomes the vehicle of a mythologizing idealism on Troilus's behalf. This remarkable speech, so clearly "out of character" according to mimetic criteria of character consistency, decisively marks the displacement of Ulysses from a metadramatist in his own right to a mere interpreter of a pageant not of his staging. His reply to Agamemnon's query about the identity of the sad-looking Trojan so completely captures that pageant that it deserves quotation in full:

> The youngest son of Priam, a true knight,
> Not yet mature, yet matchless, firm of word,
> Speaking in deeds, and deedless in his tongue,
> Not soon provok'd, not being provok'd soon calm'd;
> His heart and hand both open and both free,
> For what he has he gives, what thinks he shows,
> Yet gives he not till judgment guide his bounty,
> Nor dignifies an impare thought with breath;
> Manly as Hector, but more dangerous,
> For Hector in his blaze of wrath subscribes
> To tender objects, but he in heat of action
> Is more vindicative than jealous love.
> They call him Troilus, and on him erect
> A second hope, as fairly built as Hector.
> Thus says Aeneas, one that knows the youth
> Even to his inches, and with private soul
> Did in great Ilion thus translate him to me.
>
> (4.5.96–112)

Thus Ulysses, whose initial response to Cressida has already made him a translator of Troilus's text (to borrow his own term), all but formally places his stage-managing and interpretative powers at the beck and call of the young man's heroic destiny. He becomes, indeed, the translator of a translation.

In a sense it is Troilus, rather than Cressida, who "goes over" to the Greeks with his foray into their camp, since he is now playing their game—the war game that will end in the destruction of himself, his city, and his society. But he is doing so in a way that co-opts the tragic momentum and, in effect, defers the closure that Ulysses envisages and that history (including all other versions of his own story) decrees. He succeeds, to this extent, in stopping the march of time and entering the eternal present of romantic mythology. Instead of dying onstage, and so becoming "alms for oblivion," he is permitted to exit at the zenith of his grandeur, having just taken upon himself the role of Hector's successor. For only through his great brother's death, evidently, can he attain the role of Troy's *first* "hope," as we are reminded even in his concluding speeches. First he proclaims Hector's death and its dire implications so insistently as to provoke the rebuke of Aeneas, "My lord, you do discomfort all the host" (5.10.10); he then rhetorically expands his heroic presence to fill the very vacuum he has defined: "I do not speak of flight, of fear, of death, / But dare all imminence that gods and men / Address their dangers in" (5.10.12–14). Now he marks Achilles as his match and assumes the idiom at once of command and of tragic closure: "Strike a free march. To Troy with comfort go; / Hope of revenge shall hide our inward woe" (5.10.30–31).

It is in response to Pandarus's attempt to thrust himself back into this tragic text, from which he has effectively been excluded—"But hear you, hear you!" (5.10.32)—that Troilus pronounces his malediction, thus confirming his hegemony over discourse and time itself ("live aye with thy name" [5.10.34]). As will be shown in subsequent chapters, there is a parallel between this squelching of Pandarus and closural elements in the other Problem Plays: the Duke's exposure, silencing, and punishment of the intrusive Lucio in the last scene of *Measure for Measure*; the final appearance of Parolles in *All's Well*, who seeks to get his own back by recounting his role as Bertram's go-between, only to be shunted aside by the King. That Pandarus gets the last word after all in his bizarre address to the audience constitutes at one level a satirical thrust at the expense of the heroic strain generally, and so partly of the hero himself. But the nature of this epilogue equally marks Troilus's success in detaching himself from the sordidness that once served him well. In order to be efficacious, a scapegoat must appear surcharged with sins, as Pandarus now does. Left to his own devices, removed from the courtly context that somewhat mitigated—even as it blended with—his obscenity, he now grotesquely embodies the play's incessant rhetoric of disease and so effects a retroactive purging. Ultimately, the very irony of his transcendence of the play world recoils upon him. For in projecting himself into the audience's time and place he precisely enacts the terms of Troilus's curse.

As for Cressida, by this point Troilus has set the seal on her destiny, too, in an act—his final *reading* of her—that possesses remarkable metadramatic resonance. To tear up her letter, delivered by a Pandarus actually displaying a touch of sympathy for "yond poor girl" (5.3.99) (albeit making a rather larger claim to pity in his own right), is not only to shut the door decisively on his amorous past but to fly in the face of dramatic convention, which dictates that an audience has the right to its own reading of such evidence: the contents of letters introduced on stage are not normally suppressed. Here what are obviously the protestations of Cressida, reflecting a "self" that we, unlike Troilus, have discerned even in her exchange with Diomedes, are relegated to "Words, words, mere words, no matter from the heart" (5.3.108). The earlier unsavory discourse of Thersites, preoccupied with the production of "matter" from a "botchy core" (2.1.6–8), ironically contaminates Troilus's rhetoric of the heart as emblem of love's Truth. Troilus now goes beyond dividing Cressida; using her discourse, conveniently provided in concrete form, as a metonymy for her subjectivity, he symbolically fragments her and banishes her to the elements: "Go, wind, to wind, there turn and change together" (5.3.110).[29] He thereby implicitly asserts control over the natural world itself, magically setting himself outside the mutability of nature—the very "Commotion in the winds" (1.3.98) cited by Ulysses as part of the chaos that waits upon the collapse of "degree." And by usurping the audience's prerogative of applying its own judgment—a conspicuous shift from the multiple perspectives available in the night scene—he signals a consolidation of his power, not only to read the script but to take over the writing of it. This effect is reinforced, in intertextual terms, by a radical break with the Chaucerian version, which records the protracted correspondence of the separated lovers.

Intertextuality and Genre

The last point will serve to introduce the complex and important question of the play's relation to previous versions of the story. According to the principle stated in my preface, there is no point in repeating here the information easily obtainable elsewhere concerning scene-by-scene analogues to, and departures from, those precursor texts that demonstrably furnished basic material for the plot—chiefly William Caxton's *The Recuyell of the Historyes of Troye*, newly edited in 1596.[30] Nor will I add to the abundant speculation on more elusive questions of secondary influence—to what extent Shakespeare drew from other mediations of the same material (such as John Lydgate's fifteenth-century verse translation of the thirteenth-century *Historia Troiana* by Guido delle Colonne), from Homer, from popular ballads about the lovers, or from the lost play on the subject known to have been written by Thomas Dekker and Henry Chettle in 1599. What seems more useful for a consideration of *Troilus* specifically as Problem Play is at once the most compelling and the most elusive relation of all—that between Shakespeare's version and Chaucer's—and even here I wish to confine myself to certain implications from the perspective of genre and metadrama, rather than to examine the question comprehensively or for its own sake.

I have devoted concentrated attention elsewhere to an exploration of Shakespeare's play vis-à-vis Chaucer's poem, taking an approach by way of intertextual theory and so circumventing the indeterminate question of influence.[31] The relation between the works has naturally engaged a number of scholars, most of whom have held Shakespeare's indebtedness to be self-evident.[32] Given the lack of universally convincing evidence of the influence of *Troilus and Criseyde*,[33] such an assumption depends on the virtual certainty that Shakespeare was acquainted with this major work of Chaucer—as he demonstrably was with many other Chaucerian texts—as well as on the strong (if elusive) imaginative affinity between the two authors' treatments of aspects of the story. In particular, the complex development of the characters of the lovers—an area in which there are fascinating parallels and divergences—connects the play more closely with Chaucer, whose technique at times anticipates the psychological realism of the nineteenth-century novel, than with any other precursor.

The situation is further complicated (and therefore enriched) by the fact that Renaissance editions of Chaucer's works included Henryson's

The Testament of Cressid as an appendix to *Troilus and Criseyde*. This relatively brief piece, at once defining and filling the gap left by Chaucer with regard to the future of Cressida, uncompromisingly but not unsympathetically serves up the dying heroine as moral exemplum. Stricken by leprosy and reduced to beggary as divine punishment for her infidelity and lack of chastity, she laments her fate yet recognizes it as righteous. Henryson was largely responsible for the popular Renaissance image of Cressida as whore—starkly imported by Thersites, who has no equivalent in Chaucer's version—as well as for promoting the proverbial association between Troilus and Truth. "O fals Cresseid and trew knicht Troylus!"[34] virtually becomes the refrain of her lament. (In Chaucer, by suggestive contrast, the quality of truth is more often claimed by, and associated with, Pandarus.[35]) To approach the play in terms of an intertextual dialogue with Chaucer's poem, therefore, is necessarily to admit the *Testament* into consideration as well, although there is no mistaking the fact, even in the early editions, that the latter is a separate poem, and a reader needed to reach only the sixth stanza in order to be informed that it represented another poet's response to the work "Writtin be worthie Chaucer glorious / Of fair Creisseid and worthie Troylus" (*Testament*, 41–42). In any case, it constitutes a supplement to *Troilus and Criseyde* that not only radically changes its focus but reopens a book sealed by one of the most decisive of literary closures.

This point, in fact, carries particular significance for a reading of the play in terms of competing scripts. Such a reading attaches value and power to the privilege of having the last word, as has already been shown in the case of *Troilus* and will also be apparent in the two other Problem Plays. The hidden triumph of Shakespeare's spurned lover is never closer to the surface than in his enunciation of a tragic closure that defers his own death and discredits alternative readings, notably those of Cressida and Pandarus. From an intertextual perspective, this involves the pointed displacement of the conclusion of Chaucer's poem. There, as in the play, Troilus's love-sorrow converts to warlike rage ("In many cruel bataille, out of drede, / . . . / Was seen his knyghthod and his grete myght"[36]), which is initially focused on Diomedes ("And alwey moost this Diomede he soughte" [*T&C* 5: 1757]). But whereas the play shows Troilus further expanding his heroic dimensions by setting himself up as Achilles' match after the death of Hector, the poem brings in Hector at the end only to qualify Troilus's stature—a reminder that "second hope" also means "second best"—and almost matter-of-factly makes an actual encounter with Achilles the occasion for Troilus's death:

> The wrath, as I bigan yow for to seye,
> Of Troilus the Grekis boughten deere,
> For thousandes his hondes maden deye,
> As he that was withouten any peere,
> Save Ector, in his tyme, as I kan heere.
> But—weilawey, save only Goddes wille,
> Despitously hym slough the fierse Achille.
>
> (*T&C* 5: 1800–6)

The pitiful inequality between Troilus and Achilles is the most striking feature of the brief mention of Troilus's death in Vergil's *Aeneid*.[37] In a scene on the wall of Dido's temple, his corpse is shown pathetically trailing in the dust, *unarmed* once and for all: "parte alia fugiens amissis Troilus armis, / infelix puer atque impar congressus Achilli" [elsewhere the fleeing Troilus, having lost his arms— unfortunate boy, unequal to encountering Achilles]."[38] The broad irony produced intertextually by this passing but potently canonical reference resonates specifically with Ulysses' glorified account of Troilus in act 4, scene 5. In the first place, the authority for this heroic tableau is none other than the hero of the *Aeneid*, whose own destiny conspicuously overshadows that of the object of his praise. Moreover, the play text effectively reapplies *"infelix,"* whose basic meaning is "unhappy," and teases out the connotations of the phrase *"infelix puer"*: it is Agamemnon's query, "What Troyan is that same that looks so heavy?" (4.5.95), that moves Ulysses to describe "The youngest son of Priam," whom he qualifies as "Not yet mature" (4.5.96–97). Most suggestively "ungrammatical," in terms of intertextual theory,[39] is Ulysses' term "impare" (the Quarto spelling—"impaire" in the First Folio). The word is recorded nowhere else in English in such a context, and its meaning is disputed: *The Riverside Shakespeare* (n. to 4.5.103) glosses it as "unconsidered" on the basis of the Latin "imparatus" ("unprepared"); the Vergilian precedent, however, strongly supports the alternative view that, as Walker puts it, "the sense 'unworthy,' 'inferior' (*Lat.* 'impar'), gives more point to 'dignifies' than any other sense suggested" (Walker, n. to 4.5.103).

At any rate, the only overt acknowledgment of Troilus's inferiority within Shakespeare's play comes early on and, significantly, is provided by Cressida: "There is amongst the Greeks Achilles, a better man than Troilus" (1.2.247–48). Even more striking is the play's complete erasure of Chaucer's forceful commentary on the death of Troilus. The poem, after bringing Troilus, in a double sense, down to earth, grants him immortality in order to interrogate the "immortality" associated with earthly fame. The ghost of the slain Troilus rises through the spheres and gains (literally) a spiritual outlook (or downlook) on the vanity of worldly concerns—especially love, but also glory, as the narrator's moralizing makes clear:

> Swich fyn hath, lo, this Troilus for love!
> Swich fyn hath al his grete worthynesse!
> Swich fyn hath his estat real above!
> Swich fyn his lust, swich fyn hath his noblesse!
> Swych fyn hath false worldes brotelnesse!
> And thus bigan his lovyng of Criseyde,
> As I have told, and in this wise he deyde.
> (T&C 5: 1828–34)

Chaucer's poem, like Shakespeare's play, may be read as involving a struggle for authority between competing perspectives, though in the poem these are identified, respectively, with the narrator and with Pandarus, who is a far more efficacious figure in the poem, while Troilus is less so. (Shakespeare's Troilus, in my view, effectively assimilates the functions of Chaucer's Pandarus, complete with their ambiguities.) To summarize (and necessarily to oversimplify), the contest in Chaucer is between the exaltation of courtly love according to the chivalric code— the orientation of Pandarus—and the more strictly Christian condemnation of terrestrial, as opposed to celestial, love—*amor* as opposed to *caritas*. In this context, the final two lines of the excerpt above suggest the firm recovery of textual control and moral bearings by the narrator, who has elsewhere shown signs of being seduced by the attraction of the love story and its attendant trappings of romantic idealism. In displacing Chaucer's ending, therefore, the Troilus of Shakespeare is, in a sense, displacing the very principle of authorial containment—that is, denying that he is Shakespeare's "creation" at all.

This is part of what might be seen as the stubborn anachronism of the character: he resists (however imperfectly) the text's broad project of translating its inherited Medieval material into a "modern" mode. One may quibble about the depth and pervasiveness of the satire, but unquestionably the tendency is to reduce and undermine, not the heroic ethic of the *Iliad* itself, which is remote enough to retain a pristine quality even in Chapman's translation, but those high chivalric accretions, in the spheres of both love and war, that were grafted onto the material by Medievalizing mediations. The idealism of Medieval romance, especially as represented by Chaucer, was regularly subjected to more or less deflationary treatments on the Elizabethan stage: Shakespeare's oeuvre, after all, is virtually bracketed by *A Midsummer Night's Dream* (1595–96) and *The Two Noble Kinsmen* (written in collaboration with John Fletcher in 1613), and even his history plays continually interrogate chivalric attitudes in relation to the mechanisms of power. This preoccupation and the ambivalence with which it is imprinted mark a complex cultural phenomenon, especially given the political uses to which chivalric revivalism was often put in the Tudor and Stuart courts: hence there has recently been a renewed interest from a New Historicist perspective in the venerable reading of *Troilus* as figuring the Earl of Essex in the character of Achilles.[40]

Chaucer's poem is itself, I have suggested, of two minds about courtly love, and this is reflected in its sardonic treatment of various extremities of feeling and behavior. But by and large the work stands as an epitome of Medieval idealizing in the high style, privileging the courtly code of honor and nobility. Shakespeare's Troilus lays claim to uncontaminated continuity with that heritage. Thus, for instance, he incorporates sexuality into his idealism—a position presented as natural (if ultimately delusory) in Chaucer's fictional world, but which in the world of the play entails blatant, sordid, and hypocritical contradiction. And where his primary pretextual model lets him down most seriously, in the form of Chaucer's skeptical conclusion, the later Troilus effectively leaps over the barrier imposed by the major narrative of his amorous history into the interpretative supplement that is the next text in the book—the model of Henryson's "trew knicht Troylus."

Troilus, as we have seen, has been skewing his self-image (and Cressida's destiny) towards Henryson's model from the start, and, as if under the hero's own influence, the Chaucerian script has been increasingly modified. On the intertextual level, too, Troilus's visit to the Greek camp constitutes a liminal experience and a turning point, as the narratives, not only of Henryson, but of Caxton and Lydgate, with their emphasis on the postamatory heroics of Troilus, emerge as the dominant precursor texts and support the realization of his epic self-image, as retailed by Ulysses.[41] In Chaucer's version, Troilus remains passively within Troy, hoping, pining, and finally despairing—both reading *and* *writing* letters; the heroic sequel is only briefly sketched and, I have suggested, qualified in itself, as well as by the epilogue. Nor, significantly, does the narrator follow Criseyde after her departure or describe her subsequent actions authoritatively. They are allowed to retain the ambiguity and indeterminacy that they would also possess in the play, if they were allowed to speak for themselves.

To the extent that this approach to the play, at once metadramatic and intertextual, produces a Troilus seeking refuge in fantasies of an exalted intertextual past from the corrupt realities of the textual present, including the dubious implications of his own actions, the specifically sexual ambivalence posited by psychoanalytic readings blends smoothly with the existential terms in which the text more openly conducts its business. The latter amount to a Renaissance commonplace—the challenge of "self-fashioning" (to invoke Greenblatt again) in the face of devouring time. From such a dual perspective, it appears natural that the anxiety-laden declaration of Troilus to Cressida just before the consummation of their love ties amatory "staying power" (in both the sexual and a broader sense) to the fundamental human condition of entrapment within temporality itself: "This is the monstruosity in love, lady, that the will is infinite and the execution confin'd, that the desire is boundless and the act a slave to limit" (3.2.81–83).

Such a combining of problematic issues of sexuality, heroic action, and self-definition within the framework of an idealized past, a sordid present, and a menacing future may be usefully related to the nearly contemporaneous "Problem Tragedy." The protagonist of that play is far more self-probing—to the point where he spends much of the play as if trying, at least, to respond to the sentinel's challenge that opens it: "Stand and unfold yourself" (*Hamlet*, 1.1.2). Hamlet informs the prying Rosencrantz and Guildenstern that "Denmark's a prison" (*Hamlet*, 2.2.243) yet claims that he "could be bounded in a nutshell, and count myself a king of infinite space—were it not that I have bad dreams" (*Hamlet*, 2.2.254–56). It is in the same scene that, as discussed in the previous chapter, he defines his melancholy in terms of the disillusioning contrast between the theoretically godlike nature of man ("how noble in reason, how infinite in faculties" [*Hamlet*, 2.2.304ff.]) and the mortal condition as he perceives it ("yet to me what is this quintessence of dust?" [*Hamlet*, 2.2.308]). Moreover, Hamlet goes on to take the smiles of his interlocutors, when he affirms that "[m]an delights not me" as an occasion for extending his disaffection to include women ("nor women neither" [*Hamlet*, 2.2.309]), thereby denying Polonius's preferred explanation for his distemper.

To elaborate the point made earlier, in thus invoking the traditional positioning of mankind between the angels and the animals, Hamlet positions himself between two conflicting readings of the human condition, which may be roughly identified, respectively, as conservative and radical, optimistic and pessimistic. The former view, still influential within Elizabethan ideologies, especially Anglo-Catholicism, looks backwards to late Medieval and early Renaissance concepts of the privileges accorded humanity within the divine creation; the latter outlook, here coded as melancholic, reflects the burgeoning skepticism and pessimism, strongly tinged with a Reformist sense of human corruption, of the period of the Problem Plays. There is an obvious correspondence between this doubleness and what Hamlet himself presents as his existential dilemma, torn as he is between being and not being— between, on the one hand, the action demanded of him by an idealized representative of a heroic past and, on the other hand, the moral complexities and emotional counterclaims of the world he actually inhabits, including the claims of love.

That world, like the world of Troy, is at once under siege from outside (at least initially) and undermined from within. The ideal of a comprehensive self, capable of reconciling contradictory identities—"The courtier's, soldier's, scholar's, eye, tongue, sword" (*Hamlet*, 3.2.151)— gives way under pressure to a fragmented "madness of discourse" that focuses on female sexual menace and betrayal. Finally, Hamlet achieves a sense of integration that reenables the fulfillment of a heroic destiny within the suspended framework of that destiny's futility. The Mousetrap is not the only play-within-the-play that Hamlet helps to script; he is ultimately responsible for a larger scenario that at once presupposes his death, defers his consciousness of it, and elevates it to the level of immortalizing myth (in Horatio's narrative and Fortinbras's benediction). And a key part of the self-image thus taken out of temporality remains an idealized dedication to the now safely absent, definitively silenced "love" object. "I lov'd Ophelia" (*Hamlet*, 5.1.269), Hamlet loudly proclaims, as he jumps into the grave he has helped to dig for her.

Giving the Last Word to Cressida

What exposes such behavior as grotesquely hypocritical, such rhetoric as excessive and defensive (except for diehards of the "wounded Prince" school of criticism), is the status of Ophelia as Hamlet's innocent victim, whose death carries tragic import in its own right and so impinges on Hamlet's pretentions to tragic exclusivity. In this respect, the metadramatic "enginer" is, indeed, "[h]oist with his own petar" (*Hamlet*, 3.4.206–7). As raw material from which to fashion a "pure" heroic identity, *Hamlet* offers its protagonist a ready-made instance of female sexual weakness and incapacity for loyalty. There is plausibility, at least, in concluding from Gertrude's case, "Frailty, thy name is woman!" (*Hamlet*, 1.2.146). Nevertheless, as the ghost makes clear in enjoining him to "Taint not thy mind, nor let thy soul contrive / Against thy mother aught" (*Hamlet*, 1.5.85–86), this is an outlook to move on from, not to wallow in. And when Hamlet focuses his misogyny on Ophelia in the nunnery scene—"wise men know well enough what monsters you make of them" (*Hamlet*, 3.1.138–39)—he conspicuously taints himself with the fear that Troilus successfully projects outward: "O, let my lady apprehend no fear. In all Cupid's pageant there is presented no monster" (3.2.74–75).

If Hamlet exposes and discredits his manipulations through failing to distinguish not only shades of guilt but guilt from innocence, Troilus succeeds at the more difficult maneuver of constructing an emblem of female corruption from the sole woman in his life—in effect, transforming Ophelia into Gertrude—while keeping his "mind" (or "soul") untainted. Hamlet's temporizing "I lov'd Ophelia" makes a lame rearguard action in defense of his pure feelings, compared with Troilus's confident and conclusive self-assessment: "Never did young man fancy / With so eternal and so fix'd a soul" (5.2.165–66). Hence, until the advent of feminist and psychoanalytic criticism, commentators have had little hesitation in accepting Troilus as the incarnation of Truth. He may have fallen, even ludicrously in some views, into the traditional emotional trap blamed by the murdering Othello ("one that lov'd not wisely but too well"[42]), but such entrapment merely reinforces his status as victim, hence his innocence.

Yet one must take into account the fact that Troilus, though he may not have a Gertrude to hand, has the "benefit" of working with even more deeply tainted raw material in the form of a virtual emblem of female betrayal: the whole trajectory of his development from romantic idealist to tragic victim is pre-inscribed. And from this perspective, Cressida's very silence and disappearance actually constitute a kind of subversive presence, a dangerous loose end, akin to the challenge posed by Ophelia's corpse. For while Shakespeare's Troilus smoothly appropriates the glorious destiny bestowed on him by Henryson, amongst others, and so implicitly endorses the punishment of his lover in the *Testament*, the fact remains that Cressida comes no closer than her ambiguous remarks about the "error of our eye" (5.2.110) to fulfilling the role assigned her in that poem, whose raison d'être, after all, is her *testament*—

essentially, her self-condemnation. She is pointedly not allowed, in the script imposed by Troilus, to speak for herself, and her last words (in the torn-up letter) are obviously not confessional. It will be a useful principle to keep in mind, in considering the other Problem Plays, that to impose silence manifests not only power but also the limits of power, given the implication that acquiescence remains beyond reach: hence the legal torture of pressing to death, to which Pandarus jocularly alludes, for those who, by refusing to plead innocence or guilt, presumed to place themselves beyond the reach of judgment.

It remains inconceivable, moreover, that, if Cressida did speak, she would speak with the voice of Henryson's leper-beggar. Instead, she remains, in her absence, fragmentation, and ambiguity, a living *testament* to the view of character and identity illustrated in the play—that is, as constructed and produced, not as inherent and essential. Hence this testament problematizes the proverbial outcomes, notably Troilus's identity as fixed signifier of Truth, the stable eminence on the satiric landscape, by throwing into relief the contingency and artificiality of all connections between signs and signifieds. The paradoxical consequence is that Cressida herself (or her*selves*) becomes a truer emblem of Truth—which is traditionally, after all, gendered as feminine, as in Donne's satire—as it figures within the play: multivalent, tentative, improvisatory, subject to manipulation, *not* at the center.

This recognition takes us back to the beginning of the action, to the scene scripted by Pandarus on Troilus's behalf, in which Cressida is shown the pageant of warriors, complete with interpretative commentary:[43] "Here, here, here's an excellent place, here we may see most bravely. I'll tell you them all by their names as they pass by, but mark Troilus above the rest" (1.2.181–84). Her response to Pandarus's hyperbolic celebration of Troilus is mockery. Superficially, her soliloquy at the end of the scene reveals that her disparagement has been pretended—the first sign, if we like, of her falseness. But at a deeper level, she reveals that she is able to detach sign from signified. It is *true* that the Troilus that she loves is no match for Achilles. Tragically, however, to love at all is, as she ultimately realizes, to succumb to the "error of our eye": "But more in Troilus thousandfold I see / Than in the glass of Pandar's praise may be" (1.2.284–85). Insofar as the play presents such susceptibility as the "fault" of a woman, then makes that woman representative of her sex, it suggests that only women are genuinely capable of love. In the final analysis, Cressida pays the price, not only of threatening Troilus's mythology of Truth by desiring the true Troilus but of fatally imagining that there is such a thing.

Chapter Three
All's Well That Ends Well
(Re)Enter the Intertextual Ghost of *Hamlet*

Thanks to their protagonists' status as metadramatists, which in a sense renders visible and therefore contentious the process of character production, both *Troilus* and *Hamlet* offer analyses—in the literal sense of a resolution into component parts—of the convention of military misogyny. That convention figures throughout Shakespeare's oeuvre in a variety of forms, none of them simple. One thinks first of those later tragic protagonists—Othello, Coriolanus, Macbeth, Antony—whose very status as warriors entails, in more or less destructive ways, a potently ambivalent involvement with a female figure. Less fully developed, if no less problematic, warrior-lovers appear in a wide range of earlier plays—from Richard III to Claudio in *Much Ado about Nothing*. Arguably closest to *Hamlet* and *Troilus* in analytical depth, as in the sorts of problems it raises, is *All's Well*, where the motifs of love and war shift and intertwine elusively. Yet there is also a telling difference: here the young female "lead" is the active wooer—and metadramatist—and she at last succeeds in overcoming, at least on the level of plot, the misogynistically tinged reluctance of a professedly honor-seeking, and certainly military-minded, young man, who has declared himself the "lover of [Mars's] drum, hater of love."[1]

In this process, moreover, Helena enlists the support of the play's ultimate authority figure—the King of France—as well as that of the mother of her beloved. This marks a radical departure from the typical romantic-comic scenario, in which parental, especially paternal, opposition to youthful desires largely generates the plot. That Ophelia, too, had the support of Hamlet's mother is among the things we learn at her graveside: "I hop'd thou shouldst have been my Hamlet's wife" (*Hamlet*, 5.1.244). But of course Gertrude, according to Hamlet's script, is thoroughly discredited from the start, as surely as Ophelia is disempowered by the patriarchal social structure so aggressively represented by her brother and, especially, her father. That disempowerment extends to subjectivity at the most basic level: the audience lacks direct access to Ophelia's desires—a lack all the more striking because of the indirect access eventually afforded through her madness.

Helena, like Hamlet himself and in contrast with Ophelia, is a soliloquizer, especially at the outset. Her increasing reticence as the play proceeds is an index of power, not of impotence. After all, she performs the remarkable feat of attaining, if not the kingdom's heir apparent, at least Bertram, the Count of Rossillion, whose social superiority to her might plausibly attract a warning such as Polonius delivers to Ophelia concerning "a prince out of thy star" (*Hamlet*, 2.2.141). Indeed, Helena first presents the situation to herself in the same metaphorical terms:

> 'Twere all one
> That I should love a bright particular star
> And think to wed it, he is so above me.
> In his bright radiance and collateral light
> Must I be comforted, not in his sphere.
> (1.1.85–89)

Not only does Helena know precisely what, or at least whom, she wants, but she has no male guardian to enforce patriarchal impossibilities for her. On the contrary, she is freed from immediate masculine domination, thanks to the recent death of her father. And the burden of patriarchal authority is actually replaced by the support of feminine sympathy, for she stands in a daughterlike relation to her guardian, the widowed Countess, who is prepared to foster her desires.

That Helena's situation is closer to Hamlet's than to Ophelia's is supported in the first scene through further echoes of the Problem Tragedy, which insistently confirm its presence as intertext. In enjoining Helena to mitigate her ostentatious grief over her father's death, "lest it be rather thought you affect a sorrow than to have—" (1.1.52–53),[2] the Countess occasions a retort similar to Hamlet's distinction, in response to his mother's challenge, between "that within which passes show" and "the trappings and the suits of woe" (*Hamlet*, 1.2.85–86), although Helena's "I do affect a sorrow indeed, but I have it too" (1.1.54) is enigmatic in the short rather than the long term. Lafew's conventional admonition against "excessive grief" (1.1.56) picks up the sentiments of both Gertrude and Claudius regarding Hamlet's mourning. If these associations threaten to problematize the Countess more than her sympathetic role should warrant, comparing her advice to Bertram with the analogous "precepts" (*Hamlet*, 1.3.58) delivered by Polonius to the departing Laertes amply highlights the contrasts in attitude and situation. Against the intertextual background of Polonius's cliché-ridden pomposity, the Countess's manner emerges as genuinely judicious:

> Love all, trust a few,
> Do wrong to none. Be able for thine enemy
> Rather in power than use, and keep thy friend
> Under thy own life's key. Be check'd for silence,
> But never tax'd for speech.
>
> (1.1.64–68)

Her advice, moreover, will turn out to have far more specific applicability to Bertram, especially given his susceptibility to Parolles, than does that of Polonius to the quite self-sufficient Laertes. Finally, in the most significant contrast of all, the Countess will shortly turn her attention to Helena, as Polonius turns his to Ophelia, but with a precisely contrary purport—the encouragement of her socially transgressive match.[3]

Helena's first soliloquy, which discloses the inward scope and focus of her outward sorrow, as does Hamlet's ("O that this too too sallied flesh would melt" [*Hamlet*, 1.2.129]), contains the most striking mixture of parallels and telling departures. Her supposed obsession with her father turns out to be, if not a sham, at least a misreading that she has not rectified, and her frankly avowed forgetting of him is all the more shocking when set off against Hamlet's attack on his mother's forgetting and his enshrinement of filial duty within "the table of my memory" (*Hamlet*, 1.5.98), in keeping with the Ghost's injunction, "remember me" (*Hamlet*, 1.5.91). Helena, in rejecting the role of bereaved daughter, is almost brutally matter-of-fact:

> I think not on my father,
> And these great tears grace his remembrance more
> Than those I shed for him. What was he like?
> I have forgot him.
>
> (1.1.79–82)

She proceeds to transfer to the role of despairing lover the full force of Hamlet's idealizing rhetoric; in particular, she echoes his apotheosizing *blazon* of his father's qualities, designed to awake Gertrude's memory, and with it her conscience, in the closet scene:

> See what a grace was seated on this brow:
> Hyperion's curls, the front of Jove himself,
> An eye like Mars, to threaten and command,
> A station like the herald Mercury
> New lighted on a heaven-kissing hill.
>
>   (*Hamlet*, 3.4.55–59)

It is in her "heart's table" (1.1.95) that Helena has drawn Bertram's "arched brows, his hawking eye, his curls" (1.1.94), thereby quite erasing *her* father's memory.

Both Hamlet's and Helena's speeches at these points smack of conjuration, and the former's is actually followed by the appearance of Old Hamlet's ghost, which, however, effectively marks Hamlet less as a magician than as a man possessed. Even in her despair, Helena retains a certain distance on her own "idolatrous fancy" (1.1.97) and so implicitly recognizes its distorting propensity. Comparing Helena with Hamlet on this point offers a useful reminder that Hamlet spends the better part of the tragedy in painful service to his father's spirit, unable to generate, despite his abundant soliloquizing, any alternative subject position. The burden of perceiving that "The time is out of joint" and that he was "born to set it right" (*Hamlet*, 1.5.188–89) entails enslavement to the past—the more clearly because it is logically futile to imagine undoing the past's effects. Helena reduces the past, as represented by her father's "will," to something tangible and serviceable—the medical prescription—that will aid her in shaping a future to her own liking. The trappings both of magic itself, as her cure of the King makes clear, and even of magical thinking, prove to be grist to her materialist mill.

To return to the state of social relations at the commencement of the play, Helena's love object is himself, thanks to his father's death, in the all-but-helpless position of ward to the King,[4] whom, it soon emerges, she has the power at once to cure and to charm. Thus the element of dependence in Hamlet's position is largely detached from Helena and assigned to Bertram, though without the special moral and sexual complexities raised by Claudius's murder and Gertrude's perceived betrayal of the Prince's father. When Lafew assures the Countess, reluctant to see her son go off to the court, "You shall find of the King a husband, madam; you, sir, a father" (1.1.6–7), his words intertextually recall Hamlet's tragic situation as if to confirm that, as is more in keeping with comedy, these relations here remain at the symbolic level. This is not to say, of course, that the relations among the Countess, the King, and Bertram are without moral or sexual complexities of their own, as may easily be gathered from the Countess's view of her son's parting as a deathlike birth and from her equating of son with husband: "In delivering my son from me, I bury a second husband" (1.1.1–2). For the moment, however, what stands out is that the situation at the beginning of *All's Well* pointedly redistributes some important raw material of the potently present *Hamlet* intertext, especially its power relations, so as to invest the female protagonist with both subjectivity and the capacity for action. And in the Renaissance cultural context, granting Helena these qualities also inevitably makes her the focus of considerable ambivalence, given the threat posed by a woman's appropriation of male prerogatives, beginning with desire.[5] Even some twentieth-century commentators would appear to register such feelings in charting Helena's lapses from their particular standards of romantic hero(ine)ism.

Obviously, in *All's Well* the dice are loaded in favor of the virtuous and sympathetic Helena to an extent quite implausible in terms of Elizabethan social structures and practices, according to which she might have reasonably expected some less extreme version of Ophelia's fate. As in *Troilus*, the "modern" element signalled by (though by no means limited to) the intertextual presence of *Hamlet* is laid upon a still-visible pretextual foundation, with which it remains in problematizing tension. The tension is actually registered by Lafew in connection with Helena's apparently miraculous cure of the King: "They say miracles are past, and we have our philosophical persons, to make modern and familiar, things supernatural and causeless" (2.3.1–3). In contrast with *Troilus*, however, the fantastic world of Medieval romance here furnishes a simpler plot— one of frank wish fulfillment with a strong folkloric tinge—and it does so in a more straightforward way. There is no doubt that the main plot (apart, that is, from the Parolles subplot, for which no obvious precedent exists) derives in outline from the story of Giletta of Narbona, which first appeared in Boccaccio's *Decameron* as the ninth tale told on the third day. Scholars incline to identify the actual "source" as the French translation made by Antoine le Maçon or the English version in William Painter's *The Palace of Pleasure* or (most probably) both.[6] (Certainly, it would be strange if Shakespeare ignored the latter work, that storehouse of sensational fictions popular enough to achieve three editions [1566, 1569, 1575] and freely plundered by Elizabethan dramatists.)

Much attention has also been devoted, beginning with Lawrence's pioneering work on the Problem Comedies, to the folktale affiliations of the story, which possesses basic elements of the narrative types known as

Fulfillment of the Tasks or Impossibilities (more particularly, the sub-species featuring the so-called Clever Wench) and the Healing of the King (Lawrence, 48–68).[7] The motif of the virtuous, long-suffering maiden who finally gets her man had great appeal for readers and audiences in the Renaissance—as much, no doubt, because of the romance element of wish fulfillment itself as because the motif fits, neatly if obliquely, with the ideology of male dominance.[8] Thus there is a fundamental affinity, despite the difference between the activity and passivity of the two heroines, between the story of Giletta and the enormously popular tale of Patient Griselda, which was also told by Boccaccio and which made its way into several Elizabethan narrative and theatrical adaptations, chiefly by way of Chaucer's rendering (in *The Clerk's Tale*) of Petrarch's Latin.

Because, for all practical purposes, a single source can be identified for the main body of *All's Well*, it becomes possible (as it is not in the case of *Troilus*) to trace the play's handling of its inherited characters and plot material in some detail and with some confidence. This project has, of course, been taken up elsewhere, and with a variety of emphases reflecting—naturally enough—various readings of the play.[9] I prefer to face the fact of this interpretative circularity squarely by citing departures from the story of Giletta as they arise in the course of a discussion of the play on its own terms. But we may as well have the most basic differences in mind: besides the Parolles business and the clowning provided by Lavatch, Shakespeare invented the figure of the Countess—symbolically, at least, the source of the play's empowerment of the feminine; he also increased the gap between Helena-Giletta and Bertram (Beltramo in the original) in two respects—by making Helena poor rather than rich (though still of humble birth), as in the original, and by making the male protagonist so thoroughly unattractive that scarcely any commentator has had a good word for him.[10]

Far from pointing towards a resolution of problems, and contrary to the presumption that authors attempt to incorporate source material, however diverse, into a coherent vision, these changes would appear to work in opposite directions, accentuating the split between romance and realism, Medieval and "modern." On the one hand, the element of fairy tale, with its simultaneous insistence on Impossibilities and the certainty of overcoming them, is strengthened: in a double reduction of realism, Helena's situation is made more extreme than Giletta's, even as, paradoxically, she is visibly equipped with more of the tools that will ensure her success. (These include a much more highly developed mystical element in her healing of the King.) On the other hand, both the presentation of Bertram and the material introduced through Parolles and Lavatch reinforce the countertendency toward down-to-earth treatment of characters and situations—a tendency from which, in the view of most modern critics, Helena herself is far from exempt. Indeed, all intertextual roads lead to Helena in a way that tends, with the aid of her name—a further suggestive departure from the source—to overdetermine her. As in the case, again, of Hamlet, who is faced with the challenge of adapting his inherited role as ideal prince to a radically different world, she mediates the text's ethical and stylistic contradictions, at once defining and filling gaps on both levels. She is simultaneously absent and present, passive and active, already inscribed within her text yet rewriting it—and with it, inevitably, herself—from the outside.

Self-Managing Apotheosis

> Here will I dwell, for heaven is in these lips,
> And all is dross that is not Helena.
> —Marlowe, *Faustus*, 18.104–5

These lines, once they are recognized as expressing the blind devotion of Marlowe's Faustus to a devil in the angelic form of Helen of Troy, may be seen as capturing a contradiction between romantic inflation and subversive reality that applies, mutatis mutandis, to *All's Well*. In the third scene of the play, Lavatch seizes the occasion of the Countess's summoning of Helena to recite derogatory verses about the legendary Helen, as if to ratify the audience's readiness to associate the protagonist with her (in)famous namesake. Yet the effect is less to predetermine this Helena's character than to foreground the problematic of interpretation. We recall the dual perspective established in the council scene in *Troilus*, where Helen's "real" danger and worthlessness (in keeping with the debased character given her in direct presentation) is juxtaposed with her elevated status—especially in the eyes of Troilus and even at the cost of Troy's destruction—as "a theme of honor and renown" (*Troilus*, 2.2.199). This parallel with *Troilus* leaves room for irony at Helena's expense, but it more conspicuously prepares us for the glaring inadequacies of Bertram. For once, the venerable conflict between "love" and "honor" will be presented from the former's point of view.

Helena's predilection for, and skill in, scriptwriting, bolstered by the reference in her first soliloquy to "Th' ambition in my love" (1.1.90), have led twentieth-century commentary further and further away from nineteenth-century idealizations of her essentially passive "womanhood"— essentially the view that disgusted Katherine Mansfield[11]—to the point where one recent critic presents her as cynically and successfully plotting virtually every step of the action.[12] Helen as heavenly paragon has threatened to degenerate into Helen as femme fatale, if not witch, even if her capacity for action now appears self-justifying, as it did not even to Joseph G. Price in 1968, who defended her against the charge of being "the aggressive female condemned by so many critics."[13] Extreme readings of Helena as either passive or active are easily recognized as (futile) attempts to erase the text's central "problem."[14] Although they frequently betray antifeminist prejudice, such swings of the critical pendulum ultimately delineate the gender-neutral paradox familiar from *Troilus* (and, with variations, important in both *Hamlet* and, I will suggest, *Measure for Measure*): the role of love's helpless devotee carries within it the potential for the exercise of tyrannical power. Nevertheless, there is a crucial difference between Troilus and Helena: Troilus adopts the role as a sort of stepping-stone to another; love's devotee modulates into love's martyr, as he assumes the heroic mantle of Hector and his immortality as emblem of Truth. Such a progression is hardly open to Helena, so pointedly powerless in consequence of gender and social status; for her, desire and fulfillment must be circumscribed within the sphere of love, made coterminous with the amorous quest that her sighs, like those of Troilus, initially establish as her trajectory. Accordingly, her beloved must prove true, not false; if he is unwilling, she must impose truth upon him, then—again paradoxically—ratify that quality by her submission. In terms of genre, this means that the script she is writing can only be that of a comedy—traditionally the form in which female desire, among other Impossibilities, can be realized.

Helena's much-discussed "ambition" is revealed in this light as a far more complex and profound phenomenon than the crude social-climbing impulse it is sometimes taken to be. I have drawn attention elsewhere to the specific element of class fantasy present in the wish fulfillment served up by the Griselda story, certainly as told by Chaucer and by English Renaissance authors (*Intertextuality*, 87–88). This dimension would help to account for the popularity, too, of the romance of Giletta. But even in this respect, Shakespeare's handling of the story is self-contradictory. True, the gap between Helena and Bertram is made greater (and the fairy-tale appeal accordingly enhanced) by Helena's poverty in a way that matches the altered social conditions of Shakespeare's day, when noble status itself might not have formed the same absolute barrier to marriage with a physician's daughter as it would have for Boccaccio's audience (Zitner, 48–52; Bullough 2: 384). At the same time, her poverty becomes a factor in her eligibility points to the contamination of nobility by mercenary considerations—the stock-in-t(i)rade of Elizabethan satirists—and more generally supports the stylistic shift to realism. As part of this shift, Bertram is made to insist upon the social gap in unflattering ways and seen to lay claim to (or take refuge in) a nobility he scarcely merits.

Even in the matter of the physician's status, realism may have obtruded upon fairy tale for the original audiences more than would appear from the prestige and wealth associated with the medical profession in much Renaissance documentation. Such associations were apparently due, in part, to the "intense interest in medicine of some of the nobility, especially of aristocratic women" (Zitner, 50). Yet it is worth setting side by side with this elevated impression the sardonic comments on some female practitioners made by Thomas Powell (as it happens, the author of *Loues Leprosie*, cited in chapter 2). Powell's 1631 pamphlet, *Tom of All Trades; or, The Plaine Path-Way to Preferment*, administers practical advice to middle-class parents, accompanied by a strong dose of satirical social commentary. If, as is certainly possible, the situation with regard to physicians had altered since the turn of the century,[15] *All's Well* emerges all the more clearly as reflecting, like the other Problem Plays, a period of social and cultural transition. In any case, Powell is at pains to distinguish the objects of his contempt from the exalted variety of healer, whose claims he acknowledges. Given the rarity of the text, the relevant section is worth quoting at length:

For it [the medical profession] is growne to be a very huswives trade, where fortune prevailes more than skill. . . . And the cure of them [common maladies] is the skill of every good old Ladies cast Gentlewoman; when she gives over painting, shee falls to plastering, and shall have as good practize as the best of them for those kind of diseases. . . . Hitherto I speake nothing in disrepute of the more reverend and learned sort of *Phisitions*, who are to be had in singular reverence, and be vsefull to mankind next to the Divine. Indeed, I rather pitty them; and pittying, smile to see how pretily these young gamesters, *Male* and *Female*, lay about them, and engrosse the greater part of *Patientrie* in all places wheresoeuer.[16]

Now Helena, although she is indeed the Gentlewoman of the "good old" Countess of Rossillion, has hardly been "cast" (that is, "dismissed"), but Powell's description remains relevant, especially given its emphasis on the number of medical women at the lower end of the social scale. Helena might plausibly fit into this picture not as one of "the more reverend and learned sort of *Phisitions*"—a status clearly possessed by her father—but as one of the "young gamesters," invoking divine inspiration to support her "skill" yet dependent upon mere "fortune."[17] Yet again, Helena seems poised between "high" and "low" readings of her character and actions.

More directly to the point is that Helena's "ambition" is presented as a matter not of wealth and class but of achieving her goal—that is, of power. Never does she evince material longings, and the play contains no hint of the satirical treatment of bourgeois aspirations so widespread in the Citizen Comedies. Moreover, Shakespeare expunges from his version the detail that, after her unconsummated marriage and her husband's parting for the wars, Giletta takes up her position as lady of the estate of Rossiglione, which she administers with great success. By contrast, and with the help of the Countess—who, paradoxically, in this way *does* serve as a "blocking" figure keeping the heroine from her full fairy-tale triumph—Helena's status is made wholly a private matter involving her personal standing with her husband. But then in Shakespeare's work generally, rising above lowly origins is a very limited aspect of the larger drives for self-realization coded as ambition: perhaps most prominent in this regard are Edmund in *King Lear* and Cardinal Wolsey in *Henry VIII*, and even in these cases the desire for power is paramount. Elsewhere, advancement in terms of wealth and class scarcely enters the ambitious picture.

Helena's wish for "a military policy how virgins might blow up men" (1.1.121–22) confirms that ambition is normally a tragic impulse, functioning in the military-political rather than the romantic sphere and only indirectly exercised by women. (Ambitious women include Lady Macbeth, Volumnia in *Coriolanus*, and the Queen in *Cymbeline*; even more ominously, *King Lear*'s villainesses Goneril and Regan, who manifest an aspect of their mutual jealousy and hunger for power by pursuing Edmund amorously, cross some of the same boundaries as Helena does.) The closest verbal resemblance to Helena's most explicit articulation of her ambition is, somewhat disquietingly, furnished by *Julius Caesar*—a play roughly contemporary with *All's Well*—when Cassius stirs ambition in Brutus by adopting the language conventional for "atheistic" freethinkers on the Elizabethan stage: "Men at some time are masters of their fates; / The fault, dear Brutus, is not in our stars, / But in ourselves, that we are underlings."[18] In her second soliloquy, which expresses her resolution, in effect, to "take arms" against her "sea of troubles" (*Hamlet*, 3.1.58)—the "slings and arrows of outrageous fortune" (*Hamlet*, 3.1.57) perceived as overwhelming in the first soliloquy—Helena begins as follows:

> Our remedies oft in ourselves do lie,
> Which we ascribe to heaven. The fated sky
> Gives us free scope, only doth backward pull
> Our slow designs when we ourselves are dull.
> (1.1.216–19)

These are lines that at least guarantee our surprise when, a few scenes later, she emphatically presents her cure to the King as heaven's remedy, not her own.

To pursue, finally, the oblique but provocative instance of Hamlet, his "sea of troubles" is obviously congruent with the "bad dreams" (*Hamlet*, 2.2.256) and nebulous sense of imprisonment that Rosencrantz and Guildenstern misguidedly, if not malignantly, are eager to reduce to "ambition" of a narrow (and culpable) political kind. They make a clumsy attempt to "get a handle" on a phenomenon so elusive as to be out of reach of Hamlet himself, even after he thinks he knows his grievance (which does, after all, have a political dimension). Like "that within which passes show" (*Hamlet*, 1.2.85), the "heart" of Hamlet's "mystery," which he accuses his old friends of trying to "pluck out" (*Hamlet*, 3.2.365–66), is loudly proclaimed but never expounded. The insistence on "ambition" by Rosencrantz and Guildenstern points up the way in which, wherever it appears in the Shakespearean canon, that term is inevitably an approximation, a sign for an indefinite signified. All in all, the effect of such analogues on a reading of *All's Well* is to make it clear—even while muddying the moral waters—that Helena, rather than aspiring to wealth and status, is chafing against a fundamental, if imperfectly recognized, condition of powerlessness in her life.

Necessarily problematic, as a consequence, is the very erotic drive with which Helena's ambition is amalgamated (although the surface meaning of "Th' ambition in my love" is probably "the ambition *entailed* in my love"). Clearly, we need to broaden our concept of sexuality in Helena's case, just as we need to recognize Troilus's "desire" for Cressida as the sexual expression of a response to the basic terms of his existence. Paradoxically, such recognition is easier because Cressida's default and absence are built into Troilus's desire, whereas the project of Helena depends on securing (that is, not just obtaining, but making fast) Bertram's faithful presence; precisely this achievement is comprehended in his final words—and, one may argue, acknowledged as such, not just made ironically contingent, by his conditional expression: "If she, my liege, can make me know this clearly, / I'll love her dearly, ever, ever dearly" (5.3.315–16).

That the sexual conquest of Bertram is a means to an end is a premise of the action, in keeping with the plot type: the Fulfillment of the Tasks. But that the end has little to do with continuation of a sexual relation for its own sake is suggested in ways reminiscent of *Troilus*. The mid-play going to bed of Troilus and Cressida marks the successful completion of the first phase of Troilus's self-construction; its status as a turning point, even as (on its own terms) a bed trick, is reinforced by the sudden chill introduced into the amorous climate by Troilus, who is eager to be gone even before he knows he must be. The sexual encounter in *All's Well* is, from Bertram's point of view, precisely the sort of casual, quasi-military conquest that Cressida fears—a fear that, I have argued, actually helps make her the "all-time" loser by a different route. Helena's trick turns Bertram's sexual aggression against him, surreptitiously reversing the balance of power so as to fix the future (represented by her pregnancy) to her advantage, as she perceives it.

The true counterpart of Troilus's postcoital victory chill, therefore, is not Bertram's locker-room bravado—the joke, which proves to be on him, about "fearing to hear of [the business] hereafter" (4.3.96–97)— but Helena's rueful commentary, which echoes Cressida's worldly wisdom in the morning-after scene ("You men will never tarry" [*Troilus*, 4.2.16]), and then, in its conclusion, undercuts Bertram's boast in advance:

> But O, strange men,
> That can such sweet use make of what they hate,
> When saucy trusting of the cozen'd thoughts
> Defiles the pitchy night; so lust doth play
> With what it loathes for that which is away—
> But more of this hereafter.
>
> (4.4.21–26)

Many critics have seen Helena's detachment and skepticism here as marking, if not exactly disillusionment, at least a step away from her idealization of Bertram, with whatever feelings this is taken to entail (such as, for Asp, a remarkably Troilus-like "psychological masochism" [Asp, 57] and "narcissism" [Asp, 59]). Even in recent criticism concerned with the problem of feminine subjectivity, there is a tendency to reimpose the optimistic teleology that commentators have commonly resorted to in order to justify the ending as comic in a more than formal way: Helena, and if possible Bertram, must at least *learn* something meaningful to compensate for the fact that she acquires nothing worthwhile. Thus Asp sees her as moving beyond the limits of heterosexual desire into the Symbolic Order, where "she discover[s] the power of feminine bonding" (Asp, 59); according to Barbara Hodgdon, the heroine's experience finally prepares her to join in a "commitment to their [Helena's and Bertram's] shared sexuality" in an ending that "celebrates compromise, the text's final real-izing of romance."[19] Hodgdon usefully notes, "Both Bertram and Helena turn toward the results of their experience, toward endings" (Hodgdon 61) (although Bertram is surely *trying* to turn away). When Helena reaches act 4, scene 4's concluding couplet, however, and in the process entitles the play—thus asserting control over its ending and defining "well" in her own terms—she speaks recognizably with the warrior's voice and echoes, if not Troilus, at least his predecessor (Hector) as the epitome of heroism:

> All's well that ends well! still the fine's the crown;
> What e'er the course, the end is the renown.
> (4.4.35–36)

>   The end crowns all,
> And that old common arbitrator, Time,
> Will one day end it.
>   (*Troilus*, 4.5.224–26)

Ultimately, as in the case of Troilus, it seems less useful to invent a psychological transition for Helena from desire to something else than to allow that her desire is continuing to pursue fulfillment on its own terms, which are comprehensive and flexible. In both *Troilus* and *All's Well*, the trappings of romantic idealization widely taken to denote desire are already in service to broader conditions of being and only provisionally grafted onto sexuality. Stripped of these trappings, sexuality is merely the crude province of Pandarus and Parolles (the latter services, albeit less faithfully, as go-between for Bertram); it is subject to even cruder commentary from Thersites and Lavatch. Above all, as the bed trick's mechanical nature and intimations of interchangeability imply, sexuality in these plays is impersonal, becoming personal only when characters use it as a means of negotiating power relations. Helena's comment after her anonymous tryst with Bertram has more general applicability, as well as more specific relevance to her own subjectivity, than commentators have noticed: "lust doth play / With what it loathes for that which is away" (4.4.24–25). According to psychoanalytic theory, "that which is away" makes perhaps the most accurate definition possible of the object of desire.

All of this goes to show that Helena never really *wants* Bertram any more than he wants her. Ironically, to recognize this is to remove the largest "problem" in the way of reading the play in terms of romantic illusion and disillusion (or compromise or transcendence)—namely, the fact that she never displays the slightest sign of caring whether or not *he* wants *her*. Accordingly, she is not nearly so concerned as are his other virtuous acquaintances by his moral and judgmental lapses, and this has nothing to do with her idealization of him, which is confined to his physical appearance. After the consummation Helena merely adapts to her new and far more satisfactory situation the same distance on her emotional investment that is evident in her first soliloquy: "But now he's gone, and my idolatrous fancy / Must sanctify his reliques" (1.1.97–98). Indeed, Bertram makes a safe focus for a project of self-construction precisely because of both his indifference and his lack of distinction. The example of Cressida shows—and Cressida herself knows—the danger of emotional susceptibility ("more in Troilus thousand-fold I see" [*Troilus*, 1.2.284]) for a woman otherwise powerless within a patriarchal social structure. Bertram may be seen as filling for Helena the sudden vacuum of authority created by a father's absence, but on terms that enable her to regain a form of control over her existence; the same circumstance begets the self-destructive commitment of Cressida to Troilus, and, for that matter, of Hamlet to revenge.

The element of the arbitrary and the personally (not merely, as in the source, socially) inappropriate in Helena's fixation on Bertram is therefore, paradoxically, the key to her production of a conventionally comic ending. The fairy-tale structure of the story, its Impossibilities, are in this way, too, brought down to earth: the heroine's machinations match the quality of her love. And in practical terms, the capacity for strategic thinking underlying her "warmth" offers her an enormous advantage over the muddled responses of the "cold" Bertram. In fact, what the text and its critics generally take as Bertram's "coldness," thanks in part to Helena's sympathetic allies, contains the most potent emotionality in the play: he experiences sheer revulsion at the idea of marrying Helena, and he is reduced to quivering jelly in the final scene—features added by Shakespeare to the equivalent episodes in the story of Giletta. In contrast, Helena's self-control in both instances, as elsewhere, remains intact.

This element of self-restraint as a means of self-protection recalls Cressida, especially her answer, taking up the imagery of combat, to Pandarus's question about her "ward": "Upon my back, to defend my belly, upon my wit, to defend my wiles, upon my secrecy, to defend mine honesty" (*Troilus*, 1.2.260–62). Sexual "intactness," coded as virginity ("intact" derives from the Latin for "untouched"), is the supreme token of vulnerability because, as recent feminist analyses have made clear, virginity is the primary source of value for women within the economy of patriarchal exchange.[20] Helena's achievement involves converting this vulnerability into a source of power, exploiting, in such a way as to exert maximum leverage, its status as what both feminist discourse and Parolles term a "commodity" (1.1.153)—a status even more clearly defined later through Diana, whose name marks her as incarnating virginity itself. The question of how virginity may be turned from liability into asset is the subject—pursued if not initiated by her—of Helena's bantering prose dialogue with Parolles (the rough equivalent of Cressida's with Pandarus).

The conversation with Parolles in act 1, scene 1, mediates between the scene's two soliloquies—between, in effect, the onslaught of the "sea of troubles" and the resolution to "take up arms" against it. Here Helena translates her sense of the "slings and arrows of outrageous fortune" into the terms of sexual politics, lamenting women's passive vulnerability to male sexual aggression: "Man is enemy to virginity; how may we barricado it against him?" (1.1.112–13). Yet once the issue of sexuality as power is out in the open, power is up for grabs. In the exchange that follows, she enacts in her rhetorical procedures the very practice she describes, as she subverts Parolles' reference to the technique of mining in siege warfare by suggesting the possibility of countermining, the turning of the tables on the aggressor through the use of the same weapon:

> *Par.*   . . . Man, setting down before you, will
>   undermine you and blow you up.
>
> *Hel.*   Bless our poor virginity from underminers
>   and blowers-up. Is there no military policy how virgins might
>   blow up men?
>
> (1.1.118–22)

The insinuation of subterfuge would be more strongly present for an Elizabethan audience thanks to the term "policy," which, like "politician," carried negative connotations. And when "blowing up" is recognized as alluding to pregnancy, as well as sexual arousal—Parolles' reply is "Virginity being blown down, man will quicklier be blown up" (1.1.123–24)—the specific relevance of this discussion to Helena's final satisfying of Bertram's "impossible" conditions becomes evident.

Parolles continues to remind Helena of female sexual and social dependency by making witty arguments, on economic and moral grounds, that virginity has value only in its loss.[21] What he does not see is that the concept of self-defense remains attached to her question, "How might one do, sir, to lose it to her own liking?" (1.1.150–51), and modulates into self-assertion as she parries his gesture of mock-seduction:

> *Par.* . . . Will you any thing with it?
> *Hel.* Not my virginity yet: . . .
> (1.1.163–65)

This enigmatic last line is generally taken to be incomplete as a result of textual corruption, and to be followed by an accidental gap in sense, although rationales can be supplied for the disjunctive effect.[22] In any case, Helena ends the exchange by returning to the romantic vein, but in a way that incorporates an admixture of frank sexual thinking and projects at once a far more realistic appraisal of Bertram and an imagined reversal of the balance of power; she now laments the fact not that she cannot gaze worshipfully at him but that she cannot keep an eye on him for other reasons:

> *Hel.* There shall your master have a thousand loves,
> . . . .
>   Now shall he—
> I know not what he shall—God send him well!
> The court's a learning place, and he is one—
> *Par.* What one, i' faith?
> *Hel.* That I wish well. 'Tis pity—
> *Par.* What's pity?
> *Hel.* That wishing well had not a body in't.
> (1.1.168–81)

The new dimension of self-interest, sexual aggression, and possessiveness signalled here feeds into the confident sense of mission expressed in the soliloquy that concludes the scene:

> Who ever strove
> To show her merit, that did miss her love?
> The King's disease—my project may deceive me,
> But my intents are fix'd, and will not leave me.
>   (1.1.226–29)

It is curious that Helena's interest and skill in bawdy discourse—by answering (truthfully) "Ay," she immediately matches the aggression of Parolles' cheeky opening gambit, "Are you meditating on virginity?" (1.1.110)—have not led commentators to such conclusions about her "looseness" as are commonly drawn from Cressida's manner of speaking. After all, although virginity as such is never made an issue in *Troilus*, the play introduces Cressida as chaste; moreover, she is seemingly not a widow, as in Chaucer's version—a change that removes the implication of unruly sexual appetite and loose morals stereotypically associated with that status. Helena is, in fact, far more aggressive emotionally and sexually than Cressida, yet even in the prudish nineteenth century her reputation for purity generally survived, indeed increased. One might attribute this estimation of her character not only to her status as a fairy-tale heroine, as opposed to Cressida's legendary reputation for female falseness, but also to her effectively agreeing, in playing the sexual game, to play by the patriarchal rules, which do not allow for women's desire. From the patriarchal perspective, a genuine sexual impulse would constitute a degrading flaw, as is evinced by the remark of E. K. Chambers in 1908 that the bed trick "is a measure of the spiritual straits to which the instinct of sex has reduced the noblest of women" (cited in G. K. Hunter, Introduction, xlix). In other words, the majority of commentators unwittingly may have been responding to Helena's lack of genuine sexual interest in her love object, to the primacy in her project of, in effect, the domestication of Bertram, which will render him respectable. More specifically, her project will result, not only in his reform but in his taking his place within the patriarchal structure—and so both renewing and revalidating it. We should not forget that the child-to-be that enables the fulfillment of Helena's romantic dream will also provide an heir for Rossillion. It is in these respects that Helena furnishes the sharpest contrast with Cressida.

Because the first scene closely charts Helena's emotional position and developing resolution, when the Countess confronts Helena with her discovery of the secret passion in act 1, scene 3, a discrepancy in understanding is apparent beneath the surface of harmony and sympathy. This gap, which problematizes the superficially idealized picture of female bonding, is reflected in contrasting attitudes toward time—a major issue in the play, as will later become more evident. We have just witnessed Helena shifting in orientation from the past to the future: rather than worshiping the relics of her departed saint, much less remembering her father, she is taking the future into her own hands. Yet the Countess remains committed to the past, in keeping with her attitude at the opening of the play that her son's future means a doubling of her loss. From the vantage point of a sort of suspended animation, she measures Helena's feelings by her "remembrances of days foregone" (1.3.134), with a nostalgic emphasis on the sense of being fully alive that accompanies romantic love. As is the case elsewhere in Shakespeare, the imagery of natural growth throws into relief her resistance to time and change:[23]

> Even so it was with me when I was young.
> If ever we are nature's, these are ours. This thorn
> Doth to our rose of youth rightly belong;
> Our blood to us, this to our blood is born.
> It is the show and seal of nature's truth,
> Where love's strong passion is impress'd in youth.
>   (1.3.128–33)

The temporal dimension at once complicates and simplifies the much-discussed incest motif introduced in this scene—or, rather, picked up from the Countess's reference to Bertram as a "second husband" in the play's first lines. Psychoanalytically oriented critics regularly notice that Helena's extreme resistance to the Countess's casting herself in the role of mother ("When I said 'a mother,' / Methought you saw a serpent" [1.3.140–41]) appears to issue from a level deeper than that on which both Helena and the Countess are dealing—that is, beneath the logical implication that Bertram is Helena's brother and therefore ineligible to be her husband. The suggestion of buried incestuous feelings lends itself to teleological readings in terms of character development; it has been taken to indicate the need of Helena or Bertram or both to free themselves from various psychological entanglements in order to realize a "mature" sexual relationship.[24] As is necessarily the case with such approaches, however, the more specific the analysis, the more dependent it becomes on extratextual assumptions.

It may help instead to broaden the picture by considering the implications of the idea of incest for the play world as a whole: it is an idea, after all, built into the plot structure, thanks to the series of symbolic substitutions set in motion at the opening. There the Countess's husband is linked not only with Bertram but with the King—a connection soon confirmed by the latter's melancholic nostalgia about his friend: "Would I were with him! He would always say— / Methinks I hear him now" (1.2.52–53). As a result, incestuous overtones accrue to the King's sexual feelings for Helena, which obviously figure in his intense sponsorship of the match with Bertram. (Note the indirect allusion to these feelings in Bertram's protest, "But follows it, my lord, to bring me down / Must answer for your raising?" [2.3.112–13].) The complete pattern that emerges, however, carries broader significance relating to the division between past and present, age and youth. What may be thought of as the incestuous initiative flows from the older generation, beginning with the opening exchange between Lafew and the Countess; it involves recasting the younger generation in terms of the older—Helena as the Countess's daughter, Bertram as her (and the King's) son. The motif serves as an index, therefore of that generation's backward and inward lookingness; its attempts to reproduce the past are highlighted as at once a futile response to, and a measure of, its own entropy.

Thus, when Helena, whose links with the past world are the key to her acceptance by the Countess and the King, has supposedly died, a substitute match for Bertram is also "dug up" from amongst the old crowd—a hitherto unmentioned daughter of Lafew, whose betrothal, moreover, comes complete with a previous royal sanction that was itself an act of "remembrance":

I mov'd the King my master to speak in the behalf of my daughter, which in the minority of them both, his Majesty, out of a self-gracious remembrance, did first propose.

(4.5.71–74)

Indeed, by comparison with such a pedigree, Helena's position as parvenue is recalled, and even though the Countess precedes this discussion by praising her again as a virtual daughter ("If she had partaken of my flesh, and cost me the dearest groans of a mother, I could not have ow'd her a more rooted love" [4.5.10–12]) the elegiac distance, the contrary-to-fact condition, and the hint of obligation contrast with the insistent immediacy with which she initially imposed herself in this role: "I say I am your mother, / And put you in the catalogue of those / That were enwombed mine" (1.3.142–44). In keeping with Lafew's benediction—"We may pick a thousand sallets ere we light on such another herb" (4.5.13–15)—the "best" of Helena has been smoothly garnered in the form of memory, safely absorbed into the not displeasing mythology of the past.

Or so they think. The abrupt introduction here of an unsuspected and superconvenient substitute for the dead Helena is a recognizable romantic-comic plot device that might be expected to serve as prelude to, and "cover" for, her revival. Thus, in *Much Ado about Nothing* Leonato arranges for Hero to return to life by obliging Claudio, the misogynistic soldier-aristocrat (with a strong family resemblance to Bertram) whose unkindness has supposedly been the death of Leonato's daughter, to accept his niece instead—"Almost the copy of my child that's dead."[25] Since the scheme being formulated by Lafew and the Countess, with the abettance of the King, has no such covert aim, yet Helena will be restored notwithstanding—to their great joy, undoubtedly, but also to some degree at their expense—the structuring of *All's Well* in terms of competing scripts becomes starkly apparent. Beneath the surface of a community of interests, the scenario that is the vehicle of Helena's project clashes with that of the older generation, according to which the young merely take on their elders' identities. Theirs is the scenario, moreover, to which Bertram, despite his disobedient rejection of Helena, essentially conforms in so strongly defending the family heritage: the revised proposal, however accompanied with reproaches, in effect rewards him with precisely the sort of "noble" match he has held out for.

Far from abandoning the theme of generational conflict characteristic of romantic comedy, therefore, *All's Well* deepens and problematizes it. On the one hand, an alliance is struck at the start—not just grasped in retrospect, as in most examples of the genre—between the cause of romantic love and that of social renewal, here figured in the motif of the Healing of the King. On the other hand, since Helena's project not only cuts deeper than the fulfillment of such love for its own sake but actually runs contrary to the interests of her allies, she faces the complex challenge of pursuing her goal without allowing her efforts to be appropriated, her self-construction placed in service to that of others.

This brings us back to Helena's violent objection to the Countess's attempt to inscribe her as daughter in act 1, scene 3. What Helena most basically refuses to accept is not that role in itself but the particular symbolic order that it entails, according to which, in perhaps the ultimate form of incest, she would be called upon to enact a parent's possessiveness. The gap in communication, according to which the Countess presumes Helena's vulnerability and malleability, her abjection in the throes of romantic love, finally serves to illustrate that Helena is far from alone in using sexuality as a source of power—that, indeed, these are the terms in which her society habitually functions. Helena is, in other words, fighting fire with fire, and she manages her weapon shrewdly enough to enlist, by the end of the scene, not only the Countess's practical aid ("Means and attendants, and my loving greetings / To those of mine in court" [1.3.252–53]) but her prayers—the spiritual dimension that is the text's index, here as elsewhere, of a romantic overlay upon the mechanisms of power. Moreover, she will play by the play world's rules even in wooing Bertram through his sponsoring parent figure and taking him, in effect, as the King's stand-in.

Yet the bond thus sealed with the Countess is conspicuously missing the fine print: Helena admits that she loves Bertram, that she aims to cure the King, and that the two points are connected in her mind; she certainly does not communicate her more dubious intention to maneuver the very emblem of patriarchal power into enforcing her marriage. As Zitner insists (Zitner, 96), she is not actually deceiving the Countess. Still, this is the first of a series of withholdings that culminates in Helena's cruelly keeping the older woman ignorant of the fact that she is alive. Arguably, then, she practices such withholding not despite but precisely because of the Countess's bestowal of "a mother's care" (1.3.148). It is also notable that Helena fails from the start to share full details of her plans with the audience in soliloquy: "The King's disease—my project may deceive me, / But my intents are fix'd, and will not leave me" (1.1.228–29). Already, she has passed beyond Hamlet's handicap of substituting talk for action.

That sexuality is bound up with the exercise of power is abundantly evident from Helena's modus operandi even before the bed trick crystallizes the fact. Her effect, first on Lafew, then on the King, is reminiscent of the feigned prescription for animating the supposedly moribund protagonist of Jonson's satirical play *Volpone* (1606)—the proximity of female flesh "Lusty, and full of juice."[26] The phallic suggestions in Lafew's speech ("araise," "pen") lead the King to intimations of orgasm ("spend our wonder"):

> *Laf.*   I have seen a medicine
> That's able to breathe life into a stone,
> Quicken a rock, and make you dance canary
> With spritely fire and motion, whose simple touch
> Is powerful to araise King Pippen, nay,
> To give great Charlemain a pen in 's hand
> And write to her a love-line.
>
> . . . .
>
> *King.*   Now, good Lafew,
> Bring in the admiration, that we with thee
> May spend our wonder too, or take off thine
> By wond'ring how thou took'st it.
>
>   (2.1.72–89)[27]

In serving as go-between in this quasi-sexual transaction, Lafew develops a passing resemblance to Pandarus (besides anticipating the pandering activities of his own bête noire—and to some extent shadow self—Parolles). Helena, like Troilus, thus enjoys the practical benefit of mediation on the sexual level while retaining her purity; she, too, is free to pursue her interests exclusively in terms of idealism and spirituality. And as in the case of Troilus, this division continues a dichotomy between expressions of romantic longing and a counterdiscourse of down-to-earth achievement.

Helena, however, like shrewd soldiers before and after her (including some prominent Shakespearean ones[28]), consistently couches her "policy," which is already beginning to "blow up men," in terms of doing heaven's will ("But most it is presumption in us when / The help of heaven we count the act of men" [2.1.151–52]), despite her premise that "Our remedies oft in ourselves do lie, / Which we ascribe to heaven" (1.1.216–17). Her manipulation of heaven is nowhere more apparent than when she is engineering the final "miracle." Having paid the Widow and engineered the supposed encounter between Bertram and Diana, Helena assures the Widow,

> Doubt not but heaven
> Hath brought me up to be your daughter's dower,
> As it hath fated her to be my motive
> And helper to such a husband.
>
>   (4.4.18–21)

An unsettlingly close echo here is Hamlet's covering of his bloody tracks on the less happy occasion of the killing of Polonius: "heaven hath pleas'd it so / To punish me with this, and this with me, / That I must be their scourge and minister" (*Hamlet*, 3.4.173–75).

To take Helena as an embodiment of divine grace, then, as a strain of allegorizing commentary has been wont to do, beginning with G. Wilson Knight,[29] is actually to take her on her own terms. Helena's divinity, however, is not simply a symbolic means to a substantial end; it is part of the end itself, which involves not just acquiring Bertram but consolidating a kind of magically realized identity and transcendent power through him. Her role as heaven's minister is more than a method of getting the King to try her cure ("Of heaven, not me, make an experiment" [2.1.154]); the cure's ultimate success, the remedy she seeks for herself, depends on the experiment's having been conducted in these terms, so that she emerges not just as the instrument of her "dear father's gift" (2.1.112) possessing, again, a derivative identity but as a miracle worker with a power to awe that goes beyond more sexual attraction. (Sexuality in itself, as subsequent events make clear, is quite anonymous.) And, indeed, it is a kind of miracle to give birth to oneself. We may compare, in this respect, the way in which Portia in *The Merchant of Venice* initially chafes under the restraints of her father's "will" (in a double sense), then adapts it to her own romantic will, investing the process with supernatural overtones. It is Helena's only possible strategy, therefore, to approach the King like Helen of Troy enchanting Faustus, with "heaven," if not quite in her lips, at least in her prescription pad.[30]

In light of the parallel with Troilus, it is all the more striking that Helena establishes her bargain with the King not merely in terms of her own transcendent "truth" (recoded as heavenly grace) but also in terms of the precise consequences Cressida incurs—and agrees to incur, at Troilus's instigation—for betraying such truth. In the story of Giletta, the heroine merely stakes her life; in Shakespeare's text, Helena interposes a very different, and surprising, answer to the King's question, "What dar'st thou venter?" (2.1.170):

> Tax of impudence,
> A strumpet's boldness, a divulged shame,
> Traduc'd by odious ballads; my maiden's name
> Sear'd otherwise; ne worst of worst—extended
> With vildest torture, let my life be ended.
>
> (2.1.170–74)

Again, we are reminded that virginity, whose "flip side" is whoredom, is the battlefield on which, faute de mieux, Helena is choosing to fight.[31] In effect, she must adapt the vulnerability of Cressida to her Troilus-like project of erotic aggression.

The precedent of Cressida confirms that, even as Helena appears to establish the rules of the game, there is no way she can truly make it her own. Consequently, thanks especially to the text's not remaining at the level of fairy tale in its treatment of Bertram, winning will also mean losing. In this context, the confusingly elaborate concluding scene scripted by Helena emerges as a means of acquiring moral and psychological leverage over the man whom she has already "achieved" as, paradoxically, her legal lord and master. Again, a comparison may be made with Portia, a fairy-tale heroine who does not consummate her marriage with the man of her choice—despite his willingness, in that case—until she has conducted an elaborate stratagem, also turning on his compromising gift of a ring, by which she imposes an unfulfillable obligation upon him.[32] But equally significant is the resemblance of *All's Well* to *Troilus*, where the two successive stages of the protagonist's self-construction involve possessing his beloved, then proving her unworthy.

This point returns us to the Troilus-like element of love-martyrdom that figures in Helena's presentation. Even after she has discarded, in the second soliloquy, the image of passive sufferer defined in the first, she allows others to impose this role on her, beginning with the Countess. The discrepancy between such an image and the new reality is focused in the scene where she makes her public choice of Bertram.[33] Here not only does she possess "power to choose, and they none to forsake" (2.3.56), as the King establishes, but she herself structures the scene so as to create suspense and build towards a climax—a foretaste of the final episode, which does not prove similarly anticlimactic—by eliminating the other eligible prospects one by one before turning to Bertram. Each of these lords welcomes the possibility that he is her choice (unless their demeanor contradicts their words—a "problem-solving" staging that is sometimes adopted). Yet the onlooking Lafew, accompanied by Parolles, misreads the situation, evidently responding to Helena's mournful manner: "Do they all deny her? And they were sons of mine, I'd have them whipt" (2.3.86–87). This makes for a curious reversal of the situation in the night visitation scene in *Troilus*, where the female figure, courted by a male and responding ambiguously, is the victim rather than the beneficiary of a rival male who casts himself in the martyr's role; again,

Helena, from the position of Cressida, appropriates at least some of the prerogatives of Troilus.

When Helena is refused by Bertram, her public martyrdom actually strengthens her moral and emotional hand, which she employs so as to confirm her gain, however qualified. Bertram's effective reminder that love cannot be compelled—"I cannot love her, nor will strive to do't" (2.3.145)—seems momentarily to stymie the King: "Thou wrong'st thyself, if thou shouldst strive to choose" (2.3.146). By intervening at this point with an indirect reminder of the King's obligation and her pitiful state—"That you are well restor'd, my lord, I'm glad. / Let the rest go" (2.3.147)—Helena provokes him to an angry resolution: "My honor's at the stake, which to defeat, / I must produce my power" (2.3.149–50). Accordingly, he compels the match, though with an alienating tyranny that recalls Old Capulet's anger towards Juliet and anticipates King Lear's attempt to impose his will on his recalcitrant daughter Cordelia; indeed, Bertram benefits, in passing, from the sympathy usually accorded by an audience to female victims of love-controlling patriarchs. His subsequent churlishness, with the contempt he has clearly earned from Lafew—contempt that immediately issues, significantly, against Parolles—tends to restore the balance in favor of Helena. But her regression to the role of martyr, now again internalized, is so extreme as to forestall the audience's thorough identification with her.

Certainly, the excessive humility in her abject soliloquy at the conclusion of act 3, scene 3, has disturbed many critics:

> Poor lord, is't I
> That chase thee from thy country, and expose
> Those tender limbs of thine to the event
> Of the none-sparing war? And is it I
> That drive thee from the sportive court, where thou
> Wast shot at with fair eyes, to be the mark
> Of smoky muskets? O you leaden messengers,
> That ride upon the violent speed of fire,
> Fly with false aim, move the still-peering air
> That sings with piercing, do not touch my lord.
> Whoever shoots at him, I sent him there;
> . . . .
>   Come night, end day!
> For with the dark, poor thief, I'll steal away.
>   (3.2.102–29)

Part of what disturbs the critics, I think, is that lurking behind, or rather within, the overwhelming self-pity lies a new sense of potency: it is *she* who has done all this, after all, including removing Bertram from the vicinity of court ladies—the potential rivals she feared in the first scene (1.1.166ff.). In this backhanded way, Helena has acquired imaginative power over life and death, which she freely indulges. Hostility and anger at her rejection cannot be expressed directly, as in the case of Troilus; nor can she move on to another subject position: these are male prerogatives. Rather, her feelings must be adapted to recovering the lost object. By leaving, she says, she can induce him to return home; but we soon learn—not directly from her, however—that she leaves in order to bring him home herself, on her own conditions. And her ability to do this continues to depend on the position she occupies, in the eyes of all but Bertram himself, of love's martyr. Getting him to accept her in that role will involve a triumph not merely over his freedom to choose but over his will to do so.

Bertram and the Subplot

The process by which Helena arrives at her goal appears straightforward, once the nature of the goal is grasped, compared with the mechanisms that render Bertram even superficially suitable as a match for her. That very superficiality throws into relief Helena's "unworthy" choice by way of a simple but sharp contrast between the extraordinary and the ordinary. For Bertram takes further than any other male "lead" in Shakespearean romantic comedy the tendency present in all of them towards sheer banality. This banality is more striking, in the final analysis, than Bertram's lapses in propriety and simple decency; thus it is an uphill struggle—both for critics and, more important, for interested characters—to make much of his reformation. It is less that the raw material is so resistant to molding than that there is so little of it to work with.

Even in the first scenes, there is a sense of Bertram as appendage to the action, as object rather than subject. The indications of youthful promise that romantic heroes conventionally inherit from illustrious fathers—the extreme case is Orlando in *As You Like It*—are only dimly present, couched in skeptical terms that insinuate a "falling-off." This is to return momentarily to *Hamlet*, the intertext that informs the opening, by borrowing the phrase of the Ghost (*Hamlet*, 1.5.47)—an expression that, though it immediately refers to Gertrude's remarriage, also suggests the broader moral and spiritual diminution in which Hamlet himself notably participates. He, too, introduced as a background figure, is called upon to play a role for which he is doubtfully fit, though his heroism happens to be of the tragic variety.

When Bertram actually speaks, his ignorance of the King's illness seems to us as strange as Lafew obviously finds it ("I would it were not notorious" [1.1.36]); the pattern of social gaffe and rebuke in this exchange is clear.[34] Bertram's mother's advice has a most un-Polonius-like note of real concern. And in receiving him at court, the King exclaims, "Thy father's moral parts / Mayst thou inherit too" (1.2.21–22), longing wistfully rather than confidently expecting. This attitude is soon broadened to include the general decline of the younger generation as the King and others perceive it. It seems that a sterling model such as Bertram's father could at best serve (even as he does in the King's memory) merely to expose the nonentities of the present age; to rouse them to emulation is evidently out of the question:

> Such a man
> Might be a copy to these younger times;
> Which followed well, would demonstrate them now
> But goers backward.
>
> (1.2.45–48)

It says much that Bertram approaches the capacity to engage an audience in his subjectivity only when he says no to the King and when, in his petulant letter to his mother, he reports his oath to "make the 'not' eternal" (3.2.22)—a pun that will finally be turned against him. Similarly negative is his setting of conditions that seem to guarantee he will "never" (3.2.60) be a husband, as well as his remarkably self-defeating, if not self-denying, declaration in the letter to Helena, "Till I have no wife, I have nothing in France" (3.2.75 and 99). In bringing this line to the attention of the Countess, Helena sets the seal on the mother-child alliance between the two women. This alliance no longer poses a threat to Helena, not only for the obvious reason that the "incestuous" match has been made but also because only his mother can effect the dispossession and disempowerment of Bertram—a necessary condition of his eventual reinstatement on Helena's terms and under her authority: "He was my son, / But I do wash his name out of my blood, / And thou art all my child (3.2.66–68).

The Countess's own negativity here may seem excessive, imbued with

a suggestion of the tragically tyrannical, self-deluded actions of disin-
heriting parents elsewhere—especially Gloucester (provoked by a *forged*
letter) and Lear, who, having earlier disowned Cordelia for responding
with "nothing"[35] to his proffer of dower and husband, is reduced to
attempting to prefer Goneril to Regan: "thou art twice her love" (*Lear*,
2.4.260). In *All's Well* there is just a touch of the sympathy evoked for
outcast children in that later tragedy—enough, at least, to make the
point that Bertram is consistently an entity defined, by others as well as
himself, in terms of lacks and negatives; this negativity is an awkward
drag on the role of romantic hero that the genre has cast him in.[36] It will
take an internal dramatist to revivify the comic mechanism and reinte-
grate him into that role. Therein consist both Helena's challenge and her
opportunity. What finally makes Bertram a match for Helena as part of
a conventional romance conclusion is precisely the fact that in all other
respects he is not one.

Nevertheless, critics have often found in the subplot indications of at
least a symbolic working out of Bertram's defects. In this view, the
exposure of Parolles' empty pretenses to "manhood," even if it does not
produce a discernible change of heart in Bertram, at least enacts a process
of self-discovery, even of sexual maturation, on the hero's behalf. Parolles
is constituted as a scapegoat, and in expelling him from his influential
position as Bertram's companion the play world indicates the displacement of destructive internal influences.[37] The obvious difficulty with
this reading is that it depends largely on interested characters within the
text, who appear to strain the evidence. More significant, however, is the
fact that such an interpretation runs counter, paradoxically, to Helena's
own script. For by the time of Parolles' "capture" and humiliation,
Helena's project has reached the point of requiring her supposed death,
while the "purified" Bertram appears destined for a substitute match
acceptable to all other parties.

Even in devising their play-within-the-play in order to expose the
"counterfeit" (4.3.34) Parolles—a goal that extends to curing Bertram's
general moral blindness, which they also blame for his treatment of
Helena (4.3.1ff.)—his friends effectively set themselves up as rival
dramatists. There is a striking juxtaposition between the close of act 3,
scene 7, and the opening of act 4, where their plot is vividly set in motion
("He can come no other way but by this hedge-corner" [4.1.1–2]). The
previous scene concludes with Helena's final preparations to enact a
scenario invested, as her paradoxical language suggests, with an almost
mystical power to transcend ordinary moral categories:

> Let us assay our plot, which if it speed,
> Is wicked meaning in a lawful deed,
> And lawful meaning in a lawful act,
> Where both not sin, and yet a sinful fact.
>
> (3.7.44–47)

Her preparations, it should be noted, involve paying the actors generously—another obstacle to overemphasizing the power of female bonding. Virginity's status as a commodity exploitable by Helena is never more obvious than in her use of money to procure, through the Widow, Diana's feigned assent to Bertram:

> Take this purse of gold,
> And let me buy your friendly help thus far,
> Which I will over-pay and pay again
> When I have found it.
>
> (3.7.14–17)

This bed trick, then, like that in *Measure for Measure*, is effected by a version, however virtuous in intention, of bawdlike mediation. There is another disturbing hint in the fact that Helena most immediately owes her status as "great in fortune" (3.7.14) to the unsuspecting Countess, whom she has deceived by pretending to undertake a mortifying pilgrimage ("barefoot plod I the cold ground upon" [3.4.6]). In effect, she helps herself freely to the practical benefits of this alliance while violating its emotional terms. Helena even undertakes to exercise a power like that previously wielded by the King in her own case ("honor and wealth from me" [2.3.144])—the ability to transform a poor virgin into a marriageable commodity: "After, / To marry her, I'll add three thousand crowns / To what is pass'd already" (3.7.34–36). In this context, the honest but poor Widow's assent—"I have yielded" (3.7.36)—has a distinct air of being against her better judgment.

The scene in which Parolles is induced to abuse Bertram and the other lords (act 4, scene 3) is another involving the issue of "reading" the significance of a staged action. The issue is focused by the prominent role of language—the nonsense that Parolles takes for sense, his dependence on an "Interpreter," the reading aloud of his letter to Diana, and of course his name itself: a true "reading" of his character will reveal that he is nothing but words (*paroles*). His initial fear when ambushed, "I shall lose my life for want of language" (4.1.70), proves groundless; it is his volubility that undoes him, stripping away the image that language alone had constructed and sustained. His acknowledgment of this undoing pays an indirect tribute to the power of theatricality that equally applies to the main action—including, it will become ironically apparent, his former master: "Who cannot be crush'd with a plot?" (4.3.325).

Yet when Parolles is left alone, deprived of the power of words, he insists on a distinction between words and what they represent; there is, he maintains, an essence that remains untouched and that will provide a basis for survival: "Simply the thing I am / Shall make me live" (4.3.333–34). His very capacity to soliloquize lends substance to his determination to reconstruct himself: "Being fool'd, by fool'ry thrive! / There's place and means for every man alive. / I'll after them" (4.3.338–40). And, indeed, by the end of the play he has got a "place"—as source of "sport" to Lafew (5.3.323). Parolles' is, on the most basic level, the typical resilience of the Shakespearean low-comic figure, hence of the forces such characters represent. A particularly close parallel is with the egregious miles gloriosus Pistol in *Henry V*, who, when his cowardice is exposed, instantly forms a similar resolution—one that also involves capitalizing on his very chastisement, as well as actually taking on one role (that of bawd) that Parolles has forfeited:

> Old I do wax, and from my weary limbs
> Honor is cudgell'd. Well, bawd I'll turn,
> And something lean to cutpurse of quick hand.
> To England will I steal, and there I'll steal;
> And patches will I get unto these cudgell'd scars,
> And swear I got them in the Gallia wars.[38]

More immediately revealing, however, are the analogues in the other Problem Plays. I have suggested that the thorough impotence of the spurned Pandarus in *Troilus* shows abundantly through his vision of the future in his final address to the audience. That "misleader" of a "noble" youth is so decisively squelched by the youth himself that there is nothing left of him but the diseases that will shortly carry him off. In *Measure for Measure*, moreover, the slandering Lucio is conspicuously crushed—and silenced—beyond recovery.

From this perspective, the resilience of Parolles, with its implication of an essence ("the thing itself") lying untouched behind the demolished wall of words, becomes a comment on the limited efficacy of the scapegoating scenario in *All's Well*. For it is striking that unlike Helena in the scenes of husband-choosing, secret trysting, and final disclosure, the instigators of this plot fail to remain in control of their material or to effect the ultimate result they intended. On the one hand, Parolles, in the course of exposing himself, slings his mud more abundantly and vigorously than might have been expected, blurring the edges of what was supposed to be a clear-cut object lesson. On the other hand, Bertram, the purported object of that lesson, conspicuously fails to "read," even in Parolles' letter warning Diana against him as exactly what he is—a casual seducer—the slightest criticism of himself. Rather, he shrinks from confrontation with his unflattering mirror image, withdrawing into solipsistic anger—a move that carries the stamp of infantile regression: "I could endure any thing before but a cat, and now he's a cat to me" (4.3.237–38).[39]

As Parolles' self-assessment makes explicit, he has been made a *fool* of, and this is a role that cuts two ways. A fool's truth telling is always foolish by definition—this is what allows the option of dismissing it (and hence affords the fool his "license"); as the master-fool dynamic in *King Lear* demonstrates, the measure of openness to self-knowledge is whether or not one chooses to take such truths to heart despite their origin. Here, even the Interpreter reads Parolles' disclosures in such a way as to deflect their tenor, and he does so by way of the standard obverse of military misogyny—the chivalrous defending of women's honor, although it is hardly women who have been shamed: "If you could find out a country where but women were that had receiv'd so much shame, you might begin an impudent nation" (4.3.326–28). Such interpretation reveals that the stigmatizing of Parolles, by purporting to separate false words from "true" things, serves not only Bertram's self-image but that of the society at large. Scoured of the tarnish associated with Parolles, the quality of "honor" shines more brightly than ever. This is to stop well short of the theater's ultimate power, as Helena wields it, to destabilize and reconstruct "simply the thing" itself. Yet the broader context is kept present by one statement Parolles makes that resonates with an irony, accessible to neither of them, at Bertram's expense: the characterization of Bertram as "a whale to virginity" that "devours up all the fry it finds" (4.3.220–21) is a reminder that there is a bigger fish yet that has already (literally) got him in her belly, having found out the "policy how virgins might blow up men" (1.1.121–22).

Critics who take this scapegoating exercise as justifying Bertram's rehabilitation are following the line laid down by the figures of authority within the play world. Act 4, scene 5, opens in the midst of a conversation between Lafew and the Countess, who are cementing the substitute match between Bertram and Lafew's daughter. To this match the King has now lent his endorsement, not only "stop[ping] up the displeasure he hath conceiv'd" (4.5.75–76) but returning to the original order of things. Lafew's first words, "No, no, no, your son was misled with a snipt-taffata fellow there" (4.5.1–2), are obviously a response to the residual blame attached by the Countess to her son, but the negative iteration also suggests, as elsewhere in Shakespeare,[40] the impulse to deny unwelcome truths. The King's reception of Bertram in the final scene confirms that this is a world seeking, now that Helena is tragically but safely dead, to put an uncomfortable interlude behind it, renewing itself—for the pressure of time and mortality remains intense—in its own ("incestuous") way:

> All is whole,
> Not one word more of the consumed time.
> Let's take the instant by the forward top;
> For we are old, and on our quick'st decrees
> Th' inaudible and noiseless foot of time
> Steals ere we can effect them.
>
> (5.3.37–42)

This is, ironically, to redeem Helena, whose counterplot is about to thwart his "quick'st decrees," from "consumed time," by casting her in the role of time itself—a medium that does, in fact, lie within the (meta)dramatist's prerogative.

Lafew's bantering exchange with the Clown Lavatch, as he and the Countess plan Bertram's wedding and elegiacally consign Helena to the misty past, brings out the limited efficacy of "fooling," which has been less directly demonstrated by the exposure of Parolles (previously linked with Lavatch as fool [2.4.32ff.]).[41] This is the Clown's last appearance and the nadir of his subversiveness, which has been expressed, as is typical of his role, in sexual terms.[42] Early in the play, Lavatch presents himself as both sexually and diabolically "driven" in his desire to marry Isbel: "I am driven on by the flesh, and he must needs go that the devil drives" (1.3.28–30). After exposure to the world of the court, he "begin[s] to love, as an old man loves money, with no stomach" (3.2.15–16), and although he appears to blame this change, in conventional satirical fashion, on the promiscuous behavior of courtiers ("Our old ling and our Isbels a' th' country are nothing like your old ling and your Isbels a' th' court. The brains of my Cupid's knock'd out" [3.2.13–15]), there is also a sense of infection by the pervasive ennui of that milieu. By the time of the act 4 encounter with Lafew, Lavatch is still claiming to be the devil's follower, but only for the sake of the warmth offered by his "good fire" (4.5.48–49)—typically a concern of age rather than of youth. Lavatch has lost what little disruptive energy he ever possessed. He is merely, in Lafew's phrase, "a shrewd knave and an unhappy" (4.5.63); according to the Countess, even he lives in the shadow of the past where "real life" is enshrined: "My lord that's gone made himself much sport out of him. By his authority he remains here" (4.5.64–65). On these terms, he fits comfortably into Lafew's view of the world: "I like him well; 'tis not amiss" (4.5.68).

What we may think of as the taming of emblems of folly over the course of the play functions in two ways, each corresponding to one of the competing scenarios. From the perspective of Lafew and the Countess, the exposure of the false upstart Parolles and the retreat of the Clown from subversive self-assertion into sour and pallid commentary are part of a process of making the world more homogeneous; its anomalies—the departed Helena among them—are being absorbed into a coherent order, one that makes reassuring moral sense. The unsuspected survival of Helena, on the other hand, reveals this flattening of the dramatic landscape as equally serving her own hegemonic purposes. We should not forget that it is Lavatch who first calls attention to Helena as Helen of Troy. This reinforces his structural correspondence to Thersites, the figure of crude satire and debased sexuality who is relegated to silence as the heroic script of Troilus works towards its conclusion. In this way, too, Helena effectively enlists the present figures of authority on her behalf despite themselves, preparatory to the final confrontation. And at that point, she stages the power of the miraculous so as to acquire authority in her own person and her own right.

Conclusion: Is There Life after the Bed Trick?

Bertram's unworthiness functions, I have already suggested, on several levels at once. Perhaps its most basic significance—apart from the usual romantic premise of the irrationality of erotic passion—involves the common Shakespearean insinuation that, as the popular saying has it, "a good man is hard to find." That saying itself comes complete with the patriarchal corollary—and perhaps with an ironic acknowledgment of it—that finding a man is a woman's necessary business. Given her social dependency, which is only slightly (though significantly) less extreme than Cressida's, finding a man would appear to be a necessity for Helena. Yet in her capacity to fashion such unpromising raw material, Helena differs notably from the many other female characters in Shakespeare who wind up with inferior mates. The usual bittersweetness of such endings converts in Helena's case to sweet bitterness, according to the almost universal critical response, which is effectively sanctioned by the deferral and conditionality that dominate the King's exit lines: "All yet seems well, and if it end so meet, / The bitter past, more welcome is the sweet" (5.3.333–34). To adapt the title of Price's study, the "comedy" remains "unfortunate."

A particularly clear contrast exists between Helena and her namesake in *A Midsummer Night's Dream*. The heroine of the earlier comedy (circa 1595) similarly begins by doting over the scornful Demetrius even while she knows that love's delusory power is at work ("Things base and vile, holding no quantity, / Love can transpose to form and dignity"[43]); she also displays an instinct for manipulating the role of love's martyr: "I pray you, though you mock me, gentlemen, / Let her not hurt me. I was never curst" (*MND*, 3.2.299–300). Yet she notably fails to recognize that role as such; she mistakes it, one might say, for her essential self, and this makes the fairies' imposition of confused identities symbolically appropriate, as well as practically necessary, if Demetrius is to "see the light." When he does so, incidentally, he offers the same explanation— that he is returning to his first, instinctive choice—as the smug Bertram provides to the King in welcoming the match with Lafew's daughter and justifying his original aversion to Helena.[44] In Demetrius's case, the element of artifice and compulsion is allowed to remain in ironic suspension within his volubly displayed "natural taste" (*MND*, 4.1.174). By contrast, Bertram's asserted subjectivity will shortly collapse into speechless helplessness ("O pardon!" [5.3.308]). But then for Bertram, the wielder of natural magic who manipulates him is identical with his destined mate—and the play is not, as he supposes, over.

Closer to home, from this study's perspective, is the case of Mariana in *Measure for Measure*, whom the problematic human equivalents of fairy manipulators—the Duke and Isabella—put almost precisely into Helena's position: thanks to a bed trick, she gets to marry the man she wants, who had refused to fulfill the terms of his marriage contract with her. Her sexuality likewise becomes "a policy how virgins"—again, there are two at work—"might blow up men" (1.1.121–22). Without anticipating the next chapter in detail, it is worth noting here the complete separation between power and will evident in the portrayal of Mariana. She pines helplessly, in isolation, until action is devised for her. Her victory does not mean that Angelo's feelings towards her have changed; he offers neither word nor token of reconciliation. Moreover, her gain remains conspicuously contingent on the power of those who have helped her: when Angelo is threatened with execution, she must beg the Duke, "O my most gracious lord, / I hope you will not mock me with a husband!" (MM, 5.1.416–17), and implore Isabella's intervention with the vow, "Lend me your knees, and all my life to come / I'll lend you all my life to do you service" (MM, 5.1.431–32). In the context of her thorough powerlessness, most centrally her incapacity to make Angelo respond to her, her pitiful articulation of her condition— which, in less extreme form, is the condition of most Shakespearean female lovers—throws into relief the extraordinary achievement of Helena: "O my dear lord, / I crave no other, nor no better man" (MM, 5.1.425–26).

Such abject emotional dependence is, in effect, Helena's starting position; her resolution entails not merely getting her man, or even making him "better," but rather making him so thoroughly hers *by nature* that he ceases to possess a moral standing at all. The true alternative to a mere bundle of negatives—"no other, nor no better" reincarnates Bertram's "no" and "not"—is not a freely affirming (or for that matter desiring) subject, despite Bertram's vow to "love her dearly, ever, ever dearly" (5.3.316), but an entity whose subjectivity has been replaced by a helpless compulsion to affirm. Beneath the comic surface, this compulsion disquietingly aligns Bertram with the Helen-enchanted Faustus: "Her lips suck forth my soul" (*Faustus*, 18.102).

But the comparison that perhaps sheds most light on both the ending of *All's Well* and an important aspect of its structure is, again, with Portia in *Merchant*—the only other Shakespearean comic heroine whose machinations render her (doubtfully worthy) mate "doubly won" (5.3.314), as Helena puts it. Not only must Portia assume male disguise in order to achieve such power, rather than turning her true gender (in the form of virginity) to account, but she must also retire to an isolated world coded as feminine in order to retain her position. In an adaptation of the standard "two-world" structure of Shakespearean romantic comedy, Portia's fairy-tale Belmont, the site of the love plot, is contrasted throughout the play—and sometimes disturbingly paralleled—with the "masculine" world of commercialism and power represented by Venice. But whereas in most such comedies characters return to the "first world" of the city or court—or at least anticipate such a return—once the pastoral alternative has produced romantic closure, *Merchant* concludes with a decisive withdrawal from Venice and a confirmation of the romantic atmosphere. Belmont has reached out to enfold the characters worth "saving"; it now extends to fill the entire space of the theatrical universe—that is, to adapt the punning reference to Shakespeare's theater in a later play, of "the great globe itself" (*Tempest*, 4.1.153). The larger text thus actively and visibly supports Portia's rescripting of her world and of her place in it. But partly as a consequence, even in the multiple triumph over Shylock the hegemony of Belmont carries nagging reminders of what has been excluded and of the moral limitations defined through such exclusion.

Like the other Problem Comedies, *All's Well* wrenches the two-world pattern askew. Helena initiates the action by leaving a position of quasi-pastoral isolation for a court world that is contiguous with the masculine sphere of "honor." Even the first stage in her self-construction—the curing of the King and the engagement of royal authority on behalf of her desire—involves reshaping that sphere to her own design. When she undertakes her secret expedition to the very ethical core of that world—the equivalent of Portia's excursion to Venice—she does so not so as to retrieve power and take it elsewhere but rather so as to extend her hegemony. She transforms the play world at large, not just a piece of it (or a night of it, as in *A Midsummer Night's Dream*), into fairy tale. Bertram is not drawn into a "second" world under Helena's control; he is brought home, which, as the saying goes, "is where the heart is"—except that he is made to undergo a heart transplant.

That operation takes place in the final scene, in such a way as to highlight not only the issue of "reading"—the contingent relation between words and things—but the problematic identity of things themselves, as is epitomized in the shifting significance of the rings. Appropriately, the self-contradictory evidence of Parolles regarding Bertram's behavior begins the process of destabilization:

> *Par.* He lov'd her, sir, and lov'd her not.
>
> *King.* As thou art a knave, and no knave. What an equivocal companion is this!
>
> *Par.* I am a poor man, and at your Majesty's command.
>
> (5.3.248–52)

Determining reality itself is the ultimate prerogative of power, but the power here is shown to have shifted from the King to Helena, by way of Diana. He is well on his way to the subordinate postures he assumes in the last lines: first, that of an auditor dependent upon narrative continuity ("Let us from point to point this story know, / To make the even truth in pleasure flow" [5.3.325–26]); next, that of tentative interpreter ("All yet seems well"); finally, in the Epilogue, that of "beggar" (Epi.1).

In reducing not only Bertram but also Lafew and the King to helpless confusion, Diana vividly manifests, on behalf of the wife who has lost her virginity "to her own liking," the power of that commodity to "blow up men."[45] The King is driven to an infantile petulance that echoes Bertram's distaste for cats: "Take her away, I do not like her now" (5.3.281). Such a transparent fantasy of omnipotence merely exposes his loss of control. Diana's web of riddling words—the equivalent of the unintelligible language that ensnared Parolles—extends even to Lafew: "I am no strumpet, by my life; / I am either maid, or else this old man's wife" (5.3.292–93). To "abuse" the "ears" (5.3.293) of the company thus extremely is to prepare them to accept as authoritative the solution that, cutting the Gordian knot ("not") that binds them all, purports to restore the connection between sign and signified: "Now behold the meaning" (5.3.304).

When Helena triumphantly plays her card of love's martyr for the last time—"'Tis but the shadow of a wife you see, / The name, and not the thing" (5.3.307–8)—that card is decisively trumps; her humility barely conceals her transcendent, even God-like, power, as, rising from the dead, she offers the very possibility of fixing essence again, of re-creating the universe out of chaos. Bertram's abjection is unmistakable as he leaps at the chance, embracing the "reading" of him that she determined long ago: "Both, both. O pardon!" (5.3.308). This power to refashion not only her world but its inhabitants is the key to the divine overtones so often perceived in Helena's role. But in keeping with the play's propensity for posing problems rather than resolving them, such a recognition becomes the fountainhead of further difficulties. What does it mean to make something out of nothing if nothing is the source of everything, and everything is a staged illusion? If her self-construction depends on her construction of Bertram, is she not the primary victim of the illusion she has manufactured, a more fitting object than Troilus himself for that character's bitter realization, "How my achievements mock me!" (*Troilus*, 4.2.69)? And this point returns us to Dr. Johnson's (and most readers' and spectators') visceral distaste for her chosen romantic costar. If

Bertram, at the end of the play, *is* no more than what he *seems*, because there is no distinction between all's *being* and all's *seeming* well, his new role ineluctably includes, from the audience's perspective, the desperation (not to say ailurophobia) of a cornered rat bolting for the glimmer of any way out.

Chapter Four
Measure for Measure
Intertextual Ironies

When, in act 2, scene 2, of *All's Well*, the Clown Lavatch serves up a string of similes in praise of his "answer that fits all questions" (*AWW*, 2.2.15–16)—the courtier's infinitely empty, "O Lord, sir! (*AWW*, 2.2.41ff. *passim*)—he satirically alludes to the hypocrisy that Protestant Elizabethans habitually attached to the Roman Catholic religious orders: "As fit," he says, ". . . as the nun's lip to the friar's mouth" (*AWW*, 2.2.21–27). It is remarkable that what is probably Shakespeare's next and final comedy (excluding his final Romances) virtually stages this passing allusion in its concluding tableau. Not that Isabella is technically a nun—she has not yet taken her final vows. Nor is Duke Vincentio at all, in fact, a friar. Nor, notoriously, does the text furnish any indication of what the reaction of Isabella, in facial expression and gesture, is meant to be when the Duke declares his interest in marrying her—a surprise to the audience as well as to her, since, as far as we are concerned, his last word on love has been his early denial "that the dribbling dart of love / Can pierce a complete bosom."[1] Whatever her reaction, she gets, one might suppose, ample opportunity to display it, and the audience to observe it, since the Duke first broaches the subject before turning to deal with Lucio, the "loose cannon" who has become the plot's "loose end," then returns to it in his final words. What Isabella conspicuously does not get, however, is an opportunity to speak: the Duke precludes speech in both instances, the first time by announcing a change of subject, later by imposing on her the role of listener ("Whereto if you'll a willing ear incline" [5.1.536]). This is ostensibly to grant her a power of choice that is, however, simultaneously foreclosed by his continuing control of the dramatic situation: "So bring us to our palace, where we'll show / What's yet behind, that's meet you all should know" (5.1.538–39).

The fact that the Duke effectively imposes silence on Isabella—as indeed on all the other characters present—somewhat mitigates the problematic quality granted to that silence in much critical discussion of the play.[2] Not that her silence is insignificant—on the contrary—but, since it is not voluntary, it need not be taken to signify Isabella's ambivalence (a point I shall return to). And whereas directors have the challenge of making stage sense of the character here, as elsewhere, the rigid terms of the Duke's public spectacle, including the social decorum that Shakespeare's audiences would have taken for granted, should perhaps be understood to restrict her compass for self-expression. It seems all but out of the question that the original production chose (any more than do most modern ones) to put Lavatch's irreverent simile into action. Still, the joke in the saying—that there should be nothing so *un*fit—was and is inevitably brought to life on the visual level, unless directors artificially avoid the issue be secularizing Isabella's dress. Moreover, the Duke's wording, when he first mentions the match, indirectly but explicitly raises the question of fitness by abruptly censoring his own love discourse—a discourse that, strangely, is almost unmatched in Shakespeare for simple romantic power: "and for your lovely sake, / Give me your hand, and say you will be mine, / He is my brother too. But fitter time for that (5.1.491–93).

In addition to *All's Well*, a second dramatic intertext bears intriguingly on this offer of marriage to a would-be nun. Contemporary audiences might well have recalled the crudely melodramatic climax of one of the first romantic comedies on the Elizabethan public stage, Robert Greene's *Friar Bacon and Friar Bungay* (1589–90?).[3] There Margaret of Fressingfield, the Keeper's daughter who supposes herself rejected by her aristocratic suitor, is confronted with a moral dilemma when he unexpectedly turns up and renews his request for her hand just as she is about to take the veil. Lord Lacy, it is revealed, has only been testing her love—news that, again, comes as a surprise also to the audience. There is a parallel with the less focused "testing" of Vincentio, who has made Isabella's pleading, on her own behalf as well as Mariana's, an uphill affair and who has withheld the fact of Claudio's survival. Greene's text focuses on Margaret's silence as she makes up her mind, weighing her choices in terms that parodically anticipate Isabella's position. That silence, however, is decisively resolved in her decision to embrace the romantic offer of the nobleman:

> The flesh is frail. My lord doth know it well,
> That when he comes with his enchanting face,
> Whatso'er betide, I cannot say him nay;

> Off goes the habit of a maiden's heart,
> And, seeing Fortune will, fair Framingham,
> And all the show of holy nuns, farewell.
> Lacy for me, if he will be my lord.[4]

Margaret's dilemma is far less problematic than Isabella's: virginity had not been her first love, after all, and she owes nothing to anyone but herself. Still, Lacy's companion, Ermsby, defines the issue in terms as blunt as those that *Measure for Measure* builds into its silence:

> Choose you, fair damsel; yet the choice is yours,
> Either a solemn nunnery or the court;
> God or Lord Lacy. Which contents you best,
> To be a nun, or else Lord Lacy's wife?
>   (*Friar Bacon*, 14.81–84)

The clear implication that Margaret is substituting a secular devotion for a spiritual one feeds provocatively into *Measure for Measure*, especially given the God-like status accorded Duke Vincentio, not merely by a good many critics but, more to the point, by Angelo: "your Grace, like pow'r divine, / Hath look'd upon my passes" (5.1.369–70). The prospect of marrying the Duke not only curtails but subsumes Isabella's intended vocation as Bride of Christ. His effective restriction of her ability to make her will known ironically suggests the "more strict restraint" (1.4.4) she initially sought, with the crucial difference that in this new order, the rules limiting her power of self-expression in the presence of men will serve not to help her withhold herself sexually but to transfer her sexuality to male control:

> When you have vow'd, you must not speak with men
> But in the presence of the prioress;
> Then if you speak, you must not show your face,
> Or if you show your face, you must not speak.
>   (1.4.10–13)

All in all, a large aspect of the "problem" presented by the Duke's abruptly revealed desire to possess the near-nun to whom his friar's role has given him privileged access is precisely the intertextually focused question of "fitness."

Intratextual Ironies

Nor is the question of fitness absent from the subversive discourse of *Measure for Measure* itself, thanks largely to the slander so liberally dispensed by Lucio, who, for this reason, deserves sustained attention at this point, despite—or rather because of—his marginal role in the text. In fact, I wish to use his oblique relation to the primary textual forces as my principal avenue of approach. In keeping with the metadramatic association of the power to speak with the power to control events, the final scene pointedly reverses the dynamic of his intercourse with the disguised Duke, whose *un*willing ears once had no choice but to hear scurrilous abuse of himself—in effect, a rewriting of the Duke's character and role. The reversal is figured in the conclusion's recapitulation of the whole relationship: Lucio's comic interpolations mocking, if not menacing, the Duke's carefully crafted script are incorporated into that script despite himself then made the instrument of revealing the friar's *true* identity—that is, the Duke's image of himself—before the slanderer becomes the final victim-beneficiary of the Duke's corrective attention. Only then, it seems, is the Duke actually free to speak to Isabella. Lucio's unruly presence interposes between his ruler's two mentions of his desire and, in the first instance, is perceptibly part of the need to defer speech until a "fitter time" (5.1.493).

Superficially, in this final phase Lucio is also the occasion for recapitulating the broad ethical movement within the play from strict justice to mercy—from the retributive outlook epitomized in the Duke's application of the title phrase to Angelo ("Like doth quit like, and *Measure* still for *Measure*" [5.1.411]) to the forgiving message of the biblical text from which the phrase derives, Christ's Sermon on the Mount: "Ivdge not, that ye be not iudged. For with what iudgement ye iudge, ye shal be iudged, and with what measure ye mette, it shal be measured to you againe. And why seest thou the mote, that is in thy brothers eye, and perceiuest not the beame that is in thine owne eye? . . . Hypocrite, first cast out the beame out of thine owne eye, and then shalt thou se clearely to cast out the mote out of thy brothers eye."[5] However, the gift of mercy that Lucio receives—he will be spared whipping and hanging but forced to marry the prostitute he has impregnated—appears to him a mixed blessing, much as the reprieve accorded Angelo and even the rewards dispensed to Isabella and Mariana appear to the audience: "Marrying a punk, my lord, is pressing to death, whipping, and hanging" (5.1.522-23). His allusion to the torture employed for compelling accused persons to plead, like that of Pandarus ("which bed, because it shall not speak of your pretty encounters, press it to death" [*Troilus*, 3.2.208–9]), focuses the issue of speech as an index of power. So does the name of Lucio's wife-to-be, Kate Keepdown, which also has obvious sexual connotations. This is the last time Lucio will call, if not a spade a spade, at least a spade a pickaxe, and so perhaps dig up something besides dirt.

To the extent that the Duke's mercy conveniently comprises a more *telling* punishment for Lucio's misspeaking of him, as his "last-word" rejoinder to Lucio would seem to grant ("Slandering a prince deserves it" [5.1.524]), the biblical context ironically places him in the hypocritical camp—that is, if one regards him at all in a mortal light. The joke is on Lucio when he applies to the supposed Friar Lodowick the proverb concerning false appearances, "*Cucullus non facit monachum* [The cowl does not make a monk]" (5.1.262), as when he (the lamb going to the slaughter) demands, again in commonplace terms for accusing the Roman Catholic clergy of hypocrisy, "Show your sheep-biting face, and be hang'd an hour!" (5.1.354–55).[6] But Lucio also speaks the truth despite himself. The Duke's cowl, after all, very dubiously confers the right to the specific friarly functions that he appropriates to serve his purpose—including the speech-based privileges of hearing confession (Mariana's) and administering the last rites (although Barnardine does not make a willing enough listener in the latter case). What is at issue, thanks to Lucio, is nothing less than the power to make and remake the self and others. The Duke's triumphant mock, "Thou art the first knave that e'er mad'st a duke" (5.1.356), is turned back on him, less by Lucio's subsequent appeal ("Your Highness said even now I made you a duke; good my lord, do not recompense me in making me a cuckold" [5.1.515–17]) than by the reverberation of his proverb. Once such meanings are in circulation, they are impossible to control; the boundaries are blurred between lies and truth, "essential" identities are up for grabs, and Lucio and the Duke do indeed, in some sense, "change persons" (5.1.336), to adapt the latter's phrase.

The elusive nature of truth is, in general, the key to the paradoxical truth-telling effect of Lucio's slanders. But there is a particular point on the Duke's pristine image where the mud slung by Lucio consistently sticks, thanks in part to the example of the Duke's primary opponent and foil. Angelo's obsessive concern with his reputation for moral purity is first subjected to scrutiny through Lucio's slandering exaggeration, the gist of which is the deputy's lack of humanity:

Some report a sea-maid spawn'd him; some, that he was begot between two stock-fishes. But it is certain that when he makes water his urine is congeal'd ice, that I know to be true; and he is a motion generative,[7] that's infallible.

(3.2.108–12)

To call Angelo a "motion"—that is, a puppet—is implicitly to raise the question of who serves as puppeteer. And Lucio effects an effortless transition at this point to the supposed "feeling of the sport" that "instructed" the Duke himself "to mercy" (3.2.119–20). The obvious lies that follow with such fertile ingenuity make the same basic point, mutatis mutandis, as do both Angelo's career and the biblical text, not to mention Pompey's salacious "realism" ("they will to't" [2.1.233])— namely, that immunity to the basic conditions of physical existence is an impossibility, and that to fail to recognize one's own participation in those conditions is hypocritical self-delusion. Such recognition is forcibly brought home to Angelo, well before his final public humiliation, in those struggles with himself that produce his soliloquies in act 2 (scenes 2 and 4). The second of these speeches, moreover, includes recognition not only of the weakness itself but also of the pride involved in denying it—the primal sin, in Christian theology, and that which "goeth before a fall." The concept enters via a subordinate clause, one thought begetting another so as to denote a process of self-discovery: "my gravity, / Wherein (let no man hear me) I take pride" (2.4.9–10).

In this context, it is all the more striking that despite paying lip service to his responsibility for the current state of affairs in Vienna, the Duke continues to foster an image of himself as the perfect wise ruler. It becomes pointedly ironic that his interest in hearing Escalus's praise of him after Lucio's abuse should elicit an affirmation that the absent Duke was, according to Escalus, "One that, above all other strifes, contended especially to know himself" (3.2.232–33). Escalus goes on to deny the Duke's capacity for the "feeling" of any "sport":

> Duke. What pleasure was he given to?
>
> Escal. Rather rejoicing to see another merry, than merry at any thing which profess'd to make him rejoice; a gentleman of all temperance. But leave we him to his events.

(3.2.234–38)

The audience would certainly accept these terms as approbative. Yet they also reveal themselves as the orthodox moralistic translation of Lucio's condemnation of Angelo as a "cold fish." Moreover, they carry the intriguing implication, which suits the Duke's role in the play world—especially as interpreted by some psychoanalytical critics[8]—that he takes (or at least projects) his pleasure by proxy.

As if assured that this image of himself is still viable, the Duke concludes this central slandering scene with a soliloquy that, in contrast to those of Angelo—and indeed contrary to the premise of soliloquy generally—keeps him both pure and undisclosed. Yet he evidently lays claim to the self-knowledge required to sustain the role of heaven's deputy:

> He who the sword of heaven will bear
> Should be as holy as severe;
> Pattern in himself to know,
> Grace to stand, and virtue go;
> More nor less to others paying
> Than by self-offenses weighing.
> (3.2.261–66)

Beneath its smooth aphoristic surface, polished by rhyming trochaic couplets—a form normally reserved by Shakespeare for discourse on a ceremonial or magical plane[9]—the soliloquy is subtly self-subverting in least two respects: the Duke's reference to "my vice" ("Twice treble shame on Angelo, / To weed my vice and let his grow!" [3.2.269–70]) and his inexplicable decision to descend to Angelo's level of secrecy, if not immorality ("Craft against vice I must apply" [3.2.277]). More generally, the balanced antithetical clauses, with their homogenizing hegemony of voice, take us back, even as they insist on presenting the Duke as Angelo's opposite, to the irreverent multivocal banter over moral and physical states, similarity and difference, in the play's second scene, where it is evident that "there went but a pair of shears" (1.2.27) between Lucio and the First Gentleman.[10]

There is, after all, a sort of ritual involved in Vincentio's stately cadences—an attempt to purge the air of slander and restore his self-image to its transcendent lustre. That lustre depends on exclusiveness. It is precisely the Duke's resemblance to Angelo, insofar as both maintain an image of transcendental purity, that Lucio functions to insinuate by way of his outrageous accusations of corrupt sexual appetite. The very extravagance of his slanders becomes an index of the Duke's refusal to recognize his mortal fallibility. Lucio explicitly confronts the Duke with what he had most directly sought to avoid in appointing Angelo, "Who may, in th' ambush of my name, strike home, / And yet my nature never in the fight / To do in slander" (1.3.41–43). Insofar as the confrontation extends to a repudiated side of that "nature," the experience parallels Angelo's sudden perverse susceptibility to an emblem of purity, when "Never could the strumpet, / With all her double vigor, art and nature, / Once stir my temper" (2.2.182–84). It is a standard principle of Shakespearean drama, both comedy and tragedy, that characters are brought face-to-face with what they have shunned or excluded, and that the proportions of their experience reflect the severity of their denials. What stands out about *Measure for Measure* is that the Duke eventually contrives to bring this retributive element within his control and to exclude it again, this time decisively.

This feat is the more notable because of Lucio's heritage as a character type. More fully than any of the subversive figures in the other Problem Plays, he participates in the cultural archetype known to anthropologists as the Trickster, which came to Shakespeare largely through the tradition of the Vice figure of earlier English drama.[11] Not only does Lucio, with Pompey, continue the balancing of what might be called High and Low Clowns that exists in the other Problem Comedies (Pandarus/Thersites in *Troilus*, Parolles/Lavatch in *All's Well*); he also takes to an extreme several tendencies evident in his counterparts. (So, for that matter, does Pompey, who, as the only *professional* bawd in the trio of texts, epitomizes the commodification of the appetite he so wittily defends.) If Lucio never actually plays a bawd's part, he surpasses Parolles and even Pandarus in sheer abstract enthusiasm for bawdry. The affected and mechanical wit of Parolles, which is never truly subversive, pales beside Lucio's gift for slanderous invention, sustained as it is by a commitment to speaking "out of turn": thus Parolles' mildly risqué salutation of Helena, " 'Save you, fair queen! . . . Are you meditating on virginity?" (*AWW*, 1.1.106, 110), contrasts sharply with Lucio's blasphemous parody of the Annunciation when he first greets the novice Isabella: "Hail, virgin, if you be" (1.4.17).

The conjunction between Lucio and Isabella here is telling, not least for the fact that he actually does stand in a kind of awe—comic in itself, of course, but not the mere mockery she assumes it to be—of her withdrawal from sexuality, which he, like Pompey, takes to be a basic human condition:

> I hold you as a thing enskied, and sainted
> By your renouncement an immortal spirit,

And to be talk'd with in sincerity,
As with a saint.

(1.4.34–37)

The ambiguous relation thus established develops provocatively in the
first scene of Isabella's pleading with Angelo. Viewed schematically, the
tableau recalls the allegorical mechanisms of the Medieval Morality
Plays, with Isabella in the position of the human soul poised between
emblems of Vice and Virtue, evil and good angels. Moreover, Lucio's
whispered urgings of Isabella to make a case for her sinful brother despite
her clear reluctance (she begins with "There is a vice that most I do
abhor, / And most desire should meet the blow of justice" [2.2.29–30]),
resound with sexual overtones that suggest the bawd's function: "You
are too cold" (2.2.56); "Ay, touch him; there's the vein" (2.2.70); "O, to
him, to him, wench! he will relent. / He's coming; I perceive't"
(2.2.124–25). And it is, in fact, not the "sense" she speaks but the
"sense" (2.2.142) she arouses, to use the pun through which Angelo's
doubleness first dawns on him and us,[12] that ironically fulfills her
brother's expectation of her: "in her youth / There is a prone and
speechless dialect, / Such as move men" (1.2.182–84).

On the other hand, the impeccable Christian "sense" of Isabella's
argument for mercy rather than justice, coupled with the audience's
natural sympathy for Claudio, lends a positive cast to Lucio's role even
before the "outward-sainted deputy" (3.1.88), as Isabella explains to her
brother, belies both name and appearance to reveal himself as "yet a
devil" (3.1.91). And there remains the fact that Isabella makes her
second approach to Angelo, when she is unaccompanied by Lucio, in
terms as suggestive as Lucio's own: "I am come to know your pleasure"
(2.4.31). She and Angelo, from this perspective, no longer need Lucio as
aphrodisiac go-between. Her agility in parrying Angelo's guarded proposition ("Your sense pursues not mine" [2.4.74]) suggests, to us as to
him ("Either you are ignorant, / Or seem so craftily" [2.4.74–75]), an
alertness to double meanings, the more so because she is finally driven to
declaring, "I have no tongue but one; gentle, my lord, / Let me entreat
you speak the former language" (2.4.139–40). Such a statement signals
that she at least intuits the "sense" of Angelo's second language. Indeed,
it is in response to Angelo's developing sexual overture that Isabella
displays a genuine, if contrary, eroticism of her own, virtually telling
him under what circumstances she *would* take off her clothes:

> were I under the terms of death,
> Th' impression of keen whips I'ld wear as rubies,
> And strip myself to death, as to a bed
> That longing have been sick for, ere I'ld yield
> My body up to shame.
>
> (2.4.100–4)

To have learnt Lucio's bawdy lesson, in effect, so quickly and so well suggests, even before her own "sainted" image visibly cracks under the strain of her predicament, that, like the friar-seeming Duke, she has been confronted through Lucio with aspects of her humanity that question the "fitness" of any such image.

Lucio's revelatory promotion of the sexual substratum of virtuous pretenses is supported by a further subversive quality in which he far exceeds, not only Pandarus and Parolles but every other Shakespearean Trickster derivative. Pandarus crosses class boundaries only in the sense that, in a way alien to his Chaucerian forebear, his manners and preoccupations are felt to degrade his social standing: the upshot is his ultimate degeneration into a member of the "hold-door trade" (*Troilus*, 5.10.51). Parolles, of course, tries and fails to make the leap from servant-companion to soldier-courtier. Lucio, however, displays enormous social range within the play world—a world that is as concerned as any in Shakespeare, in keeping with its "realism," with making fine class distinctions. (Witness the importance attached by both Pompey and Escalus to establishing Master Froth as a "gentleman" [2.1.146,147] with an income of "fourscore pound a year" [2.1.123].)

Ethically and by habitual association part of the unsavory underworld, Lucio first appears as a "man-about-town" in a mingled discussion of state and sexual affairs with *"two other* Gentlemen," according to the Folio text's introductory stage direction to act 1, scene 2. He is the friend of the hitherto respectable Claudio, but also the intimate (and fickle patron) of Pompey. He introduces himself to Isabella as one of the "gentlemen" that had hoped to see military action (1.4.51–52) and appears unchallenged before Angelo as her companion in the supplication scene. He pays two visits to the prison, asking for the Provost on the second occasion (4.3.149). In the concluding scene, as he thrusts himself into the doings of the genteel characters, he is variously a "gentleman" (to Isabella at 5.1.84), "Signior Lucio" (to Escalus [5.1.260] and Angelo [5.1.324]), and the Duke's "knave" (5.1.356) and "sirrah" (5.1.214 and 500) (the latter being a contemptuous form of address often applied to servants). He ends up punished as befits a "lewd fellow" (5.1.509). Such mixed messages regarding class support the presentation of Lucio as remarkably unfixed and mobile; he is "here, there, and everywhere" in a way that reflects his unusual label in the Folio's dramatis personae: whereas virtually all of the other characters are designated according to function or social position, he is identified solely as "a fantastic" (*Riverside*, 550).

From Intratext to Intertext Again

If Lucio's extraordinary capacity to transgress class boundaries is unique in Shakespeare's oeuvre, it reinforces his affiliation with the sort of Vice figure found in drama of the earlier Tudor period, in particular those hybrid plays—all but unknown to modern readers and audiences—that loosely combine Morality Play elements with romantic extravagance in matters of character and plot. One such work is *Promos and Cassandra*, by George Whetstone, published in 1578, which is widely recognized as Shakespeare's primary source for *Measure for Measure*. The basic story was a popular one, and there is evidence that Shakespeare also knew other versions of it; in particular, *Measure for Measure*'s thematic opposition between Justice and Mercy would seem to have been inspired by the handling of the material in the Italian tragicomedy *Epitia*, by G. B. Giraldi Cinthio (published in 1583).[13] Criticism has traditionally—and quite understandably—focused on the striking fact that in all versions other than Shakespeare's, the heroine not only accedes to the demand of the corrupt deputy but is approved of for doing so. However, as my discussion of source issues previously has sought to demonstrate, the conventional activity of comparing plots, characters, and themes does not constitute the limit to the usefulness of intertextual analysis. If one approaches Shakespeare's text by way of the notion of "ungrammaticality," the anomalous role of Lucio reaffirms the importance of *Promos and Cassandra* as an intertext bearing on problems other than the ethical or those involving "meaning" in a narrow sense.

In "The Epistle Dedicatorie" prefacing *Promos and Cassandra*, the author, in terms that would appear to have influenced Sidney's *An Apology for Poetry*,[14] decries breaches of decorum in the English drama of his day, especially the violation of the classical unities: "in three howers ronnes he throwe the worlde: marryes, gets Children, makes Children men, men to conquer kingdomes, murder Monsters, and bringeth Gods from Heaven, and fetcheth Divels from Hel."[15] Also a target, however, is the very freedom to cross class boundaries on which the traditional Vice figure depends: "they make a Clowne companion with a King: in theyr grave Counsels, they allow the advise of fooles" (*Promos*, 443). With regard to the historical condition of English drama, then just at the threshold of the era of the Elizabethan public theaters, more than the scholarly scruples of Renaissance humanism are at work here; the development of a more fully mimetic drama depended on the presentation of stage societies that claimed to mirror actual social structures, as well as on new forms of characterization, in which individual identity and plausible psychology supplanted symbolic significance. A king was no longer, or at least not primarily, a generalized Everyman figure, and the influences upon him—among which the traditional "misleaders" continued to figure prominently for moral reasons—needed to be garbed in greater verisimilitude. (Shakespeare's *Richard II*, predating *Measure for Measure* by about 10 years, is interesting for its visible mixture of modes: the corrupting influences on the King are given dramatic embodiment in the persons of his "favorites"—Bushy, Bagot, and Green—but these figures are displaced by purely psychological forces, as Richard takes on the status of tragic hero.) Increasingly, the Vice figure or figures were squeezed into various quasi-mimetic molds. This is what makes Lucio, to the extent that he stands out against the background of Shakespeare's "modern" urban setting, a conspicuous throwback.

As it happens, Whetstone was rather far from practicing what he preached. *Promos and Cassandra* is a lengthy secular Morality Play, which, while avoiding the more ridiculous excesses associated with the dramatic romances of the period, nevertheless features a bizarre gallimaufry of characters, a freewheeling treatment of time and setting, frequent recourse to song and spectacle, and action that sprawls loosely, though within a coherent overall program. Even in the main structural feature that *Measure for Measure* seems to have adapted from its predecessor—the shifts between court and low-life scenes, with sexual and social degeneracy the common thread (Bullough 2: 407)—Shakespeare's text is, by comparison, highly formal and controlled. Not only is there a far greater variety of low-life characters in *Promos and Cassandra*, but the plethora of very short scenes, many involving single speeches, makes for a nearly chaotic effect. This chaos, it should be noted, at least partially serves the purpose of mirroring the state of morals in the state of "Julio" and is rendered more orderly in part 2 of the play, as the King of Hungary (note the casual allusion to such a monarch at *MM*, 1.2.2 and 5) arrives on the scene to impose moral order on society at large and his corrupt officials in particular. The dichotomous structure of Whetstone's play is the key to its didactic method, as the extended title insists: "In the fyrste parte is showne, the unsufferable abuse, of a lewde Magistrate: The vertuous behaviours of a chaste Ladye: The uncontrowled leawdenes of a favoured Curtisan. And the undeserved estimation of a pernicious Parasyte. In the second part is discoursed, the perfect magnanimitye of a noble Kinge, in checking Vice and favouringe Vertue: Wherein is showne, the Ruyne and overthrowe, of dishonest practises: with the advauncement of up-right dealing" (*Promos*, 442).

An analogous effect, of course, is built into the structure of *Measure for Measure*, but with significant differences. The retributive fifth act of Shakespeare's play is wholly under the Duke's control: its elaborate twistings and turnings all take place within the single scene that he has devised; even when he is briefly offstage, and certainly when he is onstage in his friar's disguise, he is never truly absent. But then he has remained a superintending presence all through the previous action, which, more-over, he himself set in motion by deliberately putting Angelo to the test: "hence shall we see / If power change purpose: what our seemers be" (1.3.53–54). There is no such motive behind the appointment of Promos as the representative of the King of Hungary, who does not appear at all until the final scenes of resolution—and who does not, incidentally, form any personal relationship with the victimized, yet *still* "chaste," Cassandra.

The very embodiment of the compositional fluidity of Whetstone's play, as of the corruption it depicts, is the character of Phallax, whose designation as the "pernicious Parasyte" and, consistently, as a flatterer, marks him as a Vice figure, despite the author's prefatory distancing of himself, by implication, from such dramatic conventions. Of course, a Vice figure is as a Vice figure does, regardless of labels, and beneath his mimetic "cover" as a subordinate of the guilty deputy Phallax's subver-sive energy in promoting wrongdoing in many directions, including the sexual, clearly evokes the character type. So does his speech, which, in a typical way, is full of mocking irony and expressions of self-interest, besides displaying a lively use of proverbs and Latin tags. These include one, when he distances himself from Promos's violation of Cassandra, that recalls Lucio in both a specific and a general way: "*Non bonus est, ludere cum sanctis*" (*Promos*, 463). One may translate this saying, with Bullough, as follows (allowing for the slippage of "*bonus*," literally "good man," towards an impersonal meaning): "It is not good to jest at sacred things" (Bullough 2: 463n.). But "*bonus*" *is* personal, and "*sanctis*," which may also apply to persons, is the standard term for "saints"—hence, Isabella's lines in pleading with Angelo: "Great men may jest with saints; 'tis wit in them, / But in the less foul profanation" (2.2.127–28). Further, "*ludere*" more broadly signifies "make sport" or "play" (and is also the word for dramatic *play*ing). In any case, Lucio's irreverence regarding the text's true and false "saints" and sacred things is implicated, as is his profession of awed respect for the "enskied, and sainted" Isabella: "I would not—though 'tis my familiar sin / With maids to seem the lapwing, and to jest, / Tongue far from heart—play with all virgins so" (1.4.31–33).

There is further evidence (to speak for the moment in terms of "influence") that Phallax lies behind Shakespeare's invention of Lucio. Like the latter character, only Phallax, amongst the dramatis personae, crosses the boundary between high and low life: while serving as Promos's right-hand man—the counterpart of Escalus in *Measure for Measure*—he proves the bawd Rosko (the original of Pompey) right in surmising that "he lov[es] lase mutton well" (*Promos*, 449) (that is, "laced mutton" or prostitutes). He proves "a double knave . . . / A covetous churle, and a lecher too" (*Promos*, 491). For he enters into a parody of a romantic love relation with Rosko's mistress, the prostitute Lamia, who thereby conflates the roles of Mistress Overdone and the woman whom Lucio promises to marry, gets with child, and is sentenced to wed.

In the general distribution of penalties and rewards, Phallax receives no such sentence from the King, although his liaison with Lamia is brought into the open. (He comments later [*Promos*, 506] on her "carting"—the common public punishment accorded prostitutes—as part of the general cleanup of the city.) Yet it is at this point that the resemblance of Phallax to Lucio is most specific. The King anticipates Duke Vincentio in bidding him, "speak for thyself," and when he plays for time presses him, "Why? to devise a cloke to hyde a knave? / Friend, *veritas non querit angulos* [truth does not seek corners]" (*Promos*, 497). These lines enter into dialogue with the abundant discourse of knavery, concealment, and disclosure in *Measure for Measure*, including Lucio's reference to the "Duke of dark corners" (4.3.157) and his injunction to the friar, at the moment of discovery, to "[s]how your knave's visage" (5.1.353). As the Duke spares Lucio whipping and hanging, so the King informs Phallax, "Because thou didst thy faultes at first confesse, / From punishment thy person I release" (*Promos*, 498). Finally, when the disgraced Phallax, stripped of goods and office, contemplates his condition in soliloquy, he presents, in terms especially appropriate to

Shakespeare's play, the standard declaration of his character type that he is "down but not out" (we may compare Parolles, Pandarus, and, as before, Pistol):

> Fie, Fie, the Citie is so purged nowe
> As they of none but honest men allowe,
> So that farewell my part of thriving there:
> But the best is, flattrers lyve everie where.
> Set cock on hoope, *Domini est terra* [the earth is the
>   Lord's],
> If thou can not where thou wouldest, lyve where thou
>   maye.
> Yes, yes, *Phallax* knoweth whither to go:
> Nowe, God b'wi' ye all honest men of *Julio*;
> As the Devilles likes the company of Friers,
> So flattrers loves as lyfe to joyne with lyers.
>
> (*Promos*, 507)

"Whither to go" includes, perhaps, another play.

In one important respect, Lucio is Phallax turned inside out: a slanderer is the diametrical opposite of a flatterer. This change lends even greater independence to Shakespeare's character, who thereby becomes defined by his promotion of alternative "readings" rather than by a self-serving support for the dominant discourse. Hence, too, the political complicity of Phallax, "Lord *Promos* secondary" (*Promos*, 496), is split off in *Measure for Measure* and given positive form as the honest and humane Escalus, who should by right of seniority have been appointed deputy. Even Escalus, we should note, is not a wholly unequivocal figure—or at least he is not allowed to be so. He serves as foil not only to Angelo but also to the Duke, who, in directing him to examine the stories of Isabella and the friar, confronts him with a problem he cannot solve, induces him to threaten the disguised Duke with torture, and so puts him, too, in need of pardon.

To return to Lucio, a slanderer needs to pit himself against truth, rather than to ally himself with falsehood, so the focus of Lucio's activities is naturally the play's exemplar of virtue rather than of vice. Moreover, according to the familiar convention of truth-telling folly, a slanderer's lies, unlike a flatterer's, lend themselves to a revelatory function. The name Lucio, after all, derives from the Latin word for light, as does "Lucifer" (the "light bringer")—the traditional sobriquet for the primordial ill angel, the Prince of Darkness. Moreover, Lucio's slanders tend to attach his precursor's diabolic overtones to the Duke ("angulos"/"dark corners," the devilish friars), although he obviously "must change persons" (5.1.336) in order to do so. (In fact, it is precisely in "dark corners" that the Duke often lurks—and in one of them, presumably, that he hears Mariana's confession.)

Against this background, it emerges as more significant that the retributive climax of *Measure for Measure* moves the punishing of the Vice figure from its position in *Promos and Cassandra*. In the latter play, Phallax receives justice (here, too, tempered with mercy) early on in the process of bringing order to Julio; he is then decisively shunted aside from the action. He is, after all, "secondary" (in two senses). The exposure of the corrupt deputy, with the redress of his victim's injury and the revelation of her brother's survival, is the main dramatic event. So it is in *Measure for Measure*, and in a generally similar fashion, given that the preservation of Isabella's virginity has required the introduction of Mariana as her substitute, not only in bed, but also as the deputy's loving spouse and advocate for his life (a transition that Cassandra makes rather artificially). Yet not only does Lucio insist on making a role for himself in these proceedings, thereby calling attention to the already cumbersome dramatic machinery—for once, the dramaturgy of Whetstone is straightforward by comparison—but the scene actually builds towards his comeuppance. Both he and Angelo are simultaneously exposed in the instant when he "makes" the friar a Duke, but whereas Angelo is dealt with right away Lucio's case is saved for last. This order follows both social and thematic precedence, but an audience is not about to forget that Lucio is still there, waiting to be dealt with. The Duke's concise arrest order at once invests this anticipated confrontation with a sense of closure, makes it a matter of language, and provides a physical emblem of "keeping" Lucio "down": "Sneak not away, sir, for the friar and you / Must have a word anon.—Lay hold on him" (5.1.358–59). Given the change to the primary intertext, then, a decided "ungrammaticality" accrues to the fact that Lucio is the last character to be silenced. One might say that the Duke's final act, which coincides with the play's, is to "weed" his *"vice"* indeed.

The climactic moment of the tortuous scene comprising act 5—Lucio's pulling off of the false friar's cowl—reveals, along with the Duke himself, more than the fact that Lucio and Angelo have been caught dead to rights. It shows that both of them—even Lucio at this most seemingly disruptive point in his subversive career—have been unwittingly acting parts scripted for them. Not, of course, that the Duke has anticipated or encouraged Lucio's slanders, any more than he has foreseen the details of Angelo's vicious behavior. Indeed, the latter's double-crossing of Isabella, by ordering Claudio executed after all, visibly undercuts Vincentio's confident control of the situation ("And here comes Claudio's pardon" [4.2.101]),[16] which is only restored, after Barnardine's inconvenient refusal to be executed, by the Provost's timely provision of a substitute head—a solution, moreover, that satisfies the formal prohibition against deaths in comedy.

Barnardine and Ragozine thereby divide the single part played in *Promos and Cassandra* by an anonymous executed criminal, as the roles of both Provost and Duke-as-friar are combined in that play's Gayler. The latter's pious moral regarding the survival of Andrugio (the counterpart of Claudio) is a normal part of Whetstone's discourse of divine justice: "But see how God hath wrought for his safety:—" (*Promos*, 471). What is remarkable is to find the sentiment recycled for Shakespeare's ruler— "O, 'tis an accident that heaven provides!" (4.3.77)—who otherwise so successfully takes upon himself the workings of providence. Vincentio's very discomfiture and dependency at this juncture throw into relief his general capacity, if not necessarily to provide his own accidents, at least to incorporate them smoothly within his developing design. His performance in the final scene, where he undertakes a "doubling" of parts beyond even the versatile ingenuity of Elizabethan actors, highlights his talent for quick changes and improvisation. (The ironic momentum of that scene, I think, gains from a metadramatic "in-joke," based on the obvious principle that two characters played by the same actor cannot be onstage at the same time.[17]) In sum, the Duke displays some of the same qualities as the traditional Vice; for this reason, he is sometimes regarded by commentators, in a secularized version of the deifying impulse, as a Trickster figure himself.[18]

Such a perspective suggests that in accommodating Lucio's improvisatory subversions into his own highly teleological scenario—producing a theatrical moment that makes Lucio's very theatricality serve his turn, then refocusing the drama on Lucio himself—the Duke is pitting himself against a rival creative force functioning in direct opposition to himself. Insofar as he constructs himself as God-like, not only in his omniscience and power of reward and punishment but in his concern with (re-)creating the dramatic universe, he constructs Lucio as Lucifer indeed—the rebel against divine authority, the ultimate rival to be vanquished. In Christian theology, after all, God foresees and permits Satan's evil workings in the world in order that his own beneficent power may be made manifest. Lucio's prominence as the final recipient of the Duke's attentions formally acknowledges, as it were, the centrality of his marginality. But what Lucio's status as Vice figure further implies is that the very principle of subversion within the text—its capacity for asserting contrary movement, initiating challenges, rewriting itself—is being co-opted, not merely squelched. In taking the wind out of Lucio's sails, the Duke is stealing some of it for himself. Some contemporary politically oriented criticism would argue that the Duke reproduces the strategy of authority generally by actually producing a subversiveness through which that authority is revalidated.[19] Yet Lucio's origins elsewhere, as the creature of another text and, beyond that, of a transtextual *function*, complicate such a model—as, perhaps, does the very principle of intertextuality, which Riffaterre, for one, would argue to be the inescapable condition of textuality itself.[20]

The special bond between the Duke and Lucio brings us back to *Promos and Cassandra*, where there is no such manipulative overseer of the action, and where, at least until the arrival of the King, heaven does the work of human beings, rather than vice versa. This time I wish to refocus the intertextual relation on the notorious disjunction within the Problem Plays—the conflict between romance content and realistic style or, as I have chiefly presented it in the preceding chapters, between Medieval and "modern" modes. In moral terms, Phallax, like Lucio, emblematizes the corruption that needs reform within his play world. But he also incarnates the theatrical conditions of that world—the near-chaotic diversity, the structural fluidity, the episodic choppiness that belong to the early Elizabethan romantic drama, with its robust appetite for fairy-tale quick changes and Impossibilities. In this respect, he parts company with Lucio, who can only carry the trace of *that* form of liberty, though this, too, contributes to his threat to destabilize the Duke's text.

Measure for Measure's main action gets under way—most directly at Angelo's instigation, but ultimately at the Duke's—with an image and lexis of confinement, as Claudio makes his way towards prison and answers Lucio's query, "Why, how now, Claudio? whence comes this restraint?" (1.2.124) with, "From too much liberty, my Lucio, liberty" (1.2.125). Scene 4 introduces Isabella longing for a "more strict restraint" (1.4.4). And in fact, instead of opening up into the "green world" common in romantic comedy as an alternative to repressive societies, the text takes us along with Claudio deep inside its sordid urban setting, where, at the core, we find Barnardine and Abhorson. Even Mariana, the only figure who at first seems placed outside that world (in her "moated grange" [3.1.264]), is emotionally bound to it and finally reconsolidated within it. This process, too, is part of the Duke's scenario.

From this perspective, the special enmity and rivalry between Lucio and Vincentio highlight not Isabella's defiant chastity but the Duke's manipulative presence as the key change from *Promos and Cassandra*—the one from which all others flow. Vincentio is revealed as attempting to take in hand the loose ends inevitably present in the dramatic experience itself, to do the job that, in effect, the author of that freewheeling drama could not, despite the regular moralizing he assigns his characters and the neoclassical affirmations of his preface. This project involves, like that of Helena in *All's Well* but on a much larger scale, the unmaking and remaking of essences and identities, with the result that subjectivity itself is exposed as contingent and artificial. Helena focuses—of necessity—all her hegemonic impulses on the reduction of Bertram to choicelessness in the final scene; *Measure for Measure*'s Duke can aim higher and wider, as manifested in the final sequence of silences, which logically culminates in that of Lucio, the spirit of the liberty to play by making (other) plays.

Even in Helena's case there is a suggestion that such power thrives on the thwarting of other characters' contrary self-images as they are promoted by competing scripts: Bertram certainly has such a script; so do, collectively, the Countess, the King, and Lafew. In *Measure for Measure*, the two other members of the central (anti)romantic triangle begin the play with particularly well-developed "selves" that run up against but also feed into the Duke's impulse to deconstruct, then reconstruct. And this places the focus again, but from a different angle, on the change made to Whetstone's "chaste Ladye" in the Shakespearean version of the story. The Duke's scenario would hardly profit from, or even be achievable with, a heroine willing, like Cassandra and her analogues in the other redactions, to sacrifice her*self* for her brother by acceding to the deputy's request. Isabella not only defines that self in terms of her chastity but defines that chastity narrowly and absolutely in terms of her virginity: "Then, Isabel, live chaste, and, brother, die; / More than our brother is our chastity" (2.4.184–85). Lucio's silencing clears the way, above all, for Isabella to be placed in a position of sexual powerlessness akin to Bertram's, although in a way consistent with a more "realistic" dynamic of gender relations, according to which, contrary to Helena's design, it is men who "blow up" virgins.

The Subjection of Angelo

It is basic to the play's participation in its subgenre that the theoretically clear-cut moral conflict at the heart of *Measure for Measure*, with the villain Angelo persecuting the innocent Isabella and being defeated by the virtuous Duke, is intensely problematic in theatrical practice. That some of this problematic coloring derives from the largely subtextual operation of a three-way power struggle has often been recognized, even if the gender-imposed passivity of Isabella has tended, I would argue, to obscure the extent of her participation: she is more than a mere pawn in the contest between the two men, though she is certainly that, too. What has also failed to receive adequate attention is the fact that the most fundamental struggle is played out at the level of subjectivity; the stakes involved extend to control, not merely over the body but, in effect, over the sense of identity itself, what we may think of as the right—even the capacity—to experience a personal interiority.[21] This issue is more clearly visible from a metadramatic perspective, which takes it for granted that plays-within-plays, like all fictions, entail the production of character, and that character is therefore always in flux. But the process of self-production is also made remarkably open to view in the case of Angelo, thanks to the relation between his desire to control Isabella and his struggle for *self*-control. For this reason, his story deserves, so to speak, pride of place.

We may start by rejecting a superficial approach, whether in moral or formal terms, to Angelo's status as villain, which should not be taken for granted. After all, serious villains—that is, figures not merely of mis-guided willfulness but of destructive malignancy—are rare in romantic comedies, for obvious reasons. (They are common, of course, in fairy tales, and hence feature in three of Shakespeare's four late romances.) Neither *Troilus* nor *All's Well* has such a villain, and even if we search through Shakespeare's entire comic canon, the list of villains is short: Shylock in *The Merchant of Venice*, Don John in *Much Ado about Nothing*, Oliver and Duke Frederick in *As You Like It*. It is suggestive that these plays all come relatively late (1596–97, 1598–99, and 1599, respectively) in the "comic period" that concludes with *Measure for Measure*, and that the characters in question—even, arguably, the enigmatic Don John—represent experiments in psychological depiction that stand out in their respective plays. In addition, each of these villains is structurally paired with an opposing positive figure—a process emphasized in *Much Ado* and

As You Like It by making the members of the pairs brothers. The inevitable suggestion that good and evil are blood relations, two sides of the same coin, is carried furthest in the latter play, where there are two such pairs. In all cases, the temporary ascendancy of evil involves an unnatural usurpation or displacement (with envy making up much of the motivation). This pattern reflects provocatively on the relation between those ostensible opposites, Vincentio and his (reluctant) deputy. Initially, however, I wish to focus on the way in which the psychological element associated with Shakespearean instances of comic villainy reinforces the sense of a generic crosscurrent, feeble and transitory as this may be in *Much Ado* and *As You Like It*. The centrality and complexity of Shylock, by contrast, virtually transform *The Merchant of Venice* into a tragicomedy. And as for *Measure for Measure*, however much responsibility for its conflicted generic status may be assigned to its antiromantic stylistic and thematic tendencies, the specifically tragic dimension depends on Angelo—not only for what he does, I propose, but for what he is.

Obviously, the villain's natural milieu is tragedy—the genre to which Shakespeare turned in a concentrated fashion around 1600 with a series of plays that specialize in the subjectivity of villains and heroes alike. In at least one case, that of Macbeth, such subjectivity is the key to uniting hero and villain in a single character. And even in the presentation of *Hamlet*'s Claudius, whose villainy is taken for granted rather than produced before our eyes, aside and soliloquy succinctly render the suffering associated with a guilty conscience. Self-division of this kind, from the time, in Judaeo-Christian mythology, of the impulse of the fallen Adam and Eve to hide from their Creator, has been coded as self-discovery, the revelation of the "self" as sinful. This is precisely the intellectual framework within which Angelo enacts his fall, but, as with other manifestations in the play of conventional Christian thinking, that framework proves difficult to hold in place, inadequate to contain the flux of the experience. We come up against the familiar point that in the context of the comprehensive Christian solution to questions of the "self," genuine tragedy is an impossibility. Whether or not they nominally exist in Christian settings, the characters of Shakespeare and his contemporaries arguably qualify as tragic to the extent that when they *do* perceive the "beame" that is in their own eyes they also discover not a soul in the divine image polluted by sin but a void.[22] The self divided becomes the self fragmented, thrown into turmoil that threatens to expose the very notion of an essential self as mere illusion.

Both *Hamlet*, which preceded *Measure for Measure* by four years or so, and *Macbeth*, which followed it by roughly half that interval, illuminate the development of such a characteristically tragic subjectivity in Angelo. The obvious specific analogue is with Claudius's futile attempt to purge his conscience through prayer—an attempt he abandons with a statement whose despair may be measured by the implicit resolution to pursue his criminal course: "My words fly up, my thoughts remain below: / Words without thoughts never to heaven go" (*Hamlet*, 3.3.97–98). Angelo begins the scene of his second encounter with Isabella by delivering a soliloquy that attributes the failure of his prayers to a similar split between outward and inward, sign and signified:

> When I would pray and think, I think and pray
> To several subjects. Heaven hath my empty words,
> Whilst my invention, hearing not my tongue,
> Anchors on Isabel; heaven in my mouth,
> As if I did but only chew his name,
> And in my heart the strong and swelling evil
> Of my conception.
>
> (2.4.1–7)

Angelo's moral fall thus entails a fall into subjectivity—ironically, by the same self-divisive route exemplified by the virtuous Hamlet, who announces, with regard to his ostentatious manifestations of mourning for his father,

> These indeed seem,
> For they are actions that a man might play,
> But I have that within which passes show,
> These but the trappings and the suits of woe.
> (*Hamlet*, 1.2.83–86)

Thus a Problem Play yet again recalls Hamlet's issue of being as opposed to seeming. This *is* precisely the question as the Duke himself has established it—"hence shall we see / If power change purpose: what our seemers be" (1.3.53–54)—and as Angelo now admits:

> O place, O form,
> How often dost thou with thy case, thy habit,
> Wrench awe from fools, and tie the wiser souls
> To thy false seeming! Blood, thou art blood.
> (2.4.12–15)

Although, as I suggested earlier, Angelo's second soliloquy goes on to portray continuing self-discovery—that is to say, self-production—it also produces a resolution to act his way out of the destabilization and fragmentation initiated in his first (in act 2, scene 2).[23] There his sexual response to Isabella first presented itself in terms of her temptation: "Is this her fault, or mine? / The tempter, or the tempted, who sins most, ha?" (2.2.162–63). Even though he paid lip service to his own responsibility ("Not she; nor doth she tempt; but it is I" [2.2.164]), and implicitly allowed the contingency of "being" ("What dost thou? or what art thou, Angelo? [2.2.172]), he clung to a sense of stable "saintly" identity subjected to diabolical assault: "O cunning enemy, that to catch a saint, / With saints dost bait thy hook!" (2.2.179–80). From the point of his second soliloquy, Angelo *subjects* himself, however reluctantly, to the reinscription of his identity by circumstance, in accordance with the arbitrary nature of moral signifiers: "Let's write 'good angel' on the devil's horn, / 'Tis not the devil's crest" (2.4.16–17). Subsequently, his villainy becomes, like Claudio's machinations against Hamlet, coldly mechanical, aggressively shameless, integrated into a fallen "self" that shuns self-awareness and seeks to recover wholeness through cynical detachment.

A liminal moment of analogous resolution is focused by Macbeth's determination, in effect, to outrun his conscience through bloody action, thereby restoring unity to a painfully divided self:

> For mine own good
> All causes shall give way. I am in blood
> Stepp'd in so far that, should I wade no more,
> Returning were as tedious as go o'er.
> Strange things I have in head, that will to hand,
> Which must be acted ere they may be scann'd.
> (*Macbeth*, 3.4.134–39)

Macbeth's conscience, of course, is continually catching up with him, "scanning" as tyrannical excesses those acts that now impose themselves as obvious (if "strange") measures of self-protection. An analogy may be drawn with Angelo's most blatantly tyrannical action—his order for Claudio's execution despite the presumed yielding of Isabella. This double cross shocks us as well as the Duke, yet it is all but taken for granted in Angelo's third and final soliloquy, which amounts almost to a scene in itself.

Angelo's third soliloquy begins and ends with the pangs of conscience, but its thematic thread is protection from exposure, and its perspective and lexis, on the subject of Claudio, recall tragic tyrants on the defensive: Claudius's guilty fear of Hamlet, Macbeth's aggressions against Banquo and Fleance, as well as Macduff's family. Except for the final vague reference to lost "grace" (4.4.33), the language is wholly secular; the framework of temptation and fall—Angelo's bulwark from before his meeting with Isabella (" 'Tis one thing to be tempted, Escalus, / Another thing to fall" [2.1.17–18])—has simply vanished. Initially striking in this speech is the primacy given by Angelo to his injury to Isabella, as opposed to the killing of Claudio; indeed, his view that Claudio's life, had he survived, would be "dishonor'd" (4.4.32) provocatively echoes Isabella's self-righteous scorn for her brother's willingness "to take life / From thine own sister's shame" (3.1.138–39)—further evidence of the compatibility of villain and heroine. Yet that Angelo shifts attention to Claudio abruptly, without even identifying the referent of "he," manifests a heavy conscience, according to familiar stage convention:

> This deed unshapes me quite, makes me unpregnant
> And dull to all proceedings. . . .
> . . . .
> . . . But that her tender shame
> Will not proclaim against her maiden loss,
> How might she tongue me! Yet reason dares her no, . . .
> . . . .
> . . . He should have liv'd,
> Save that his riotous youth with dangerous sense
> Might in the times to come have ta'en revenge,
> By so receiving a dishonor'd life
> With ransom of such shame. Would yet he had liv'd!
> Alack, when once our grace we have forgot,
> Nothing goes right—we would, and we would not.
>   (4.4.20–34)

This soliloquy, with its incorporation of subtle modulations of subject and tone into a meditative flow (note the several changes of direction within single lines), offers particularly rich material for the actor specializing in the nuanced inwardness of tragic experience—material that in performance, unfortunately, is often shunted aside by the cruder aspects of Angelo's villainy. But then there is always the danger of upstaging the Duke.

All of this may seem an overelaborate approach to a simple phenomenon. Certainly, Angelo's identity-shattering confrontation with himself
as desiring subject and the intensity of his emotional experience make
normal dramatic accompaniments to such an egregious fall into sin,
given that this is not, after all, a Morality Play universe populated by
allegorical personations of vices and virtues. On the other hand, the text's
close attention to the production of Angelo's interiority involves a
distinct overdetermination vis-à-vis the clear-cut moral issues and religious principles, which tend to brand him a villain of the garden (of
Eden) variety. There is also a pointed contrast with the lack of such
inwardness on the part of the Duke. It is, in fact, this insistent polarity
that lends the overdetermination most significance. To recognize that
Angelo's fall, like that of the first fallen angels, is part of a quasi-
providential scheme is to identify the (re)formation of consciousness
itself as the most basic level of what might appropriately be called, in the
common metaphor adapting the dramatic dynamic to military purposes,
the Duke's theater of operations.

When Vincentio reveals his machinations, Angelo's use of the honor-
ifics proper to his ruler helps to invest the moment of his greatest loss, the
public exposure and humiliation of his false self, with a sense of the
restoration of the "grace" he has "forgot":

> O my dread lord,
> I should be guiltier than my guiltiness,
> To think I can be undiscernible,
> When I perceive your Grace, like pow'r divine,
> Hath look'd upon my passes.
>   (5.1.366–70),

This is to make all but explicit the nature of the dynamic that functions
also, but below the surface, in *All's Well*, where the gracelike Helena
similarly provides essence and meaning in the place of the helpless
confusion, outward and inward, that had reigned thanks to her present-
absence. The Duke's sudden presence supplies the tragic void—
previously coded as volitional impasse ("we would and we would not")—
with unequivocal and manifest "guiltiness" befitting one who merely
sought to remain "undiscernible." Angelo is put squarely into the
position of the chastened Adam in the Garden. And as with Adam, this
recognition of a sinful soul opens the way to its redemption through
mercy. God's mercy towards mankind was exercised through the death

and resurrection of his Son; the Duke miraculously brings Claudio back to life as the mechanism of Angelo's salvation (and of Isabella's increased indebtedness): "By this Lord Angelo perceives he's safe; / Methinks I see a quick'ning in his eye" (5.1.494–95).

This statement, however, conspicuously imposes a reading upon an imposed silence, and it does not suppress the lingering trace of Angelo's all but final words some 120 lines earlier. For Angelo immediately follows his awestruck acknowledgment of the Duke's grace with a return to tragic subjectivity, redefining "grace," most unchristianlike, in terms of liberation from the intolerable pain of consciousness itself:

> Then, good Prince,
> No longer session hold upon my shame,
> But let my trial be mine own confession.
> Immediate sentence then, and sequent death,
> Is all the grace I beg.
>
> (5.1.370–74)

Nothing in the previous presentation of Angelo justifies the cynical dismissal of these sentiments that is implied in the Duke's attribution to him of a desire to live at any price. Thus to reduce him from tragic hero to contemptible and cowardly criminal is to "steal forth" the "soul" he had begun to discover despite himself. As an integral part of his "grace," the Duke sees to it that Angelo is punished by way of what his own words confirm as his worst nightmare: he will have to live with the highly public exposure of his hypocrisy. Such humiliation is reinforced, whatever the justice of the case, by the control over his sexuality imposed through his enforced marriage to Mariana. Angelo's punishment, like Lucio's, is indeed "pressing to death, whipping, and hanging," with Mariana's "virtue" (5.1.527), publicly attested by the Duke-as-friar, providing shameful leverage equivalent to that of the proclaimed vice of Kate Keepdown. Angelo has been induced to fall from seeming, only to be deprived of being. His failure as a ruler of others because of his failure to rule himself has made him the most abject of subjects—without subjectivity.

Isabella and the Bed Trick

The preceding discussion of Angelo leaves unaddressed, if not necessarily unanswered, the question that so starkly confronts that character at the outset: why is he so potently and helplessly attracted to such an emblem of virginal purity? There is an answer in the sense that merely to pose the question in these terms is to posit a response, at least on one level. And the terms are Angelo's own:

> Having waste ground enough,
> Shall we desire to raze the sanctuary
> And pitch our evils there? O fie, fie, fie!
> What dost thou? or what art thou, Angelo?
> Dost thou desire her foully for those things
> That make her good?
>
> (2.2.169–74)

Psychoanalytic criticism can press the issue by refining the relation between Angelo's sexual repression and his impulse to defile. It can only go so far, however, without finding itself outside the text. The dynamic of competing scripts extends Angelo's self-analysis in an ultimately more useful direction by linking his desire—as is consistently the case in the Problem Plays—with the impulse to dominate through possession. The Duke's grant of outward power to Angelo forces his inward power onto the public testing ground, and that power consists in sexual self-denial, coded as unrivalled virtue. Isabella, in these terms, threatens Angelo's monopoly—much, one might add, as Angelo's threatens the Duke's. In fact, this comparison is very much to the point, given the multiple exercise of power over sexuality that accompanies the Duke's reassertion of moral dominion, with Isabella's virginity his ultimate prize.

Such a view allows for an Isabella who has an agenda of her own in dealing with Angelo. This operates within and despite the limitations of gender, which affect her as they do Helena: marriage and the religious life are the two respectable female "vocations" (Cressida being consigned to a version of the unacceptable alternative). While Isabella is reluctant to become involved in the first place, the nature of that involvement, once undertaken, confirms that she is not merely doing her brother's bidding (or, for that matter, Lucio's, or even later the Duke's). Her arguments for mercy display an abstract passion that appears to have less to do with personal affection for her brother—indeed, she never shows a trace of this—than with her commitment to the role of heaven's own advocate. This commitment is surcharged with a personal intensity that helps to account for Angelo's sensual response:

> but man, proud man,
> Dress'd in a little brief authority,
> Most ignorant of what he's most assur'd
> (His glassy essence), like an angry ape
> Plays such fantastic tricks before high heaven
> As makes the angels weep.
>
> (2.2.117–22)

I have already noted (as have many others) the readiness with which Isabella's discourse of supplication modulates into double entendre, as well as the eroticism of her vision of martyrdom for virtue's sake.[24] In light of the association elsewhere of sexual desire with (to borrow Helena's imperfect term) "ambition," this undercurrent of sexuality points to more than mere repression. Perhaps oddly, given his aggressive sexual pursuit of Cressida (conducted, however, through his agent), the precedent of Troilus is to the point here: it is common to take his narcissism, with its clear link to ambivalent sexual feelings, as a mark of neurotic passivity; I have argued that his apparent helplessness masks an active program of self-construction, which will culminate in an absolute withdrawal from sexuality and the assumption of a martyr's role (an element that also figures in Helena's manipulations).

Such a withdrawal, though to a convent rather than the battlefield, is Isabella's starting point, and it should be recognized as an active rather than a passive move. We do wrong to downplay her *desire* for "a more strict restraint" (1.4.4) or her evident sense of herself as set aside from other women—the specialness that Lucio captures, in exaggerated form, in addressing her as "enskied, and sainted." She is not shocked by the news that Claudio has impregnated Juliet. Her response, "O, let him marry her" (1.4.49), bespeaks not moral outrage but rueful acceptance of such ways of the world and of ordinary mortals. The latter include a woman with whom she once, in the long-ago past, shared a naïve intimacy:

Isab. Some one with child by him? My cousin Juliet?

Lucio. Is she your cousin?

Isab. Adoptedly, as school-maids change their
     names
    By vain though apt affection.

(1.4.45–48)

"Vain" conveys an infinite distance on that former life and world. Now her identity is self-contained and depends upon self-withholding. It is also pointedly established, like Angelo's and the Duke's, in opposition to the prevailing permissiveness of Vienna.[25]

I stress the positive and active element in Isabella's initial position because it is common to take the Duke's manipulations of her, which extend to the extreme of keeping her brother's survival a secret from her for no apparent reason, as a process of education in simple humanity (and hence, for many commentators, in true religion).[26] In this reading, Isabella's withdrawal from the world, together with her moral rigidity and intolerance, manifests a lack of emotional sympathy, which renders hollow her preaching of the doctrine of mercy. The Duke—if not actually the incarnation of "pow'r divine" at least a wise patriarch along the lines of *Pygmalion*'s Henry Higgins—refines, softens, and implicitly "feminizes" her character to the point where she can kneel to beg forgiveness for Angelo on Mariana's behalf. He then falls in love with his creation, in keeping with the Pygmalion myth—and with the sentimentalizing adaptation of Bernard Shaw's play in the Broadway musical *My Fair Lady*.[27] (It may be argued that the more toughly problematic portrayal of Higgins in the original play intertextually engages more skeptical readings of Vincentio; Shaw's own view of *Measure for Measure* and the other Problem Plays as anticipating twentieth-century concerns and attitudes might be made part of such a study.)

My point, however, is not merely that such a highly teleological scenario—one, indeed, that the Duke himself might have described—displays a Broadway-like tendency to sing away the very problems that define the play and its genre. My more immediate objection is that from this standpoint Isabella is deprived of a projected scenario of her own, however isolationist it may be, with the result that the full extent of the Duke's penetration into the "dark corners" of his creations is obscured. In this view, he is merely writing his own comprehensively comic script, not rewriting the scripts of others—an activity that inevitably complicates the genre of his own. A more particular consequence is that the parallel between Isabella and Angelo, so clear from their matching rigidities (they would indeed "make a nice couple"), is abruptly curtailed at the very point when they come closest together, as figures whom the Duke keeps in the dark, then renders helpless with a blinding illumination.

Making Isabella susceptible to the Duke's apocalyptic finale entails far more than an education in human sensitivity. It involves, as with

Angelo, producing a fall from the summit of self-styled exemption from humanity—a position that the Duke alone may finally occupy—into an intensely experienced subjectivity, a condition of spiritual impasse and confusion ("And is this all? / Then, O you blessed ministers above, / Keep me in patience" [5.1.114–16]) that only the manifestation of "grace" can resolve (and supplant). To this extent, the Duke responds to the challenge implicitly posed to him by Isabella much as does Angelo himself. Indeed, such a perspective adds a dimension to the often perceived dynamic whereby the deputy does the Duke's psychological "dirty work" in unlawfully pursuing her (in the same way that Angelo is detailed to clean up Vienna without soiling Vincentio's image).

There is, however, a major difference, related to the obvious moral one, between the responses of Angelo and Isabella under pressure. For whereas Isabella does indeed display a remarkable range of emotions inconsistent with her "enskied, and sainted" status, her position as innocent victim consistently enables these emotions to be rechannelled into her self-righteousness. This phenomenon is immediately evident at the disclosure of Angelo's intentions, when her near-glee at discovering his hypocrisy exceeds the relief she might be expected to feel at the prospect of saving her brother:

> Seeming, seeming!
> I will proclaim thee, Angelo, look for't!
> Sign me a present pardon for my brother,
> Or with an outstretch'd throat I'll tell the world
> aloud
> What man thou art.
>
> (2.4.150–54)

Her leverage, as Angelo deflatingly points out, is illusory: "Who will believe thee, Isabel?" (2.4.154). For a brief moment, however, hers is the heady discourse of achieved power, and as she echoes the Duke's initial characterization of Angelo as a "seemer" she, too, effectively makes "being" a mark less of integrity than of weakness. Significantly, the position in which the Duke's last-act scenario initially puts Isabella entails a supposed recovery of the power to make such a public proclamation, then an apparently fatal undercutting, as the Duke, in his own person, pretends not to believe her. It is not only Angelo who is drawn more deeply into the Duke's trap by this device.

Isabella's outright lapses of religious composure in dealing with her situation are notorious. In earlier versions of the prison scene between Isabella and the condemned Claudio, the maiden—nowhere else a nun, we should bear in mind—is straightforwardly honest with her brother, responds sympathetically to his fearful entreaties, and yields with a sorrowful dignity. By drastic contrast, Shakespeare produces an evasive fencing match, with Isabella shrinking from disclosure of Angelo's offer ("O, I do fear thee, Claudio, and I quake" [3.1.73]) and even distorting Claudio's life expectancy ("six or seven winters" [3.1.75]); finally, she falls into an anger that again betrays the erotics of martyrdom, as she casts his will to live as sexual perversion and slanders their mother's chastity (note that their father is endowed with a Duke-like superhumanity):

> O you beast!
> O faithless coward! O dishonest wretch!
> Wilt thou be made a man out of my vice?
> Is't not a kind of incest, to take life
> From thine own sister's shame? What should I think?
> Heaven shield my mother play'd my father fair!
> For such a warped slip of wilderness
> Ne'er issu'd from his blood.
>
>   (3.1.135–42)

The upshot is a complete loss of control in violent, even blasphemous, abuse—arguably unmatched in Shakespearean drama for sheer vitriol:

> Take my defiance!
> Die, perish! Might but my bending down
> Reprieve thee from thy fate, it should proceed.
> I'll pray a thousand prayers for thy death,
> No word to save thee.
>
>   (3.1.142–46)

Against this background, it is not surprising to find Isabella omitting the grief for her brother's supposed death that is displayed by her pretextual precursors and leaping straight to the idea of revenge, which, admittedly, they also entertain. In her case, however, the leap is instantaneous and the prospect vividly personal: "O, I will to him, and pluck out his eyes!" (4.3.119). And it is followed by the Duke-as-friar's binding her to the contours of his scenario with quasi-diabolical temptations, including a reminiscence of the serpent's appeal to Eve's desire for God-like status:

> If you can pace your wisdom
> In that good path that I would wish it go,
> And you shall have your bosom on this wretch,
> Grace of the Duke, revenges to your heart,
> And general honor.
>
> (4.3.132–36)

She cannot, however, foresee in what form the Duke will supply his "grace"—the term also serves, we should remember, as his title—or to what degree her transcendent position will depend on his.

What is most significant about these multiple indications that Isabella's pretenses of superhumanity, no less than Angelo's, are giving way is the complete absence of self-conflict or introspection. Her only soliloquy applies to her predicament a logic as abstract and absolute as the Duke's—"Then, Isabel, live chaste, and, brother, die; / More than our brother is our chastity" (2.4.184–85)—even as her concessive sentence structure and overprotestation betray the fearful knowledge that its premise is false:

> Though he hath fall'n by prompture of the blood,
> Yet hath he in him such a mind of honor
> That had he twenty heads to tender down
> On twenty bloody blocks, he'ld yield them up.
>
> (2.4.178–81)

Isabella's blindness to her own "fallen self" manifests her extraordinary capacity to accommodate apparent contradiction, with the help of the basic assurance, which is undoubtedly built into the situation, that she is a victim of injustice. This is further evidence that her initial identity is not, like Angelo's, limited to a narrow and conventional image of resistance to temptation. If Angelo is plunged into the throes of soul making, a chaos in which all certainties are lost, Isabella's fidelity to a life of the soul in Christian terms appears to be overlaid on a more flexible and accommodating structure of self-belief, which in turn is founded on the rock of the conviction of her own righteousness. Her participation in this world can be justified and supported by the fact that she stands outside—and above—it. It is a perspective that highlights the paradoxical fitness of *this* "nun's lip" to *this* "friar's mouth."

To use the metaphor of the "soul" for the condition of subjectivity is not so anachronistic as might at first appear—witness the Duke's statement to Escalus that he has chosen Angelo "with special soul" (1.1.17) and his subsequent delineation of Angelo's power (and indirectly his own): "Your scope is as mine own, / So to enforce or qualify the laws / As to your soul seems good" (1.1.64–66). Here it is the conventional religious sense that obtrudes ironically. Such interplay between the meanings of "soul" sets off Isabella's difficulty in expounding her dilemma convincingly in terms of religious salvation, despite the impulse to do so that goes with her habit. This difficulty is evident in the face of the arguments of both her brother and Angelo ("I talk not of your soul" [2.4.57]): her sense of sin, of what it means to "die for ever" (2.4.108), is a manifestation of inwardness, not a function of theological doctrine, and it relates to her status in this world rather than in the next. This makes an intriguing recycling of the presentation of the heroine's dilemma in *Promos and Cassandra*, where, despite the pervasive religious ethic, Cassandra is never concerned about her salvation but only about "honor" (*Promos*, 463), in the sense of reputation. Certainly, the concept of "honor" is so central to Isabella's self-image that the Duke-as-friar makes it the cornerstone of his promise to her. It seems clear that, for Isabella, yielding to Angelo is a less appalling prospect in itself, or as a danger to her immortal soul, than for its threat to violate the identity she has staked on her purity. This is, again, an identity she can sustain—converting potential self-conflict into self-protective anger—by clinging to the fact that the fundamental challenge is outward rather than inward.

The orthodox idea of the soul also displays slippage into the concept of subjectivity in Claudio's case, when Isabella (reluctantly, because she anticipates his response) offers him a glimmer of hope. First he suggests that because Angelo is not concerned about damnation, the act cannot entail such punishment (3.1.112ff.). Then his previous acceptance of the friar's *contemptus mundi* consolation, including the proposition that in mortal existence "Thou art not thyself" (3.1.19), gives way to terror at prospective self-loss:

> This sensible warm motion to become
> A kneaded clod; and the delighted spirit
> To bathe in fiery floods, or to reside
> In thrilling region of thick-ribbed ice
> (3.1.119–22)

There is more at issue here than a mere lapse of religious faith. After all, the friar's advice—as befits both his false status and the Duke's true project—makes no mention of the promise of the afterlife, but exclusively promotes the attraction of surrendering subjectivity.[28]

By comparison with the vulnerable "seeming" of Angelo, Isabella's resistance to self-doubt, the capacity of her self-righteousness to shift its ground while remaining itself, poses a challenge to the Duke on territory closer to his own (and therefore, again, suggests an Angelo-like mechanism of attraction to her "virtue"). There is no possibility of exposing her "dark corners" by inducing a "fall" into conscience-ridden introspection; he must bait his hook (to adapt Angelo's resonant metaphor) not with a saint but with sainthood itself. Accordingly, his manipulations are calculated rather to embroil her in a plausibly impeccable (the word comes from the Latin for "free from sin") course of action that will at least have the effect, when all the circumstances are revealed, of making her completely dependent on his authority for "general honor." This course appears at the time to be unequivocally advantageous, as does his initial empowerment of Angelo, though the latter has enough intuitive self-knowledge to ask that "some more test be made of my mettle / Before so noble and so great a figure / Be stamp'd upon it" (1.1.48–49). I have already noted that the friar seductively promises Isabella revenge through a public appeal to the Duke, who then appears to leave her dangerously (and publicly) in the lurch. Nor is it too cynical to detect a hint of psychological benefit for Isabella even in the friar's major deception of her. For Claudio's supposed death surreptitiously offers Isabella a less tangible version of the concealment Angelo aims at—the promise of burying uncomfortable moral issues, of cutting off the potential for self-conflict.

Claudio's miraculous resurrection thus becomes at once welcome and disturbing in much the same way as Helena's. Conspicuously, as the news of his death elicits no grief from Isabella the revelation of his survival produces no blissful reunion. The vacuum is filled by the "reading" of the Duke, who deftly elides the feelings between brother and sister in the course of appropriating their supposed joy for his own purpose. His conditional logic ("If . . . and . . .") effectively offers such elision, convenient for all concerned, as a means of reinforcing the unrefusability of his new gift of "grace":

> If he be like your brother, for his sake
> Is he pardon'd, and for your lovely sake,

> Give me your hand, and say you will be mine,
> He is my brother too.
>
> (5.1.490–93)

For an audience, however, to bring Claudio and Isabella together
in this way is inevitably to bring back the bitterness of their last
encounter. And that Isabella joined in a plot to save Claudio and her
honor, too, thereby evading the implications of her choice not to sacrifice
herself for him, hardly erases the questionable morality of her absolut-
ism, publicly reaffirmed in her declaration a few lines before: "My
brother had but justice, / In that he did the thing for which he died"
(5.1.448–49).

This brings us to the key instance of a moral quagmire masquerading
as a way out: the friar's provision of Mariana as a substitute. Isabella
embraces this solution as if, like Ragozine's head, it were "an accident
that heaven provides" (4.3.77), and she thereby incurs a quasi-religious
obligation to the Duke. The salient moral question is one that has
troubled even critics who resolve it with reference to Elizabethan
laws and customs regarding marriage: why is it mere fornication for
Claudius and Juliet to sleep together outside of marriage, despite their
declared intention to marry and the fact that their act was committed
"mutually" (2.3.27), while it is "no sin," according to the Duke-as-friar
(4.1.72), to unite Mariana and the unwitting (but sinfully minded)
Angelo? The issue turns on the nature of precontracts and the conjugal
rights these were sometimes taken to confer. It is possible to distinguish
between the "true contract" (1.2.145) uniting Claudius and Juliet (a
verbal agreement "*de praesenti*") and, on the other hand, the "*de futura*"
"pre-contract" (4.1.71) between Angelo and Mariana invoked by the
Duke to justify the bed trick.[29] The fact is, however, that such a
distinction seems artificial within the play world—the more so because
it is promoted by a false friar and because it so neatly suits the interests of
the parties involved (with the exception of Angelo). The hairsplitting of
the rescued Isabella in the last scene, questionable on both logical and
theological grounds, glosses over the issue of intention in a way that
confirms that fine intellectual distinctions in this play lend themselves to
expedient manipulation:

> For Angelo,
> His act did not o'ertake his bad intent,
> And must be buried but as an intent

> That perish'd by the way. Thoughts are no subjects,
> Intents but merely thoughts.
>
> (5.1.450–54)

She is here, as elsewhere, measuring all causes by their effects on herself.

The deeper mechanism by which the bed trick engages Isabella in the Duke's hegemonic scenario is by appealing to the dimension of sexual power in her denial of sexuality. The friar miraculously resolves, from this perspective, the inherent contradiction in the notion of virginity as power—the fact that the exercise of that power entails its surrender. Helena needs an entire play of her own to transform the loss of virginity into a means of dominance. Isabella can gain the upper hand without doing the "dirty work" herself, and seemingly even without putting herself into the abject position of wife. The Duke offers her, in effect, the "pure" subjectivity of Mariana as a substitute for experiencing complex and conflicted feelings of her own.

Mariana's extreme and distorted subjectivity is itself the basis of a self-definition that works in the friar's favor. She feels compelled to assure him of her commitment to melancholy:

> I cry you mercy, sir, and well could wish
> You had not found me here so musical.
> Let me excuse me, and believe me so,
> My mirth it much displeas'd, but pleas'd my woe.
>
> (4.1.10–13)

Vincentio replies by projecting on music what we might take to be his own capacity "To make bad good, and good provoke to harm" (4.1.15). (He thereby recalls the equivocal relativism of Friar Lawrence in *Romeo and Juliet*, also a manipulative applier of "craft against vice": "Virtue itself turns vice, being misapplied, / And vice sometime by action dignified" [*Romeo*, 2.3.21–22].) Mariana's thirst for martyrdom through self-bestowal rather than self-withholding makes her not only the perfect tool of the Duke but the ideal foil to Isabella. That drive is left pitifully open-ended within the text, as she reiterates her desire to submit herself to a man who has multiply abused her, and who still scorns her: "I crave no other, nor no better man" (5.1.426). And the Duke continues to exercise power over her desire by threatening Angelo's execution.

This returns us, from a different angle, to Isabella's dramatic agreement to intervene with the Duke on Mariana's behalf in asking mercy for

Angelo. Isabella's decision, which is often taken to mark the triumph of merciful humanity over the impulse for revenge, may be read, on the contrary, as a final succumbing to the temptation to flaunt her moral victory before the Duke reveals her brother's survival and so opens the terms of that victory to scrutiny in a radically new light. It is significant that the Duke precipitates her action by all but inviting her to parade her own virtue and her contempt for her brother. She delivers her questionable affirmation that Claudio "had but justice" in response to the Duke's declaration: "He dies for Claudio's death" (5.1.443). In asking—with irony at her own expense—that Angelo be treated "As if my brother liv'd" (5.1.445), she begins the refocusing of the issue on Angelo's thwarted crimes against herself, and her humble assumption of responsibility only thinly conceals a sense of achieved power—with, moreover, a decided sexual dimension: "I partly think / A due sincerity governed his deeds, / Till he did look on me" (5.1.445–47).

It has been precisely on the sexual level, beginning with his attraction to her, that Isabella has defeated and degraded Angelo—"And yet," to adapt the Duke's definition of his project, her "nature never in the fight / To do in slander" (1.3.42–43). There is no more graphic demonstration of her entitlement to her "enskied, and sainted" image than her plea for mercy. Yet mercy in this case entails much the same self-aggrandizement for herself as for the Duke. Relevant here is the concern of the victorious Caesar in *Antony and Cleopatra* that Cleopatra should be treated mercifully, "Lest in her greatness, by some mortal stroke / She do defeat us; for her life in Rome / Would be eternal in our triumph" (*Antony*, 5.1.64–66). Isabella's intervention is the ultimate fulfillment of her reply to her brother's emotional remonstrance that "Death's a fearful thing": "And shamed life a hateful" (3.1.115–16). Thanks to the bed trick and its aftermath, Isabella appears to practice the art of self-withholding with consummate success. Yet all of this depends, more than she could realize, on the Duke.

In the cause of forcing this realization (and ultimately himself) upon her, the Duke may be seen as playing cat and mouse in the final scene as much with Isabella as with Angelo, beginning with his apparent abandonment of her to the deputy's judgment. And while she has nothing to lose in pleading for Angelo, it still makes a point about power that her "suit" is coolly dismissed as "unprofitable" (5.1.455)—as the Duke evidently does not expect his own to her will be. The disclosure of her brother's survival is the final strand in the web Vincentio has woven, the thread by which he draws the others tight. She had supposed the story to be over with the revelation of the Duke's identity, which was aimed at Angelo. The next revelation gets Angelo off the hook (at least superficially) and places her on it, extending the script to enfold her. The price Isabella will have to pay for her implicit challenge to the Duke's monopoly of virtue is essentially the same as that demanded (and eventually also paid) by Angelo: in yielding her virginity she will surrender control over her self in precisely the terms by which she had defined it. To what extent "general honor" as the Duke's wife will prove a consolation is a question that a Renaissance audience might not push as hard as does a modern one, given the fact that in marriages among the ruling class at the time private feelings—subjectivity itself—were understood to be absorbed into public functions, despite the discourse of amatory fulfillment with which such unions were generally invested.

The Duke and His *Subjects*

Together with the two blatant marriages of punishment (Angelo's and Lucio's), the climactic match of the Duke and Isabella pushes into the background the conventional romantic associations of marriage in comedy, which are here relegated to the anticlimactic union of Claudio and Juliet, lovers who constitute a skeptically revisionist gesture towards the "star-cross'd" (*Romeo*, Pro. 6) young innocents of Shakespeare's early romantic tragedy. Yet marriage is no less central in *Measure for Measure* than in Shakespeare's earlier comedies. Indeed, there are few of these in which the standard generic identification between multiple marriages and the (re)formation of the community is taken so far. Certainly, we may contrast these multiple marriages to the situation in *All's Well*, where Helena's marriage is the only one, though it is made so comprehensive in its implications, thanks to Helena's maneuvers, that it effectively encompasses the whole of the play world. By further contrast, the insistently mundane conditions of *Measure for Measure*'s Vienna, both its underworld and its upper world, offer no point of entry for marriage conceived as a vehicle of fairy-tale transformation. Rather, marriage emerges as an institution mediating between the personal and the collective (that is, social, economic, and political) spheres—a view that would doubtless have rung true to the experience of the original audience.

This mediating function of marriage in the text matches the connection between the personal and the transpersonal dimensions of Vincentio's project—the business of making subjects, in the political sense, by means of the control of subjectivity. The new state takes shape

by reshaping its members' interior beings—a process that entails breaking down their illusions of essential identity. Yet the framework of comic
structure and, in particular, the discourse of personal fulfillment through
marriage that sustains it enable this hegemony to be presented in terms
of the benevolent promotion of both the particular and the general
welfare. From this perspective, Shakespeare's Duke might indeed be
recognizable, for the audience of 1604, as a plausible representation of
the new monarch—a long-standing hypothesis that has recently returned to favor in less literal-minded forms[30]—although such a view, no
less than those exalting the Duke as "pow'r divine" in an allegorical
sense, has somehow to reckon with those factors that subversively display
such power as profoundly tyrannical beneath its reformist and merciful
surface.

Not only do the Duke's political gains come at the usual cost to
individual liberties, they also entail decidedly personal forms of gratifi-
cation. In this respect, all dramatic roads, including the final appropriation of Isabella, lead to the Duke's position vis-à-vis Angelo, against
whom he sets himself up from the start in terms of moral rivalry. Having
declared his political rationale, of which Friar Thomas encourages us to
be skeptical ("It rested in your Grace / To unloose this tied-up justice
when you pleas'd" [1.3.31–32]), Vincentio goes on to engage Angelo's
claims to superhuman purity, displaying an intensity—his descriptions
of Angelo are only slightly less vivid, if much more refined, than Lucio's
in act 3, scene 2—that belies his implication that the testing of the
deputy is merely one of various secondary "reasons":

> Moe reasons for this action
> At our more leisure shall I render you;
> Only, this one: Lord Angelo is precise;
> Stands at a guard with envy; scarce confesses
> That his blood flows; or that his appetite
> Is more to bread than stone: hence shall we see
> If power change purpose: what our seemers be.
>   (1.3.48–54)

The image from fencing—"Stands at a guard with envy"—not only
confirms the sense that the Duke is taking up a challenge, as in a duel,
but logically casts him in a highly dubious role: if pride is the chief of the
traditional seven deadly sins, envy is another. Indeed, the Duke's plotting here enters into intertextual dialogue with the discourse of several of

Shakespeare's envious villains, such as *Othello*'s Iago, who schemes to kill Cassio, in part because "He hath a daily beauty in his life / That makes me ugly" (*Othello*, 5.1.19–20), and the usurping Duke Frederick in *As You Like It*, who advises his daughter to accept his banishment of Rosalind because "she robs thee of thy name, / And thou wilt show more bright and seem more virtuous / When she is gone."[31]

So pressing is the personal aspect of the Duke's attitude towards Angelo throughout the play that we need to remind ourselves of the political stakes of the contest. These are real and high.[32] For if Angelo never displays the slightest disrespect for the Duke, either as a man or as a ruler, it is nonetheless apparent that against the background of the latter's avowed negligence such a transcendent reputation for righteousness in one of his high officials is bound implicitly to "do in slander" the Duke himself, with potentially dangerous practical consequences. Image and political power went hand in hand in Renaissance monarchies (even more so than in some modern democracies), and the Duke's professed indifference to politics as theater—a statement that forms part, after all, of his initial deception—makes the most ironic possible preparation for his subsequent role, especially if an allusion to King James would have been perceived by the original audiences:[33]

> I'll privily away. I love the people,
> But do not like to stage me to their eyes;
> Though it do well, I do not relish well
> Their loud applause and aves vehement;
> Nor do I think the man of safe discretion
> That does affect it.
>
> (1.1.67–72)

His triumphant fifth-act self-staging, the culmination of his metadramatic maneuvers, is precisely calculated to rally "loud applause and aves vehement" in support of the Duke's return to reincarnate what Claudio cynically terms "the demigod, Authority" (1.2.120). This point was stressed, to brilliant theatrical effect, in one recent production (by Michael Bogdanov at Stratford, Ontario, in 1985) in which the ruler in the guise of a contemporary military dictator, with dark glasses and armed guards, arrived by helicopter and displayed himself on a balcony to the accompaniment of deafening cheers and dazzling flashbulbs.[34] Unquestionably, the Duke's purging of his "vice" is part of a political dynamic, and the highly public scapegoatlike disgrace of Angelo is crucial not merely to the rehabilitation of the ruler's moral image but to his reconsolidation of power.

It remains to note, as further subverting the Duke's triumph in the audience's eyes, that various underworld elements resist consolidation. There is, of course, the straightforward question of the effectiveness of the social reforms imposed by Angelo and tacitly appropriated by the Duke. Pompey and Mistress Overdone may be suppressed, but their resilience and resourcefulness are guaranteed to keep the sex trade alive in one form or another, whether in the bawdy house or the "hot-house" (2.1.66), as long as people have sexual appetites—and as long as there is a "wise burgher" (1.2.100) unhindered by moral qualms in the pursuit of financial advantage. At the same time, Pompey's point to Escalus about instinct—"If your worship will take order for the drabs and the knaves, you need not to fear the bawds" (2.1.234–35)—fails to envisage the possible subjection of sexuality to nonsexual forces: after all, the only sexual intercourse that actually takes place within the text—the encounter of Mariana and Angelo—occurs despite the unwillingness of one of the parties. Indeed, procuring this union takes the efforts of more than common go-betweens for whom, one might say (adapting Isabella's accusation of Claudio), the "sin" is not a "trade" but "accidental" (3.1.148)—purportedly, indeed, another "accident that heaven provides" (4.3.77). Even by this route, the Duke's omnipotence, it would seem, is reaffirmed.

An even more fundamental and more intractable element, perhaps, is represented by the lowest comic character, the condemned murder Barnardine. In his untimely refusal to be executed he is responsible for the one situation that puzzles the Duke into impotence, much as Angelo is stymied (unlike Escalus) by the spirited recalcitrance of Pompey in act 2, scene 1. The threat thus posed to the Duke's control over circumstances is manifested in the only indication we get, indirect and transitory though it is, of possible self-doubt on his part: his confident assumption of the prerogatives of a genuine friar for once gives way, and, despite having undertaken to "give him a present shrift, and advise him for a better place" (4.2.207–8), the Duke must finally report to the Provost that Barnardine is "A creature unprepar'd, unmeet for death; / And to transport him in the mind he is / Were damnable" (4.3.67–69). Even this retraction is problematic: the Provost enters and requests the friar's (as it were) professional opinion—"Now, sir, how do you find the prisoner?" (4.3.66)—at the very moment when the Duke has echoed Angelo's abandonment of Pompey, Froth, and Elbow to Escalus, though on a rather more serious plane. Angelo merely throws up his hands and leaves, "Hoping you'll find good cause to whip them all" (2.1.137); the Duke drops all friarly pretenses: "Unfit to live, or die; O gravel heart! / After him, fellows, bring him to the block" (4.3.64–65).

Whether Vincentio's change of mind represents an inward faltering or a quick resumption of his role for the Provost's benefit—there is room for interpretation in performance here—he has obviously failed to extend his hegemony to the most basic manifestation of human subjectivity: the instinct for survival. It is the same point previously made by the failure to "stick" of the Duke-as-friar's advice that the condemned Claudio should dismiss life as "a thing / That none but fools would keep" (3.1.7–8). The entire execution sequence, intertwined with the sexual low-life scenes by means of the involvement of Pompey as Abhorson's assistant, sets limits to the power over life and death as Vincentio so conspicuously arrogates it at the conclusion. He can, at that point, impose or remove the death sentence with a word and without getting any in return—in contrast to Barnardine's earlier refusal to listen (which itself pointedly reversed the Duke's interruption of Pompey's expostulation at 3.2.29ff.):

> Duke. But hear you—
> Bar.   Not a word. If you have any thing to say to me, come to my ward; for thence will not I to-day.
>
> (4.3.61–63)

What the Duke cannot touch, even in his own person, is the desire to live—or, as in Angelo's case, to die. His public pardon of Barnardine, who has in no way deserved mercy and whose participation in the comic resolution is formally redundant, amounts to a symbolic extension of hegemony that clearly fails to impinge upon Barnardine's core of self, indomitably defined as an absolute moral vacuum. Against the background of their previous encounter, the Duke's remission of all "earthly faults" (5.1.483) seems less an exercise of power than a vain gesture of ratification after the fact, while his bland reference to Barnardine's spiritual state ("thou art said to have a stubborn soul / That apprehends no further than this world" [5.1.480–81]) confirms his retreat from claims to jurisdiction in that sphere. One "stubborn soul," at least, has survived his ministrations.

Such ironic qualifications of Vincentio's final position, however, scarcely impinge upon his triumph within the play world, the essence of which is that, amidst the proliferating disclosures of identity, he himself remains undisclosed, uniquely retaining the power that accrues to self-withholding. The climactic moment of revelation, as Lucio pulls off the friar's cowl, visually makes the point that the Duke never has to "show [his] knave's visage" (5.1.353)—or at least that that visage need never be made recognizable as such. As a rule, Shakespearean characters who enter into disguise—even Helena in *All's Well*—undergo some destabilization of identity; Vincentio merely destabilizes the identities of others. When, in the final scene, the mysterious friar is threatened with torture so that Escalus and Angelo may "know his purpose"—essentially, the principle of pressing to death—his denial of the Duke's power over him suggests a withholding of himself from himself, thanks to his ironic playing on his own identity (and even without the benefit of the pun on "subject" that a modern reader may supply): "Be not so hot. The Duke / Dare no more stretch this finger of mine than he / Dare rack his own. His subject am I not" (5.1.313–15). Yet the Duke-as-friar proceeds to tell the truth about the evil in Vienna, and even to suggest his own responsibility for it:

> laws for all faults,
> But faults so countenanc'd, that the strong statutes
> Stand like the forfeits in a barber's shop,
> As much in mock as mark.
>
> (5.1.319–22)

The response of the outraged Escalus is "Slander to th' state!" (5.1.322). Thus Vincentio purges the very "slander" he first determined to avoid by taking it on himself. There is, finally, no greater evidence of his metadramatic talents than this appropriation—prior to disposing of him—of the role of Lucio.

Chapter Five

Conclusion

Reputation and Influence, Onstage and Off

It would not suit my purposes to take up the stage history of the Problem Plays on its own, even if sufficient space were available to do justice to the subject. In the first place, there is no point in attempting to duplicate, much less supplant, the extensive accounts available elsewhere. Moreover, it is striking from the perspective of a very general study such as this one how close a correlation exists between trends in performance and in criticism, as far as the Problem Plays are concerned. My intention in this brief final chapter is to incorporate discussion of certain performance practices into a discursive survey—itself highly selective—of the critical reception of the Problem Plays. And what usefully stands out against this background is that productions have consistently encountered difficulties in attempting to stage some highly influential critical readings—for instance, the portrayal of *Measure for Measure*'s Duke as an allegorical figure of benevolent providence.

The preceding chapters have inevitably illustrated, in their critical biases, the premise of my discussion here—namely, that the Problem Plays lend themselves to interpretation in ways that reflect the interpreter, who is, in turn, necessarily a product of his or her culture (however self-consciousness and resistant). The same may be said, of course, of any artifact and its observer, and Shakespeare's plays generally, thanks to the status as monuments of Western Civilization projected upon them from the eighteenth century on, provide an especially sensitive barometer of changing interpretative pressures. In fact, documenting such pressures and tracing them to their roots have been popular critical activities recently, to the point where some members of the scholarly community would now dismiss textually oriented criticism (including this book) as outmoded or worse. For in the extreme versions of this view, to focus on texts (rather than contexts) is merely to serve the educational establishment, whose interests are understood to be ideological indoctrination and political inhibition if not intimidation. As it happens, however—

and some of the same critics would agree—the Problem Plays may themselves be read as provocatively engaging similar political issues.

The (Pre-Twentieth-Century) Past

The very notion of such engagement is relatively recent in Shakespearean criticism, as elsewhere. The common ground between the critical and theatrical history of the Problem Plays begins with the commonplace observation that these works have come into their own in the twentieth century, especially the late twentieth century. Needless to say, they have participated in the explosion of critical attention to all of Shakespeare's work that has accompanied the professionalization of literary studies and the proliferation of "higher education."[1] But this does not account for the increasing prominence that criticism has assigned them within the Shakespearean canon or for their newfound popularity in the theater.

To "come into their own" means particularly to come with textual integrity, their problems intact. But then historically it has been more difficult for the Problem Plays than for most of Shakespeare's work to gain an audience or readership otherwise. Accordingly, they remained in relative obscurity as Shakespeare underwent his eighteenth- and nineteenth-century metamorphosis into England's national Bard. As an established part of his oeuvre, they could not be wholly ignored, and the theater at least found ways of minimizing their problematic qualities. Yet from literary figures throughout this period (setting aside Dr. Johnson's landmark of Shakespearean criticism, cited in chapter 3), they attracted mainly superficial descriptions or scattered comments, many of the latter noncommittal or enigmatic. The most intriguing may be the remark of Goethe: "*Macbeth* is Shakespeare's best acting play, the one in which he shows most understanding of the stage. But would you see his mind unfettered, read *Troilus and Cressida*."[2]

The dominant view of the plays was reflected in their stage treatment, insofar as they were staged at all. In common with all of Shakespeare's works, they were subjected to freewheeling adaptation—most of which now looks merely absurd—in response to changing theatrical tastes. In common with the comedies generally, which rated as an inferior species and were little played until the nineteenth century, *All's Well* and *Measure for Measure* were first plundered for characters and plot devices with the object of transforming them into innocuously superficial entertainments. In the early 1660s, under the bland rubric of *The Law against Lovers*, William Davenant fantastically combined elements of *Measure for*

Measure—not, however, the low-life elements—with the characters of Beatrice and Benedick from *Much Ado about Nothing*, as well as such inventions as a dancing and singing "little girl," described by Samuel Pepys in his *Diary*.[3] Another production in 1695, probably by Charles Gildon, turned the play into a quasi-operatic spectacle, with the improbable assistance of a masque staged by Escalus for Angelo; the underworld characters are virtually eliminated, and the bed trick is rationalized by making Mariana Angelo's secret wife (Odell 1: 72–74 and 195–97). Two farcical versions of *All's Well*, centering on Parolles at the expense of the rest of the play, were mounted in the eighteenth century, and the play (or certain rudiments of it) appeared in the form of a musical extravaganza as late as 1832 (at Covent Garden) (Price, 18–22; Odell 2: 146–47).

As far as *Troilus* is concerned, the scant stage history between Shakespeare's day—presuming that it was staged then—and the twentieth century belongs exclusively to Dryden's 1679 adaptation, whose subtitle, *The Truth Found Too Late*, points to his crucial alteration: as part of his program to "remove that Heap of Rubbish under which many excellent Thoughts lay wholly bury'd (cited in Odell 1: 49), Cressida is unequivocally absolved. Dryden's faithful heroine is compelled to feign love for Diomedes as part of a scheme to escape, and Troilus tragically misinterprets her feigning. Especially given the obvious project here of relocating tragedy in circumstances rather than in the characters, it is ironic that this gesture of intertextual defiance effectively makes Cressida *truer* than Troilus and arguably disinters the very problematizing elements buried in Shakespeare's characterizations: the ambiguity of Cressida's behavior in the night scene and the misconstruction (in the fullest sense) involved in Troilus's reading of it.

The capacity of the most distorted adaptation to shed valuable light on the original text by entering into intertextual dialogue with it may be evident in the theatrical interest attracted by particular characters. To place Parolles in the foreground, however absurdly, is actually to be "on to something" about *All's Well*. By the same token, the omission of much of the low-life material from versions of *Measure for Measure* staged during the eighteenth century would appear to throw Lucio into relief by taking him out of his element. Thus, as John Russell Brown points out, a critic for the *London Chronicle* writing in 1758 accords Lucio a prominence and, implicitly, a complexity beyond what literary criticism—at least until very recently—has been willing to grant him:

> The part of Lucio . . . is, as far as I can
> judge, both for humour and nature, by many

degrees superior to any character of the same
stamp, introduced upon the stage since.[4]

More or less drastic rewritings were the rule for Shakespeare's plays
generally until the late nineteenth century, when scholarly accuracy
began to encroach upon the territory previously dominated by theatrical
expedience and moral squeamishness. In the case of the Problem Plays,
however, the mixture of romantic and realist modes created a special
situation. From the late eighteenth century on, the romantic side had
considerable appeal, based especially on the potential for sentimentalizing Helena and Isabella—parts that were taken by many famous actresses. (The fact that Cressida was not susceptible to such treatment,
being beyond the moral pale, no doubt helps to account for the complete
neglect of the third play during this period.) *All's Well* and *Measure for
Measure* were never among the most frequently staged of the comedies,
but when they were played they were stripped as fully as possible of their
problematizing elements.

Such an agenda meant at least keeping the low-life business to a bare
minimum; thus, for instance, the pendulum now swung back against
Parolles, while the underworld of *Measure for Measure*, as had been
standard procedure from the Restoration onward, underwent various
degrees of purging. But the challenge also existed of deproblematizing
the heroines themselves and the action surrounding them. A significant
transitional text in this regard is the "Bell acting edition" (so called after
John Bell, the London publisher) of 1773, which featured an introduction and notes by Thomas Gentleman. While Gentleman approves of the
prominence still accorded Parolles in this version, he precociously displays a proto-Victorian distaste for Helena's aggressiveness, coupled
with a burgeoning Romantic admiration of her love sentiments (Price,
19–20). In anticipation of Coleridge's designation of her as Shakespeare's
"loveliest character," Helena was made at once more central, more
passive, and more pitiful in John Philip Kemble's versions of 1793 and
1811 (even more so in the latter), and although the bed trick could not be
dispensed with entirely the presentation of it was softened and the
references to Helena's pregnancy were expunged (Price, 23–27).

As for *Measure for Measure*, Gentleman delivers a fascinatingly inco-
herent judgment upon even the heavily expurgated Bell text, which has
also been improved in his view by a new conclusion—five lines added to
the Duke's final speech:

> Dear Isabel, I have a motion much imports your good,
> Shade not, sweet saint, those graces with a veil,
> Nor in a nunnery hide thee; say thou'rt mine;
> Thy Duke, thy Friar, tempts thee from thy vows.
> Let thy clear spirit shine in Publick life;
> No cloister'd sister, but thy Prince's wife.
>   (cited in Odell 2: 25)

Evidently, in Gentleman's view, this speech resolves the troubling ambiguity of the ending by justifying the surprise marriage proposal (and Isabella's presumed acceptance) in moral terms—the same terms that the Duke initially uses in deputizing Angelo. Yet for all that, and despite his endorsement of this "acting edition," Gentleman concludes by relegating the play to the study on grounds that obviously, in the matter of generic uncertainty, anticipate the category of Problem Play: "upon the whole of this play, for we cannot stile it either Tragedy or Comedy, there are several great beauties, clouded with much trifling and indecent dialogue; it must always be heavy to the majority of an audience; yet, purged of impurities and superfluities, as we hope the readers will find it in this edition, it may be entertaining and instructive in the closet" (cited in Odell 2: 25). All in all, Gentleman's comments on the two plays bear convincing witness that, from early days, the problematic of genre was intertwined both with the doubtful handling of moral issues and with more obvious violations of "decency."

The (Twentieth-Century) Present

The salient fact that emerges from the Problem Plays' pre-twentieth-century critical and theatrical histories, taken together, is that to bring these texts *out* of the closet is a threatening activity unless they can somehow be deproblematized—something that Michael Jamieson, incidentally, writing in 1972, considered already to have been accomplished by dint of the sheer attention paid to them.[5] I wish to suggest that such an attitude and the sanitizing impulse that goes with it have continued to figure over the last 100 years, forming a counterpoint—sometimes in very close harmony—to the newfound interest in their problems as such. In its crudest form, this perspective was a direct extension of Victorian prudery, the bane of Shaw and other early champions of the plays. The latter prominently included William Poel, who specialized in innovative and self-consciously (if loosely) "Elizabethan" stagings. Despite the warning of his university tutor that *Measure for Measure* and *Troilus* were too indecent even to read, Poel became the first director in modern times to mount all three plays (Jamieson, 126). His production of *Troilus* in 1912 appears to have been distinguished mainly for bringing to notice a brilliant amateur named Edith Evans. That of *Measure for Measure* in 1893, despite drastic cuts to the low-life scenes (he also decided not to dress Isabella as a nun, in order to help account for the Duke's proposal [Speaight, 135]), provoked William Archer, the progressive dramatic critic and translator of Ibsen, to condemn the work for obscenity.[6] It is perhaps more disconcerting to find Odell, the author of the first major scholarly history of Shakespearean staging (1920), opining that *Measure for Measure*, together with *All's Well*, "has a revolting plot" and doubting whether it should ever be played "if its rendition necessitates the retention of much, or indeed any, of the Froth, Pompey, Elbow, Mrs. Overdone material" (Odell 2: 23–24). This is by way of praising the expurgated Bell version for being "fumigated" and "disinfected of the gross underworld folk"—especially disturbing rhetoric in view of Odell's flippant dismissal, shortly afterwards, of Jessica (in *The Merchant of Venice*) as "this Jewess" (Odell 2: 24, 26).

It is, of course, all too easy to find examples of egregiously benighted attitudes on the part of distinguished academics—one need not even hunt so far afield. But my point is not a frivolous one: it relates to the continuity of the moralistic strand of the critical tradition. Odell was for many years the colleague (at Columbia University) of Lawrence, the author (11 years later) of the first study of the Problem Plays as a group, who pays tribute to Odell in his preface (Lawrence, 12). In this context, it is easier to pick up the similar tone of moral disgust informing Lawrence's exposition of his thesis—the incongruity of romantic and realistic elements: "Instead of gay pictures of cheerful scenes, to be accepted with a smile and a jest, we are frequently offered unpleasant and sometimes even repulsive episodes, and characters whose conduct gives rise to sustained questioning of action and motive" (Lawrence, 20–21). What opens the door to productive criticism on Lawrence's part, of course, is that he comes to account for this strange mixture, not to purify it, but the gist of his argument remains deproblematizing; he sought, according to his preface to the second edition in 1958, "to dispel the perplexities which the problem comedies arouse in the minds of thoughtful readers and spectators today" (Lawrence, 9). The route he chose was a significant one: by stressing the organic power of the myths that lie behind Shakespeare's plots, he not only excused the Bard for failing to bring them cogently down to earth ("Problem comedy was never really congenial to Shakespeare's genius" [Lawrence, 202]) but also implicitly invoked the sanction of a transcendent spirituality, in whose light the sordid realism associated with the texts' problems pales into insignificance.

It is arguably this direction that one major strain of later twentieth-century criticism and production has pursued. We find it, to some degree, wherever a stylized or mythologized background is used to convey the assurance of a source of stable values. This is rarest, no doubt, in the case of *Troilus*, where the central characters, through whom such an assurance must be made to flow, are blatantly incapable of such a function; indeed, in performance they often simply "lose distinction" as individual characters (to quote Troilus on his "joys") in the general atmosphere of brutality and decadence. It takes, arguably, a director's sure sense of the connection between Troilus's love game and history's war game to realize the text's interplay between idealism and cynicism, and the attraction of the deflationary elements, which have seemed increasingly blatant as the present century has spawned war after war, has generally outweighed the interest of the hero's myth-making project. Even a pioneering pre–Second World War production by Michael Macowan (Westminster Theatre, 1938) elicited the telling comment that the play seemed to have been "*written* in modern dress" (Speaight, 163). In these circumstances, the equivalent of the evasion of difficulty by the bolstering of romance, as practiced in the other texts, may be the inflation of the satirical dimension to the point where it farcically draws the teeth of the text's realism; of this approach there are a number of recorded examples—for instance, Tyrone Guthrie's 1956 production at the Old Vic, in which "Hohenzollern Trojans and Ruritanian Greeks exposed their feet of clay" in "a field-day of satiric fun" (Speaight, 271).

On the other hand, the central figures of *All's Well* and *Measure for Measure* have often been elevated above their milieux by critics and directors alike—or, rather, not *quite* alike, since theatrical practice has had a hard time carrying off the more extreme forms of apotheosis to which some criticism has resorted. Helenas incarnating romantic love have abounded since the eighteenth century. The Christ-like Helena of Knight, however (discussed in chapter 3 above), has not presented itself to many directors as a solution to the play's insistent mixture of modes and tones. It seems to have been a strongly New Critical sense of this mixture as intractable in the theater that led Price, writing in 1968, to claim (on what verifiable basis, it is not clear) that "No really satisfying production of *All's Well* has yet been accomplished in a major theatre" (Price, 71).

By contrast, the presentation of Duke Vincentio as a figure of transcendent authority has a well-established stage history, as is clear from the detailed survey of modern productions (from 1950 through 1970) that has been made by Jane Williamson.[7] At first, within this period, Dukes tended to be preternaturally wise and virtuous yet simultaneously human. Indeed, in Peter Brook's 1950 production of *Measure for Measure* at Stratford-upon-Avon the character was evidently presented so engagingly as to make the audience forget, according to Harold Hobson, that "[the Duke] is a masquerader and an eavesdropper, a practical joker, and a liar" (cited in Williamson, 152); this is an aspect of the significant larger impression recorded by Williamson that "the problems raised by the scholars in the study seemed to disappear on the stage" (Williamson, 150). Paradoxically, the influence of academic theologizing criticism— the most obvious sort of attempt to erase the play's problems[8]—resulted in greater difficulties on stage when it made itself strongly felt in the 1960s. Those productions that deified the Duke naturally ran the risk, given his problematic behavior and motives, of producing a God "with repellent as well as attractive qualities, . . . an enigmatic, mysterious deity who controlled a universe in which happiness seemed to be achieved only through pain" (Williamson, 160). Thus, while there is consistent evidence of the deproblematizing impulse on the part of both literary scholars and stagers of productions, neither camp appears to have found the other's methods wholly satisfactory.

The mythologizing approach to the Problem Plays is, however, only half of the twentieth-century story, both critically and theatrically. For every approach to the texts that has sought to subordinate their realism there has been, beginning with Shaw, another that has insisted upon it and sought to banish the romantic aspects and spiritual overtones as vestiges, excrescences, or psychological evasions. With respect to *Troilus*, such self-conscious realism has been by far the dominant school. Along with this perspective comes a commitment to the idea of the plays' problems—not just a willingness but an eagerness to face facts. Yet a case can be made that here, too, a surreptitious deproblematizing impulse is at work, and this is not surprising, perhaps, given the grounding of most such readings in New Criticism, psychoanalytic criticism, or a mixture of both, since critics of these persuasions put a particular premium on rationalizing literary phenomena. Accordingly, instead of a retreat into myth the impulse now takes the form of an attempt to furnish thorough and coherent explanations. Among other consequences, such approaches entail the fixing of meanings, placing them beyond the reach of the very texts that produce them—in conjunction, of course, with their readers or audiences.

The first prominent literary critic who falls into this group is Tillyard, who is clearly of two minds about the plays' problematic nature, despite his decision to employ the term Problem Play, and to do so "equivocally"—an apparent sign of openness to *unfixed* meanings. Although he complains that the term is forced upon him for want of a better, "as a matter of convenience" (Tillyard 1950, 1), in fact it proves eminently convenient from the start, enabling him to distinguish between two sorts of "problem children": the "radically schizophrenic" (*All's Well, Measure for Measure*) and the brilliant but misunderstood (*Hamlet, Troilus*) (Tillyard 1950, 2). Note that in thus implicitly adopting the role of psychologist to Shakespeare's brainchildren Tillyard puts a typically New Critical premium on making things whole and unified—on, in effect, removing equivocation, or where it cannot be removed imposing the stigma of artistic failure.

The equivalent of Tillyard's project in terms of traditional psychoanalysis is socialization, the process of integrating subjects into a system of values designated as "healthy" or "mature." Throughout the sixties, seventies, and eighties, there appeared a great many critical studies applying Freudian psychology to the Problem Plays—a trend that continues, but with two major differences: first, psychoanalytic criticism is now largely text-centered rather than author- (or even character-) centered; secondly, its Freudianism has generally been modified along the lines developed by Jacques Lacan. Even in their pre-Lacanian manifestations, however, the most interesting psychological approaches went well beyond the preoccupation with the author's psyche that was figured early on in the expression "dark comedies" and against which Lawrence reacted defensively at the end of his early study ("Shakespeare's mind, we *must* believe, was singularly healthy" [Lawrence, 202; emphasis mine]). Moreover, such valuable work as that of Richard P. Wheeler demonstrates the substantial critical dividends that may be gleaned even where the concept of the author remains paramount—as, indeed, it does even in Wheeler's title (*Shakespeare's Development and the Problem Comedies*).[9]

The problematic conduct of Helena and Bertram especially, as well as of Vincentio, Angelo, and Isabella—and especially in combination—has attracted much probing psychological commentary, though often at the familiar cost of transforming fictive constructs into de facto analysands.

Psychoanalytic attention to *Troilus*—omitted from Wheeler's study (for the formal reason, he says, that the play is not a comedy [Wheeler, 2n.])—has been belated but has more than made up its lost ground in recent years, thanks mainly to feminist critics (I cited studies by Janet Adelman, Carol Cook, and Linda Charnes in chapter 2), many of whom find useful Lacan's ideas concerning the psychosocial construction of subjectivity in general and of gender in particular. Nor have such critics neglected the other two plays—especially *All's Well*, with its central problem of the romantic-aggressive heroine. In dealing with this phenomenon, discussions with a psychological emphasis, like that of Asp (cited in chapter 3), make a natural fit with those concentrating on sexual politics, such as Neely's analysis of, and extrapolation from, Helena's conversation with Parolles on the subject of virginity (Neely, 67–68). Both approaches are ultimately concerned with freeing Helena from the trappings of transcendental significance that her femininity has been made to bear since the late 1700s—a project analogous, for reasons that I hope my readings of the two plays have made clear, to the demythologizing of Cressida as an emblem of female fickleness.

The psychologizing trend in criticism of the Problem Plays, therefore, may be seen in part as a refutation of romantic myth making and may be related to the general prevalence of realism in their performance. A survey of the increasingly numerous productions over the past 30 years suggests that the majority—if not necessarily the most interesting ones—reflect the tendency, planted in the modern theater by the *real* problem plays of the turn of the nineteenth century, to have the theatrical experience make not merely sense but *common* sense for contemporary audiences. The later twentieth century is also in a position to draw on theatrical styles, ranging from Brechtian Expressionism to Absurdism to the Theater of Cruelty, that push realism so hard, so to speak, that it comes out the other end in varieties of surrealism—a mode that some would consider to have been anticipated by the Jacobeans generally, even by the Problem Plays themselves. The most provocative productions of the last few years would appear to have been those (Bogdanov's 1985 *Measure for Measure* at Stratford, Ontario, referred to earlier, is a case in point) that relentlessly pursue the idea of corruption or (for *All's Well*) jadedness so as to show that the dominant figures rise not in opposition to such a milieu but out of it—and therefore remain part of it. The paradoxical result is a restoration of the mode of myth.

This brings us, in this whirlwind tour of criticism and performance, to the self-consciously political poststructuralist positions of New Historicism and Cultural Materialism. These are the dominant modes among contemporary critics of the Problem Plays, if not of Early Modern English literature at large, and their influence is apparent in the theatrical trends I have just described—particularly the tendency to remythologize figures of authority in negative terms. Here *All's Well*, the most obvious candidate for feminist analysis, takes a backseat to the more conventionally political *Troilus* and especially *Measure for Measure*, although at least one reading of *All's Well* (that of Richard A. Levin [1980], cited earlier) ahistorically anticipates New Historicism in taking Helena's "realistic" aggressive side to a Machiavellian extreme. The premise of all such readings, although they differ in emphasis and detail, is that the dramatic texts of Shakespeare's period inscribe the dialectical opposition between authority (emanating from the ruling class) and subversion (the revolutionary tendencies of the common people). The relation between authority and subversion is taken to operate on authority's terms, however, in accordance with the principle of "containment,"[10] which provides that the forces of order actually construct disorder in order to consolidate their hegemony. Thus Dollimore, in his influential essay on *Measure for Measure*, specifically seeks to "forestall" (Dollimore 1985, 72) readings that might apply Mikhail Bakhtin's theory of the revolutionary carnivalesque[11] so as to attribute genuine subversive power to the low-life energies of the play's underworld.

A perspective such as Dollimore's produces a Duke every bit as all-knowing, all-wise, and all-powerful as that of the theologizing critics. The similarity in approaches is impossible to miss in Goldberg's observation that Lucio's early statement, "Grace is grace, despite of all controversy" (*MM*, 1.2.24–25), anticipates the Duke's eventual enactment of an absolutist and transcendent "grace" (Goldberg, 236). Arguably, to take this position, at once deflationary and inflationary, is also to be seduced by Vincentio. Certainly, Tennenhouse conspicuously adopts the Duke's own view in claiming that the play is concerned to demonstrate the eruption of disorder in the absence of the monarch (Tennenhouse, 156–59). For him, "[a]ll of those features which modern literary folk find so disturbing about Vincentio actually aim at . . . the revelation of an earlier, rarefied and magical form of patriarchy as the principle of political order" (Tennenhouse, 159). This deproblematizing argument is essentially the same as that of numerous traditional commentators who maintained that the problems presented by the Duke's conduct for historically uninformed readers and audiences simply would not appear against a background of unquestioning and absolute faith in

religious authority such as supposedly characterized Shakespeare's age.
Thus, for instance, F. R. Leavis—the mid-century conservative bane of
today's progressive political critics—discerned in the ending of *Measure
for Measure* "a consummately right and satisfying fulfilment of the
essential design."[12]

In my introductory chapter I referred to the tendency of poststructuralist critical approaches to align the Problem Plays more closely with the
remainder of the Shakespearean canon, now revealed as multifariously
problematic. A corollary of this phenomenon is that the Problem Plays,
which are, one might say, so frank about their undermining of received
values, their failure to resolve themselves convincingly, present less of a
target for analytical modes determined above all to bring to light
"hidden agendas." Such critical stances thrive on resistance, of which
these texts offer very little—except to interpreters who would smooth
out their difficulties. It is hard to accuse texts of blindness and complicity
when self-consciousness and ironic subversion are their stock-in-trade.
The most resolutely cynical perspective fails to out-cynic *Troilus*. In
conformity with its very raison d'être, therefore, New Historicist criticism has sometimes produced resistance where, arguably, there is none (a
version, ironically, of authority's role in the subversion-containment
paradigm). This tendency is evident when earlier readings of Vincentio
as a textually sanctioned wielder of power, whether specifically King
James or not, are recycled with a new proletarian orientation that
presumes such power—and therefore, ultimately, the complicit text
itself—to be negative rather than positive.

Yet there is no denying that materialist skepticism regarding
authority—essentially, the view of Machiavelli—*plays* better than does
the romantic transcendentalism that makes heavenly, rather than resolutely terrestrial, manipulators out of Vincentio and Helena and a figure
of tragic sentimental grandeur out of Troilus (if rarely Cressida). This is
partly so, no doubt, because of the basic principle, evident as far back as
the Medieval stage and certainly throughout Shakespearean drama, that
evil is more engaging and exciting onstage than is virtue. But a case can
also be made that Machiavellianism better suits the concept of
metadrama—not necessarily in the abstract but as I believe it functions
in these plays. The roughly 30-year history of metadramatic criticism—
since Barton's *Shakespeare and the Idea of the Play* in 1962—provides
ample evidence that the approach is adaptable to radically divergent
concepts of the metadramatists, that is, to both myth making and myth
breaking. Thus, for instance, Thomas Van Laan finds Vincentio full of

"the sheer delight he can derive from successfully bringing off his multiple theatrical achievement," whereas for Alexander Leggatt Vincentio's play writing is ironically exposed as incompetent.[13] Honigmann sees the moment when "the Duke has lost control of his play"—that is, Angelo's double cross—as focusing the Duke's responsibility "for its genre, and for our genre-expectations," but also as calling attention to "a more efficient dramatist who tidies up, so to say, behind the Duke, and ensures that all of the play's bits and pieces combine plausibly together" (Honigmann 167–68).

Honigmann's outlook is notable for affirming Shakespeare's secure control over his creation. It has been my working thesis, as it is my conclusion, that the internal scripts presented here, most unlike a providential scheme, involve a large element of improvisation and are, by definition and by conspicuous implication, imperfect even in their triumph. Yet I would also argue that they effectively eclipse the author as presumptive producer of such dramatic ironies, just as they preclude the emergence of a coherent moral vision or a stable set of human values. And this is to recuperate, in contrast with the idea of a perfectly hegemonic internal or external authority—and contrary to the major tendencies of criticism from its inception—the notion of the Problem Plays as precisely that.

The Future

In deference to the imperatives of symmetry, it seems fitting (if foolhardy) to conclude with a tentative remark or two on possible future directions for the criticism and staging of the Problem Plays. Implicit in my discussion of the currently dominant schools, with their "historical" remythologizing of the plays in terms of dialectical power struggle, has been my sense that such approaches have already reached their limit and offer little potential for development. Onstage and off, the corruption of these play worlds has been carried to (often convincing) extremes, their ruling classes invested with a maximum of cynicism, their manipulating figures made the very models of postmodern Machiavellians—that is, when their manipulations have been recognized as such. And this qualification points to both a limitation of materialist criticism and the further promise of an (intersecting) avenue—one that has already seen quite a lot of traffic.

My readings have suggested that Troilus and Helena can only fully join Vincentio as full-fledged metadramatists when the concept of manipulation is extended beyond the sphere of politics, beyond even the confines of action, to include the "fashioning" of both the self and others according to alternative semiotic systems. To return to one of the traditional critical problems, one must be able to accommodate within the same interpretative space—without erasing either term—both Helena's "ambition" and her passivity, her means and ends. Likewise, the triumph of Troilus must be brought into focus within the same picture as his tragic victimization. Despite the apparent applicability of Greenblatt's terminology and of the broad principle behind it, this is territory that New Historicism and Cultural Materialism are not inclined to explore, since it is not strictly historical or political.

Such territory would seem to be, however, the natural province of forms of poststructuralist feminism, given the central and pervasive role of sexual politics in the plays' character dynamics. An especially useful focus might be the precise mechanisms whereby both the active and passive female characters—in sharp contrast, say, to Portia or Rosalind— are constructed as pawns in games they cannot win, even if they get what they think they want (Helena's Bertram, Mariana's Angelo). Although no feminist critic, to my knowledge, has grappled with the Problem Plays as a group in a sustained way, the numerous feminist treatments to date of Helena and Bertram, as well as Troilus and Cressida, have produced specific insights exciting enough to whet the appetite for more systematic and comprehensive investigation. And the relative neglect, from this angle, of the quasi-love quadrangle in *Measure for Measure* further delineates the gap to be filled. This line of inquiry might also extend to engaging the shadowy interrelation between internal dramatists and offstage author—conceivably a means of addressing with some theoretical precision the question of how open these texts are to their own problems and to their more and less effective problem solvers.[14] And therein lies perhaps the best hope for a thorough revitalization of the plays as a distinctive subgenre.

If feminist approaches, among foreseeable future trends, appear to offer the most interesting possibilities for scholarly criticism, they also hold considerable potential for generating innovative versions of the plays onstage. Such a development would be in line with the vital contribution currently being made to the theatrical scene, especially in Britain, by directors and playwrights committed to exploring gender as a (patriarchal) construct—that is, precisely, as something *staged*. It appears that to date, whether or not they have been stylistically "realistic," feminist productions of the Problem Plays (as of Shakespeare generally) have largely been confined to (and by) traditional "liberal humanist" assumptions.

An exception may have been the pointedly feminist production of *Troilus* by Howard Davies for the Royal Shakespeare Company in 1985, although the published accounts (my only basis for judgment) point in different directions. Hodgdon makes a detailed and ingenious argument for this production as an exception to a well-documented pattern of recent misogynistic stagings, concluding that Davies's production "calls attention to the act of spectatorship, locating its power and value as decidedly female" and so "questions the gendered economy of inherited looking capital and renders it transgressive" (Hodgdon 1990, 271–72). The extent of the critical hostility she records is promising: many male-gazers were clearly rubbed the wrong way. Still, that hostility appears to have been centered on a textual flattening related to what Hodgdon considers the central transgressive fact—namely, that Cressida was presented not merely as "a historical subject" (Hodgdon 1990, 271) but specifically as a late nineteenth-century New Woman.

Interestingly, the same impulse seems to have underlain Peter Brook's 1979 production of a French translation of *Measure for Measure*, in which, according to Wolfgang Sohlich, Isabella figured as a "pioneering feminist" and a "devout and heroic Jeanne D'Arc," but in such a way as to "[gloss] over contradictions instead of foregrounding them."[15] Joan, of course, was one of Shaw's protofeminist heroines, though even in his hands she took on a romantic aura of redemptionism.[16] In Davies's *Troilus*, too, such a return, in effect, to the very historical source for the concept of the Problem Plays evidently reinscribed something of that age's notion of solutions, for it entailed inventing, as an excuse for Cressida's infidelity, a madness imposed by patriarchal brutality.[17] The more stimulating feminist criticism of the present day makes no such excuses, any more than does Shakespeare's text, and it would be interesting to see the theater more broadly taking up the challenge of such a perspective in all three plays—without transforming what are still, after all, female victims into caricatures of self-assertion.

I will finish by suggesting with some confidence that, whatever may happen to Shakespearean studies in the long term—and against the growth pattern of the "Shakespeare Industry" must be set the trend towards dismissing Shakespeare, above all authors, as overcanonized, ideologically retrograde, and dangerously irrelevant—the Problem Plays, once the most obscure members of the canon, have now established themselves as among the least likely of his texts to be neglected, provided only that the barrier of prudery does not reappear. This is so simply because even more actively than most of Shakespeare's works, they solicit diverse, even contradictory, interpretation. They are closest to the Histories in this respect, offering similar scope for ambiguous judgment of the political, moral, and psychological projects dramatized within them. (Indeed, the "reversibility" of *Measure for Measure*'s Duke, his ability, as dominant manipulator, to determine the overall reading of the play according to our positive or negative judgment of him, almost exactly matches that of Henry V.) At the same time, these plays remain provocative today, even threatening, in ways that the Histories have long ceased to be. As part of their mixing of modes, they combine extremes of conduct and attitude with a disquieting sense that these extremes are actual possibilities—even, in milieux ranging from urban (or suburban) wastelands to military dictatorships, current realities. The never-never land of romance in which the plays are set is always liable (unlike, say, fifteenth-century England or France) to be recognized as close to home. Whatever particular directions literary criticism in general may take, precedent suggests that the Problem Plays will readily adapt themselves, or even serve as a leading indicator. For their problematic nature ultimately consists in their capacity to demonstrate, both as objects of interpretation and (as I have argued) within themselves, the chameleon-like nature of meaning—literary and otherwise.

Notes and References

Preface

1. Jonathan Culler, *The Pursuit of Signs: Semiotics, Literature, Deconstruction* (Ithaca, N.Y.: Cornell University Press, 1981), 103.

Chapter One

1. Two facts—that it is not listed in the Folio's Table of Contents and that its position in that volume was altered during printing—are now generally held to be "red herrings" as far as the issue of genre is concerned. A more substantial puzzle surrounds the seemingly contradictory claims made in versions of the Quarto, whose printing was also interrupted for a change. In earlier copies, the play was described as having been acted by Shakespeare's company (the King's Men) at the Globe Theatre; the revision removed this statement and added a letter to the reader announcing "a new play, neuer stal'd with the Stage, neuer clapper-clawd with the palmes of the vulger" (cited in G. Blakemore Evans, textual ed., *The Riverside Shakespeare* [Boston: Houghton Mifflin, 1974], 492 [textual note to title]); this volume will hereafter be referred to as *Riverside* and will be used for citations from Shakespeare's works, although I have not followed its practice of enclosing departures from the copy-text within square brackets.

2. E. M. W. Tillyard, *Shakespeare's Problem Plays* (Toronto: University of Toronto Press, 1950), 1–2; hereafter cited in text.

3. *Macbeth*, in *Riverside*, 5.5.28; hereafter cited in text.

4. Louis Adrian Montrose, " 'Shaping Fantasies': Figurations of Gender and Power in Elizabethan Culture," *Representations* 2 (1983): 61–94.

5. This context is stressed by A. P. Rossiter in *Angel with Horns and Other Shakespeare Lectures*, ed. Graham Storey (London: Longmans, 1961), 108–10; hereafter cited in text.

6. William Witherle Lawrence, *Shakespeare's Problem Comedies*, rev. ed., Penguin Shakespeare Library (Harmondsworth, Middlesex: Penguin, 1969), 21; hereafter cited in text.

7. "He taught me how to say profound things and at the same time remain flippant and lively" (conversation with Ferrucio Busone, cited in Dan H. Laurence, Introduction to *How to Become a Musical Critic*, by George Bernard Shaw, ed. Dan H. Laurence [New York: Hill and Wang, 1961], xx).

8. George Bernard Shaw, Preface to *Plays Unpleasant* (1898; reprint, Harmondsworth, Middlesex: Penguin, 1946), 22.

9. Frederick S. Boas, *Shakspere and His Predecessors* (1896; reprint, New York: Haskell House, 1968), 345; hereafter cited in text.

10. But cf. Ernest Schanzer, *The Problem Plays of Shakespeare: A Study of Julius Caesar, Measure for Measure, Antony and Cleopatra* (London: Routledge, 1963), whose refocusing of the moral issues led him to revise the membership of the category.

11. *Antony and Cleopatra*, in *Riverside*, 2.7.42–43; hereafter cited in text.

12. Stephen Greenblatt, *Renaissance Self-Fashioning: From More to Shakespeare* (Chicago: University of Chicago Press, 1980).

13. Anne Barton, *Shakespeare and the Idea of the Play* [originally published under the name of Anne Righter] (London: Chatto, 1962), 178–80.

14. Karen Newman (*Shakespeare's Rhetoric of Comic Characters: Dramatic Convention in Classical and Renaissance Comedy* [London: Methuen ,1985], 20–29) makes some interesting observations concerning the "illusion of reality" (20) in *Measure for Measure*, especially with regard to Angelo's psychology.

15. E. M. W. Tillyard, *The Elizabethan World Picture* (London: Chatto, 1943).

16. A. L. Rowse, *The England of Elizabeth: The Structure of Society* (London: Macmillan, 1950), 532–33; hereafter cited in text.

17. Lawrence Stone's most important studies include *The Crisis of the Aristocracy, 1558–1641* (Oxford: Clarendon, 1965) and *The Family, Sex and Marriage in England, 1500–1800* (London: Weidenfeld and Nicolson, 1977). Recently, however, several scholars have issued caveats against the tendency, especially among New Historicist and Cultural Materialist critics, to accept Stone's methods and conclusions unquestioningly; see, e.g., David Cressy, "Foucault, Stone, Shakespeare and Social History," *English Literary Renaissance* 21 (1991): 121–33.

18. Mervyn James, *Society, Politics, and Culture: Studies in Early Modern England* (Cambridge: Cambridge University Press, 1986).

19. Frances Yates, *The Myth of Astraea: The Imperial Theme in the Sixteenth Century* (London: Routledge, 1975); Roy Strong, *Henry, Prince of Wales, and England's Lost Renaissance* (London: Thames and Hudson, 1986).

20. Useful perspectives on these critical approaches are provided by Montrose himself ("Renaissance Literary Studies and the Subject of History," *English Literary Renaissance* 16 [1986]: 5–12) and, especially, by Jean E. Howard, "The New Historicism in Literary Studies," *English Literary Renaissance* 16 (1986): 13–43.

21. This was the argument, e.g., of R. W. Chambers (*The Jacobean Shakespeare and* Measure for Measure, Annual Shakespeare Lecture of the British Academy, 1937, from *Proceedings of the British Academy*, vol. 23 [London: Humphrey Milford, n.d.], 3–30), who associated this view of history with the myth of Shakespeare's personal despair—a myth that Chambers needed to expose in order to replace it with his own conviction of Shakespeare's profound Christian optimism. Thus the early years of James's reign become the focus of

Rowse-like cultural panegyric: "What a Quinquennium! The Bible, Shakespeare, our free institutions, our search for knowledge [this evidently includes the first colonialist ventures]. These are the things which must hold together all who speak the English tongue" (Chambers, 27).

22. I have focused on this trend in the drama of the late Elizabethan and Stuart periods in my recent book *Intertextuality and Romance in Renaissance Drama: The Staging of Nostalgia* (Houndmills, Basingstoke, Hampshire: Macmillan; New York: St. Martin's, 1992); hereafter cited as *Intertextuality*.

23. The most extreme example of such a reading is actually relatively recent. Josephine Waters Bennett (Measure for Measure *as Royal Entertainment* [New York: Columbia University Press, 1966]) confidently identifies the Duke not only with James and God but with Shakespeare himself—a reading that conspicuously subsumes, incidentally, the metadramatic dimension. For a trenchant critique of the methodology and conclusions of this school, see Richard L. Levin, "The 'King James Version' of *Measure for Measure*," in *New Readings vs. Old Plays: Recent Trends in the Reinterpretation of English Renaissance Drama* (Chicago: University of Chicago Press, 1979), 171–93.

24. Thus Jonathan Dollimore ("Transgression and Surveillance in *Measure for Measure*," in *Political Shakespeare: New Essays in Cultural Materialism*, ed. Jonathan Dollimore and Alan Sinfield [Manchester: Manchester University Press, 1985], 72–87) argues that the Duke uses religion in a manner generally associated with Machiavelli as "a form of ideological control which worked in terms of internalised submission" (Dollimore, 81); hereafter cited in text. That such skeptical readings of the Duke are now de rigueur is evident (leaving aside the present volume) from the student-oriented guide to the play by T. F. Wharton, *Measure for Measure*, "The Critics Debate" series (Houndmills, Basingstoke, Hampshire: Macmillan, 1989); a roughly equivalent work of 14 years earlier had sustained the image of the Duke as a God- (and James-) like ruler: Nigel Alexander, *Shakespeare:* Measure for Measure, Studies in English Literature 57 (London: Arnold, 1975).

25. *Hamlet*, in *Riverside*, 3.1.127–28; hereafter cited in text.

Chapter Two

1. John Dryden, Preface to *Troilus and Cressida* (1679), cited in *Riverside*, 1848.

2. Kenneth Muir (Introduction to *Troilus and Cressida*, by William Shakespeare, The Oxford Shakespeare [Oxford: Clarendon, 1982], 20–21) justly rebuts as simplistic the argument of Oscar J. Campbell (*Comicall Satyre and Shakespeare's* Troilus and Cressida [San Marino, Calif.: Huntington Library, 1938], vii, 1, *et passim*) that this ban forced satirists to become dramatists. It is reasonable, however, to consider stage satire as, to some extent, an extension of the poetic variety. Cf. R. A. Foakes, *Shakespeare: The Dark Comedies to the Last Plays: From Satire to Celebration* (London: Routledge, 1971).

3. This is the view, e.g., of Alice Walker, Introduction to *Troilus and Cressida*, by William Shakespeare, ed. Alice Walker (Cambridge: Cambridge University Press, 1969), xv; hereafter cited in text.

4. William B. Toole, *Shakespeare's Problem Plays: Studies in Form and Meaning*, Studies in English Literature 19 (The Hague: Mouton, 1966), 137; for a skeptical opinion, see Walker, xliii.

5. Thomas Middleton, *Micro-cynicon*, in *The Works of Thomas Middleton*, ed. A. H. Bullen, 8 vols. (1885; reprint, New York: AMS, 1964), 8: 111–36, Satire 5, p. 131; hereafter cited in text as *Micro-cynicon*.

6. *Troilus and Cressida*, in *Riverside*, 5.2.165–66; all line numbers in this chapter, unless otherwise specified, refer to *Troilus and Cressida*.

7. John Donne, "Satyre III," in *The Complete Poetry of John Donne*, ed. John T. Shawcross (Garden City, N.Y.: Doubleday Anchor, 1967), lines 79–82; hereafter cited in text as "Satyre III."

8. *Virgidemiarvm, Sixe Bookes*, in *The Collected Poems of Joseph Hall, Bishop of Exeter and Norwich*, ed. Arnold Davenport (Liverpool: Liverpool University Press, 1949), book 1, Prologue: line 1; hereafter cited in text as *Virgidemiarvm*.

9. Evarard [Edward] Guilpin, *Skialetheia; or, A Shadowe of Truth, in Certaine Epigrams and Satyres*, ed. D. Allen Carroll (Chapel Hill: University of North Carolina Press, 1974), Satire 6, line 190; hereafter cited in text as *Skialetheia*.

10. John Marston, *The Scourge of Villanie*, in *The Poems of John Marston*, ed. Arnold Davenport (Liverpool: Liverpool University Press, 1961), 94; hereafter cited in text as *Scourge*.

11. See Robert Kimbrough, *Shakespeare's* Troilus and Cressida *and Its Setting* (Cambridge, Mass.: Harvard University Press, 1964), 37–39.

12. *Henry IV, Part 1*, in *Riverside*, 4.2.65–66.

13. *The Tempest*, in *Riverside*, 1611 ("Names of the Actors"); hereafter cited in text.

14. See notably Carol Cook, "Unbodied Figures of Desire," *Theatre Journal* 38 (1986): 34–52, who applies Luce Irigaray's notion of "hom(m)o-sexuality," and Eric S. Mallin, "Emulous Factions and the Collapse of Chivalry: *Troilus and Cressida*," *Representations* 29 (1990): 145–79.

15. My metadramatic application of the constructive power of gazing shares considerable common ground (though it differs in emphasis and detail) with Barbara Hodgdon ("He Do Cressida in Different Voices," *English Literary Renaissance* 20 [1990]: 254–86), who uses this meeting between Hector and Achilles as her point of departure for an approach to Cressida "as an object of exchange within male subjectivity . . . ratifying and reinforcing the very homosocial bonds that exclude her" (Hodgson, 257); hereafter cited in text. See also Paul Gaudet, "'As True as Troilus,' 'As False as Cressid': Tradition, Text, and the Implicated Reader," *English Studies in Canada* 16 (1990): 125–48.

16. For examples of criticism along these lines, see Cook; Elizabeth

Freund, "'Ariachne's Broken Woof': The Rhetoric of Citation in *Troilus and Cressida*," in *Shakespeare and the Question of Theory*, ed. Patricia Parker and Geoffrey Hartman (New York: Methuen, 1985), 19–36; and Linda Charnes, "'So Unsecret to Ourselves': Notorious Identity and the Material Subject in Shakespeare's *Troilus and Cressida*," *Shakespeare Quarterly* 40 (1989): 413–40.

17. *Measure for Measure*, in *Riverside*, 1.3.41–43; hereafter cited in text.

18. This has long been understood to involve a satirical allusion to Jonson's introduction of an armed Prologue (as an image of the poet confidently defying his detractors) in his *Poetaster* (1601).

19. Troilus is included in the stage tradition of misogynistic soldiers by Linda Woodbridge, *Women and the English Renaissance: Literature and the Nature of Womankind, 1540–1620* (Urbana: University of Illinois Press, 1984), 279.

20. Christopher Marlowe, *The Tragical History of the Life and Death of Doctor Faustus*, ed. John D. Jump, The Revels Plays (London: Methuen, 1962), 18.102; hereafter cited in text as *Faustus*.

21. *The Merchant of Venice*, in *Riverside*, 2.9.21; hereafter cited in text. Portia compares Bassanio's venture to Hercules' rescue of the Trojan princess Hesione; she feels herself similarly to "stand for sacrifice" (*Merchant*, 3.2.57), though her hero supposedly acts "with much more love" (*Merchant*, 3.2.54). Hesione's story makes an interesting analogue to that of Cressida on several levels. Hesione was condemned by her father, King Laomedon (the father also of King Priam), to be sacrificed to a sea monster in order to protect Troy; Laomedon treacherously denied Hercules the horses he had promised as a reward, so Hesione's rescuer killed Laomedon and sacked the city. In effect, her redeemer himself became a monster of destruction, she a sacrifice to his heroic stature. Moreover, there is an indirect allusion to the origins of the Trojan War, since Priam first stirred Paris to the rape of Helen in retaliation for the Greeks' possession of Hesione—see *Troilus*, 2.2.72ff.

22. Pressing to death was the torture appointed in Renaissance England for refusing to plead in criminal cases.

23. *Romeo and Juliet*, in *Riverside*, 3.5.2ff.; hereafter cited in text.

24. Janet Adelman, "'This Is and Is Not Cressid': The Characterization of Cressida," in *The (M)other Tongue: Essays in Feminist Psychoanalytic Interpretation*, ed. Shirley Nelson Garner, Claire Kahane, and Madelon Sprengnether (Ithaca, N.Y.: Cornell University Press, 1985), 120.

25. See especially Adelman, Cook, and Charnes. On the commonplace association between sexual pleasure and death as it is bizarrely elaborated in this speech, see also J. A. Bryant, Jr., *Shakespeare and the Uses of Comedy* (Lexington: University of Kentucky Press, 1986), 193–94. Bryant's reading of the love-dynamic usefully imputes destructive potency to the fact that Troilus is fundamentally in love with "the projection of an imagined purity in himself" (Bryant, 199).

26. Cf. Cook on the "concentric structure of voyeurism" (Cook, 50) in this

scene; also the Cultural Materialist approach of Jonathan Dollimore, *Radical Tragedy: Religion, Ideology, and Power in the Drama of Shakespeare and His Contemporaries* (Chicago: University of Chicago Press, 1984), 47–49, who finds that, in dealing with Diomedes, Cressida "internalises the contradiction of the war itself" (Dollimore, 48). While Jean E. Howard, *Shakespeare's Art of Orchestration: Stage Technique and Audience Response* (Urbana: University of Illinois Press, 1984), observes that the scene's "orchestration" prevents the audience from identifying totally with Troilus's point of view (Howard, 64–68), it is strange to find her using the language of essentialist mimeticism to portray Cressida as "neither the fallen goddess nor the worthless whore the men proclaim her, but simply a flirtatious, confused, and weak-willed person struggling with her own weakness and losing the battle" (Howard, 67).

27. Homer, *Homer's Iliads*, trans. George Chapman, in *Chapman's Homer*, ed. Allardyce Nicoll, 2nd ed., Bollingen Series 41 (Princeton: Princeton University Press, 1967), vol. 1, book 10, line 35.

28. Geoffrey Chaucer, *The Legend of Good Women*, in *The Riverside Chaucer*, 3d ed., gen. ed. Larry D. Benson (Boston: Houghton Mifflin, 1987), text F, lines 332–34 (this is essentially the version printed in Renaissance texts); hereafter cited in text as *Legend*. The story of Dido and Aeneas is also considered relevant to Shakespeare's play by Gaudet, who suggests that the character of Aeneas functions as a "shadow-figure of Troilus" (Gaudet, 136).

29. Cf. Hodgdon 1990, 284.

30. Walker's notes are especially thorough and useful in comparing Shakespeare and other versions, notably that of Caxton, which stands at the end of a line of Medieval translations stretching back to accounts of the Trojan War attributed to the ancient authorities Dictys the Cretan and Dares the Phrygian (Walker, xxxviii–xxxix).

31. See my book, *Intertextuality*, 58–81. The following discussion inevitably overlaps, in a general way, with the detailed argument presented there.

32. See especially R. Ann Thompson, *Shakespeare's Chaucer* (Liverpool: University of Liverpool Press, 1978), 111–65; E. Talbot Donaldson, *The Swan at the Well: Shakespeare Reading Chaucer* (New Haven: Yale University Press, 1985), 74–118; and Alice S. Miskimin, *The Renaissance Chaucer* (New Haven: Yale University Press, 1975), 215–21.

33. Walker, e.g., remains skeptical (xliii–xlv).

34. Robert Henryson, *The Testament of Cressid*, in *The Poems of Robert Henryson*, ed. Denton Fox (Oxford: Clarendon, 1981), line 546; hereafter cited in text as *Testament*.

35. See my book, *Intertextuality*, 67 and 185n15.

36. Geoffrey Chaucer, *Troilus and Criseyde*, in *The Riverside Chaucer*, gen. ed. Larry D. Benson, 3d ed. (Boston: Houghton Mifflin, 1987), book 5, lines 1751–54; hereafter cited as *T&C*.

37. The prevailing view of Troilus around the time of the play may also be

judged from the account of his death in *Loues Leprosie*, a poem published by Thomas Powell in 1598. See *Ancient Poetical Tracts of the Sixteenth Century*, ed. Edward F. Rimbault, vol. 6 of *Early English Poetry, Ballads, and Popular Literature of the Middle Ages* (1842 [Percy Society]; reprint, New York: Johnson, 1965), 63–89. This work, which is mainly concerned with presenting Achilles' downfall as a result of his helpless passion for the treacherous Polyxena, depicts Troilus, after Hector's fall, as "A second leader to the forebred fight" (Powell, 77) and blames his death at Achilles' hands on his being "ouer insolent" (Powell, 78).

38. Vergil, *The Aeneid of Virgil*, ed. R. D. Williams, 2 vols. (London: Macmillan, 1972), book 1, lines 474–76; translation mine.

39. For an explication of this idea, see, e.g., Michael Riffaterre, "Syllepsis," *Critical Inquiry* 6 (1980): 625–38, esp. 627; I discuss (and apply) the concept in *Intertextuality*, 2–3, 17, 23, *et passim*.

40. See especially Mallin. The older school finds a recent representative in E. A. J. Honigmann, *Myriad-minded Shakespeare: Essays, Chiefly on the Tragedies and Problem Comedies* (Houndmills, Basingstoke, Hampshire: Macmillan, 1989), who hypothesizes the play's suppression on these grounds in order to explain its mysterious textual and stage history; hereafter cited in text.

41. On the non-Chaucerian bases of Ulysses' heroic portrait, see Cook, 45.

42. *Othello*, in *Riverside*, 5.2.344; hereafter cited in text.

43. Hodgdon observes that despite the effort of Pandarus to "direct her gaze" in this scene, it is "not only privileged but given potential power and agency"—an effect obscured by the placement of stage directions in some modern editions (Hodgdon 1990, 263).

Chapter Three

1. *All's Well That Ends Well*, in *Riverside*, 3.3.11; all line numbers in this chapter, unless otherwise specified, refer to *All's Well That Ends Well*.

2. The note in *Riverside* is somewhat overprotesting in its insistence that the modern meaning of "affect" should be rigorously excluded, together with any suggestion of hypocrisy, in favor of "an outward show of grief in excess of what she now (after a lapse of time) feels" (n. to 1.1.53). Helena's response, which confirms that she is pretending to be grieving for her father, militates against such hairsplitting.

3. Cf. the moralizing use made of this scene by Samuel Taylor Coleridge: "Thus the Countess's beautiful precepts to Bertram, by elevating her character, elevate that of Helena, her favourite, and soften down the point in her which Shakespeare does not mean us not to see, but to see and forgive, and at length to justify" (*Shakespearean Criticism*, ed. Thomas Middleton Raysor, 2 vols., Everyman's Library 162 [London: Dent; New York: Dutton, 1960], 1: 199).

4. The implications of this position are effectively brought out by

Sheldon P. Zitner, All's Well That Ends Well, Twayne's New Critical Introductions to Shakespeare (Boston: Twayne, 1989), 42–48; hereafter cited in text.

5. For a feminist and psychoanalytic study from this perspective, and with an emphasis on the play's power relations, see Carolyn Asp, "Subjectivity, Desire and Female Friendship in *All's Well That Ends Well*," *Literature and Psychology* 32, no. 4 (1986): 48–63; hereafter cited in text.

6. See G. K. Hunter, Introduction to *All's Well That Ends Well*, by William Shakespeare, The New Arden Shakespeare, 3d ed. (London: Methuen, 1959), xxv–xxix; hereafter cited in text.

7. See also Geoffrey Bullough, ed., *Narrative and Dramatic Sources of Shakespeare*, 8 vols. (London: Routledge; New York: Columbia University Press, 1957–75), 2: 376; hereafter cited in text.

8. The latter element is stressed by Zitner, 7–8.

9. See, for the most extensive treatment, Howard Cole, *The "All's Well" Story from Boccaccio to Shakespeare* (Urbana: University of Illinois Press, 1981); see also Lawrence, 67–68; G. K. Hunter, Introduction, xxvi–xxviii; Bullough 2: 379–88; and Zitner, 1–22.

10. Johnson's scornful judgment of Bertram is famous and influential: "a man noble without generosity, and young without truth; who marries Helen as a coward, and leaves her as a profligate: when she is dead by his unkindness, sneaks home to a second marriage, is accused by a woman whom he has wronged, defends himself by falsehood, and is dismissed to happiness" (*Johnson on Shakespeare*, ed. Arthur Sherbo, vol. 7 of *The Yale Edition of the Works of Samuel Johnson* [New Haven: Yale University Press, 1968], 404). Especially notable in this assessment, given the example of Troilus, is the absence of truth. An exception to the usual critical line is Coleridge's defense of Bertram as "a young nobleman in feudal times just bursting into youth with all the feelings of pride of birth and appetite for pleasure and liberty natural to such a character" (*Table Talk*, ed. Carl Woodring, vol. 14, pt. 1, of *The Collected Works of Samuel Taylor Coleridge*, Bollingen Series 75 [London: Routledge; Princeton: Princeton University Press, 1990], 400). Better known is Coleridge's designation of Helena as Shakespeare's "loveliest character" (Raysor, ed., *Shakespearean Criticism* 2: 102), though he was troubled by both her apparent disingenuousness (1: 102) and her passion (1: 199).

11. Zitner (87–89) describes and puts into useful perspective Mansfield's early feminist critique. The staying power of the idealized reading is evident in such modern analyses as that of Bullough, who humanizes Helena's function as "ministering angel" only to the extent of deeming her "entirely good . . . gracious and shrewd and warm in her human relationships"—all the more so for her capacity to see the "moral paradoxes" of her own behavior (Bullough 2: 382–83).

12. Richard A. Levin, "*All's Well That Ends Well*, and 'All Seems Well,'" *Shakespeare Studies* 13 (1980): 131–44. A noteworthy step en route to this reading is Clifford Leech's more moderate judgment that she is "genuinely in

love with Bertram" ("The Theme of Ambition in *All's Well That Ends Well*," *ELH* 21 [1954]: 23) but driven by ambition to pursue him—an oddly contradictory notion (blamed on the "dramatist's failure in imagination" [Leech, 29]) that nevertheless recognizes ambition as catalytic and intertwined with love. Despite his highly romantic idea of feminine "virtue," G. K. Hunter also displays a sense of Helena's social position in perceiving her "search for a means by which a woman's virtue can become effective in society" (G. K. Hunter, Introduction, xli); similarly, Bryant applies what he sees as the Shakespearean comic principle that in marriage "the woman will continue to lead . . . by uncovering the redemptive potential in the submissive role that society has forced upon her" (Bryant, 219). On Helena as metadramatist, see also Arthur Kirsch, *Shakespeare and the Experience of Love* (Cambridge: Cambridge University Press, 1981), 115–16.

13. Joseph G. Price, *The Unfortunate Comedy: A Study of* All's Well That Ends Well *and Its Critics* (Toronto: University of Toronto Press, 1968), 144; hereafter cited in text. A recent reading of the play as a positive feminist statement has been contributed by Honigmann, 130–46.

14. Rossiter, for one, judges it to be insoluble: "analysis of Helena's character only results in confusion" (Rossiter, 106). He sees her as contradictorily positioned between ideas of the passionate woman and the New Woman.

15. Powell (1572?–1635?), who evidently had a satirical bent, had been a commentator on various social practices for many years (see *The Dictionary of National Biography*).

16. Thomas Powell, *Tom of All Trades; or, The Plaine Path-Way to Preferment, etc.* (London, 1631); reprinted in *Tell-Trothes New-Years Gift and The Passionate Morrice; John Lane's Tom Tell-Troth's Message, and his Pens Complaint; Thomas Powell's Tom of all Trades; The Glasse of Godly Love (by John Rogers?)*, ed. Frederick J. Furnivall (London: Trübner for The New Shakspere Society, 1876), 160–61.

17. Given the models of female involvement in medical practice at both extremes of the social scale, one must beware of anachronistically reading Helena's role as itself involving an exercise of "ambition" by virtue of intrusion into a masculine sphere, as would obviously have been the case in later centuries when medicine had become more "professionalized." This is by no means to deny the general cultural ambivalence attaching to learned women (see Lisa Jardine, "Cultural Confusion and Shakespeare's Learned Heroines: 'These are old paradoxes,'" *Shakespeare Quarterly* 38 [1987]: 1–18). Still, there is a distinction to be made between Helena's case and that of Portia, who must disguise her sex in order to act as a lawyer. While gender is certainly an issue in Helena's reception by Lafew and the King, the issue does not take the form of disallowing her expertise on this account.

18. *Julius Caesar*, in *Riverside*, 1.2.139–41.

19. Barbara Hodgdon, "The Making of Virgins and Mothers: Sexual

Signs, Substitute Scenes and Doubled Presences in *All's Well That Ends Well*," *Philological Quarterly* 66 (1987): 67–68; hereafter cited in text.

20. See, notably, Luce Irigaray, *The Sex Which Is Not One*, trans. Catherine Porter with Carolyn Burke (Ithaca, N.Y.: Cornell University Press, 1985), 186. The relation between virginity and power in *All's Well* is the main focus of a stimulating chapter in Carol Thomas Neely's feminist study, *Broken Nuptials in Shakespeare's Plays* (New Haven: Yale University Press, 1985), 58–104.

21. On the commercial imagery, see G. K. Hunter, ed., n. to 1.1.123–29.

22. See, notably, G. K. Hunter, ed., n. to 1.1.161.

23. See my discussion in *Intertextuality*, 146–47.

24. For a range of such opinions, see Kirsch, 141; Kay Stockholder, *Dream Works: Lovers and Their Families in Shakespeare's Plays* (Toronto: University of Toronto Press, 1987), 74–76; Ruth Nevo, "Motive and Meaning in *All's Well That Ends Well*," in *"Fanned and Winnowed Opinions": Shakespearean Essays Presented to Harold Jenkins*, ed. John W. Mahon and Thomas A. Pendleton (London: Methuen, 1987), 26–51; and Richard P. Wheeler, *Shakespeare's Development and the Problem Comedies: Turn and Counter-Turn* (Berkeley: University of California Press, 1981), 41–45; the last work will hereafter be cited in the text.

25. *Much Ado about Nothing*, in *Riverside*, 5.1.289.

26. Ben Jonson, *Volpone; or, The Fox*, ed. R. B. Parker, The Revels Plays (Manchester: Manchester University Press, 1983), 2.6.35; Jonson, it seems, may actually have taken Lafew's confidence and the later pessimism of the King (Lafew's "royal fox" [2.1.70 and 71]) as a model for Volpone's feigning despondency when Corvino offers his wife:

> Alas, I'm past already! Pray you, thank him
> For his good care and promptness. But, for that,
> 'Tis a vain labour; e'en to fight 'gainst heaven,
> Applying fire to a stone, [*Coughing*] uh! uh! uh! uh!
> Making a dead leaf grow again. I take
> His wishes gently, though; and you may tell him
> What I've done for him. Marry, my state is hopeless!
>   (3.7.81–87)

27. The sexual dimension of the King's cure is effectively brought out by Wheeler, 75–77.

28. Most notably Henry V, whose manipulations also extend to the amatory sphere.

29. G. Wilson Knight, "The Third Eye: An Essay on *All's Well That Ends Well*," in *The Sovereign Flower* (1958; reprinted London: Methuen, 1966), 94–160.

30. On the King as a despairing Faustus, Helena as redeemer, see Cynthia Lewis, "'Derived Honesty and Achieved Goodness': Doctrines of Grace in *All's*

Well That Ends Well," *Renaissance and Reformation/Renaissance et Réforme* new series 14 (1990): 148. Lewis's variation on the common Helena-as-grace theme accommodates the character's more and less sympathetic exercises of power in terms of contradictory attitudes towards the Calvinist concept of the irresistibility of grace. Robert Grams Hunter, *Shakespeare and the Comedy of Forgiveness* (New York: Columbia University Press, 1965), sees the allusion to Helen of Troy as balanced by one to the British saint Helena, so that the character's name embodies her double role as "a beautiful and sexually attractive girl who is also a recipient of God's grace and a means by which it is transmitted to others" (R. G. Hunter, 114)—a description that gives the distinct sense of eating one's cake and having it too. On the (redemptive) "witchery" in Helena's manipulations of both the King and Bertram, see also Bertrand Evans, *Shakespeare's Comedies* (Oxford: Clarendon, 1960), 166.

31. Cf. Hodgdon 1987, 52, whose emphasis is somewhat different.

32. See my discussion of Portia as manipulator in *Shakespearean Subversions: The Trickster and the Play-text* (London: Routledge, 1992), 103–15; hereafter cited as *Subversions.*

33. A sensitive treatment of the "charade" mounted by Helena here is offered by Robert Ornstein, *Shakespeare's Comedies: From Roman Farce to Romantic Mystery* (Newark: University of Delaware Press, 1986), 182–84.

34. Cf. the subtle analysis of the exchange with Lafew by Zitner, 46–47.

35. *King Lear,* in *Riverside,* 1.1.87; hereafter cited in text.

36. Cf. the perception by G. K. Hunter of a broad linguistic pattern within the play of "definition . . . achieved by a negative process of exclusion" (Introduction, lviii, n. 2), and the extension of this idea by Joseph Westlund in *Shakespeare's Reparative Comedies: A Psychoanalytic View of the Middle Plays* (Chicago: University of Chicago Press, 1984), 121–46.

37. Thus Neely, e.g., sees the text at large as complicit: "As Parolles attempts to protect himself by condemning his comrades and Bertram, so the characters and the play seek to exonerate Bertram by attacking and exposing Parolles" (Neely, 76).

38. *Henry V,* in *Riverside,* 5.1.84–90.

39. Price records one (university) production where, according to a reviewer, "the lords and Bertram were shamed in the vileness of the man [Parolles]; Bertram hurled himself off stage 'with a desperate need to reform'" (Price, 69). This would seem to represent a triumph of wish fulfillment over text.

40. Cf. Lear's response after the defeat of Cordelia's forces, when she proposes that they confront Goneril and Regan: "No, no, no, no!" (*Lear,* 5.3.8).

41. The ineffectuality of nominally subversive elements is the basis of my approach to the play in *Subversions,* 157–69.

42. For an account of his withdrawal from sexuality as a correlative of

Bertram's psychosexual condition, see Wheeler, 52–54. Hodgdon (1987, 50–51) sees him rather as a double of Helena.

43. *A Midsummer Night's Dream*, in *Riverside*, 1.1.232–33; hereafter cited in text.

44. For a comparative rhetorical analysis of the two characters' speeches, see G. K. Hunter, Introduction, lvi–lviii.

45. In stressing Helena's management of this scene, especially her "artful choreographing of Diana's accusations," Ornstein effectively focuses the metadramatic dimension, even observing that "Helena does not need much help from Shakespeare" (Ornstein, 190). Like most commentators, however, he does not fully pursue the implications of the comic confusion thus produced.

Chapter Four

1. *Measure for Measure*, in *Riverside*, 1.3.2–3; hereafter in this chapter all line numbers, unless otherwise specified, refer to *Measure for Measure*.

2. A recent example is the discussion of the multiple final silences by Philip C. McGuire in *Speechless Dialect: Shakespeare's Open Silences* (Berkeley: University of California Press, 1985), 63–96.

3. This parallel has often been noted; see, e.g., Louise Schleiner, "Providential Improvisation in *Measure for Measure*," *PMLA* 97 (1982): 234.

4. Robert Greene, *Friar Bacon and Friar Bungay*, ed. J. A. Lavin, The New Mermaids (London: Benn, 1969), 14. 86–92; hereafter cited in text as *Friar Bacon*.

5. *The Geneva Bible*, with an Introduction by Lloyd E. Berry (1560; fac. reprint Madison: University of Wisconsin Press, 1969), Matt. 7: 1–5.

6. The allusion is to the fable of the wolf in sheep's clothing.

7. This puzzling word is sometimes emended to "ungenerative"—i.e., "sexless" (see n. in *Riverside*).

8. See, e.g., Wheeler, 120–39; Stockholder, 81; and Richard A. Levin ("Duke Vincentio and Angelo: Would 'A Feather Turn the Scale'?" *Studies in English Literature 1500–1900* 22 [1982]: 257–70), who neatly (if sketchily) brings Lucio into the picture (Levin, 266–69).

9. Examples occur in the speech of the fairies in *MND* and the Witches in *Macbeth*, as well as the "fairies'" rhyme in *The Merry Wives of Windsor* (5.5.93ff.), the epitaph and funeral song of Hero in *Much Ado about Nothing* (5.3.3ff. and 12ff.), and the dirge for Imogen in *Cymbeline* (4.2.258ff.)—all cited from *Riverside*.

10. Cf. Richard A. Levin 1982, 260.

11. On Lucio in the context of the Trickster, see my book, *Subversions*, 150–52. For an account of the Vice tradition as an influence on aspects of Shakespeare's work, see Bernard Spivack, *Shakespeare and the Allegory of Evil: The History of a Metaphor in Relation to His Major Villains* (New York: Columbia University Press, 1985).

12. On the various ironic uses of this word, cf. William Empson ("Sense in *Measure for Measure*," in *The Structure of Complex Words* [1951; reprint, Totowa, N.J.: Rowman and Littlefield, 1979], 270–88), who perceives "an examination of sanity itself, which is seen crumbling and dissolving in the soliloquies of Angelo" (Empson, 270).

13. Cinthio had earlier (1565) included a prose version of the story in his collection of tales, *Hecatommithi*, and the story had been translated into French in 1585 (Bullough 2: 401). For a summary of the important analogues and evaluation of their influence, see Bullough 2: 399–417; see also Mary Lascelles, *Shakespeare's* Measure for Measure (London: University of London, Athlone Press, 1953), esp. 1–42.

14. See Geoffrey Shepherd, ed., *An Apology for Poetry; or, The Defence of Poesy*, by Philip Sidney (Manchester: Manchester University Press; New York: Barnes and Noble, 1973), nn. to page 134, line 12, and page 135, line 31.

15. George Whetstone, *Promos and Cassandra*, in Bullough 2: 443; hereafter cited in text, by page number, as *Promos*.

16. On this point, cf. Honigmann, 167.

17. One might add this phenomenon to the tendency of the play's theatricality to undermine the Duke's hegemonic project, as discussed vis-à-vis New Historical readings that take his success for granted by Anthony B. Dawson in *"Measure for Measure*, New Historicism, and Theatrical Power," *Shakespeare Quarterly* 39 (1988): 328–41.

18. I have made an argument for Vincentio as one of Shakespeare's most highly developed *counter*-tricksters (*Subversions*, 150–57).

19. For a strict application to the play of the so-called subversion-containment paradigm important in New Historicist and Cultural Materialist criticism, see Dollimore 1985, 72–87. I share Dollimore's view of the Duke's project as involving the resubjection of his subjects, though I read many aspects of that process differently. See also Franco Moretti, "The Great Eclipse: Tragic Form as the Deconsecration of Sovereignty," trans. David Miller, in *Signs Taken for Wonders: Essays in the Sociology of Literary Forms*, trans. Susan Fischer, David Forgacs, and David Miller, revised ed. (London: Verso, 1988), 56–61, and Steven Mullaney, *The Place of the Stage: License, Play, and Power in Renaissance England* (Chicago: University of Chicago Press, 1988), 88–115. I find Moretti's treatment of the metadramatic dimension especially congenial.

20. See, e.g., Michael Riffaterre, "Intertextual Representation: On Mimesis as Interpretive Discourse," *Critical Inquiry* 11 (1984): 142–43.

21. Cf. Mullaney, 108–11. Perhaps surprisingly, such an argument intersects with Northrop Frye's observation, from a quite different (indeed "natural") perspective, that "[t]he theme of self-knowledge is a prominent one in *All's Well* and *Measure for Measure*, where the attempted descents of Bertram and Angelo into vice are really mistaken forms of self-discovery" (*A Natural Perspective: The*

Development of Shakespearean Comedy and Romance [New York: Harcourt, 1965], 81–82).

22. The salient exception of Marlowe's Faustus, who despairs of salvation, wishes he had been "a creature wanting soul" (*Faustus*, 19.172), and is damned before our eyes, actually proves the rule.

23. For a rhetorical analysis of this soliloquy, extended to a discussion of comic conventions in the play, see Newman, 7–29.

24. Cf. Harriet Hawkins, "'The Devil's Party': Virtues and Vices in *Measure for Measure*," *Shakespeare Survey* 31 (1978): 105–13; reprinted in *Aspects of Shakespeare's "Problem Plays": Articles Reprinted from* Shakespeare Survey, ed. Kenneth Muir and Stanley Wells (Cambridge: Cambridge University Press, 1982), 89; also Carolyn E. Brown, "Erotic Religious Flagellation and Shakespeare's *Measure for Measure*," *English Literary Renaissance* 16 (1986): 259–76.

25. Cf. Marcia Riefer ("'Instruments of Some More Mightier Member': The Construction of Female Power in *Measure for Measure*," *Shakespeare Quarterly* 35 [1984]: 157–69), whose view of the Duke's undoing of Isabella's "self-defining character" (Riefer, 165) has much in common with my own, including a metadramatic perspective. However, Riefer's advocacy of Isabella leads her to deproblematize both that character and the nature of subjectivity itself.

26. See, notably, R. G. Hunter, 204–26.

27. The corresponding softening of the Duke's character thus implied may easily be made part of such a teleological reading—witness Cynthia Lewis, "'Dark Deeds Darkly Answered': Duke Vincentio and Judgment in *Measure for Measure*," *Shakespeare Quarterly* 34 (1983): 271–89.

28. That the friar's consolation is not notably Christian is demonstrated by J. W. Lever, Introduction to *Measure for Measure*, by William Shakespeare, The New Arden Shakespeare (London: Methuen, 1965), lxxxvii.

29. The most significant recent treatment of this issue is probably that of Karl P. Wentersdorf ("The Marriage Contracts in *Measure for Measure*," *Shakespeare Survey* 32 [1979]: 129–44), whose conclusion that "there is no appreciable dramatic flaw" (Wentersdorf, 144) leaves the audience's response out of the picture. Margaret Scott ("'Our City's Institutions': Some Further Reflections on the Marriage Contracts in *Measure for Measure*," *ELH* 49 [1982]: 790–804) invokes the historical state of marriage laws in Catholic Vienna, chiefly in order to rebut rationalization of the situation with reference to English practice.

30. A good review of previous opinion on this idea, which dates back to Thomas Tyrwhitt in the eighteenth century, is provided by David Lloyd Stevenson (*The Achievement of Shakespeare's* Measure for Measure [Ithaca, N.Y.: Cornell University Press, 1966], 134–66), in the course of making his own case, supported by additional evidence; this especially concerns the play's compatibility with King James's political credo as set out in the *Basilikon Doron*. See also

Bennett and Darryl J. Gless, Measure for Measure, *the Law, and the Convent* (Princeton: Princeton University Press, 1979), esp. 151–66. For developments of the Vincentio-James connection from a New Historicist perspective, see especially Jonathan Goldberg, *James I and the Politics of Literature: Jonson, Shakespeare, Donne, and Their Contemporaries* (Baltimore: Johns Hopkins University Press, 1983), 231–39; hereafter cited in text; Leonard G. Tennenhouse, *Power on Display: The Politics of Shakespeare's Genres* (New York: Methuen, 1986), 154–59; and Dollimore 1985; hereafter cited in text.

31. *As You Like It*, in *Riverside*, 1.3.80–82.

32. So thoroughly habituated are recent commentators to thinking in these terms that Wharton confidently speaks of the Duke's entire course of action as "a major political ploy" (Wharton, 79), deliberately undertaken in order to restore his image and authority. Much as I agree with the tenor of Wharton's argument, to supply the character with such comprehensive awareness seems reductive and unduly demystifying, as well as contrary to the *self*-manipulation evident in the Duke's soliloquies.

33. King James's known dislike of crowds was the focus of Tyrwhitt's argument, as is pointed out by Stevenson, 138–39.

34. Cf. the discussion of this effect by Dawson, 338. The frontispiece of the present volume provides a view of the Duke-as-friar in this production; this image admirably captures the sinister plausibility that Alan Scarfe brought to the role throughout.

Chapter Five

1. Among the Problem Plays themselves, intriguingly, there appears to be a substantial disproportion in favor of *Measure for Measure*, not only in the quantity of criticism but also in the number of anthologies of reprinted criticism directed towards students.

2. Quoted in Robert Speaight, *Shakespeare on the Stage: An Illustrated History of Shakespearian Performance* (Boston: Little, Brown, 1973), 105; hereafter cited in text.

3. Cited in George C. D. Odell, *Shakespeare from Betterton to Irving*, 2 vols. (1920; reprint, New York: Dover, 1966), 1: 26–27; hereafter cited in text.

4. Cited by John Russell Brown, *Shakespeare's Plays in Performance* (1966; Harmondsworth, Middlesex: Penguin, 1969), 241.

5. "They are no longer Problem Plays, and no longer unpopular" (Michael Jamieson, "The Problem Plays, 1920–1970," *Shakespeare Survey* 25 [1972]; reprinted in *Aspects of Shakespeare's "Problem Plays": Articles Reprinted from Shakespeare Survey*, ed. Kenneth Muir and Stanley Wells [Cambridge: Cambridge University Press, 1982], 135; hereafter cited in text). Wharton actually begins his 1989 book by asserting, with some justification, that "*Measure for Measure* is currently Shakespeare's most popular play" (Wharton, 9).

6. Arthur Colby Sprague, *Shakespearian Players and Performances* (1953; reprint, New York: Greenwood, 1969), 141.

7. Jane Williamson, "The Duke and Isabella on the Modern Stage," in *The Triple Bond: Plays, Mainly Shakespearean, in Performance*, ed. Joseph G. Price (University Park: Pennsylvania State University Press, 1975), 149–69; hereafter cited in text.

8. Thus Gless, one of the most extreme (and recent) adherents of this school, claims that his approach "resolve[s] most of the problems [the play] has presented to previous critics" and exposes "many of those problems" as "illusory" (Gless, 13).

9. Cf., however, Meredith Anne Skura's circumspect evaluation of psychoanalytic issues in relation to *Measure for Measure* in her book published the same year, *The Literary Use of the Psychoanalytic Process* (New Haven: Yale University Press, 1981), 243–70.

10. See especially Stephen Greenblatt, "Invisible Bullets," in *Shakespearean Negotiations: The Circulation of Social Energy in Renaissance England* (Berkeley: University of California Press, 1988), 21–65.

11. See Mikhail Bakhtin, *Rabelais and His World*, trans. Helene Iswolsky (Cambridge, Mass.: M.I.T. Press, 1968).

12. F. R. Leavis, *The Common Pursuit* (London: Chatto, 1952), 169.

13. Thomas F. Van Laan, *Role-Playing in Shakespeare* (Toronto: University of Toronto Press, 1978), 100; Alexander Leggatt, "Substitution in *Measure for Measure*," *Shakespeare Quarterly* 39 (1988): 358–59.

14. Thus, e.g., Riefer runs up against the "murky" relation between the playwright and his surrogate in *Measure for Measure*, given the difficulty of assessing the "extent to which Shakespeare transcends the Duke's limitations" (Riefer, 168).

15. Wolfgang Sohlich, "Prolegomenon for a Theory of Dramatic Reception: Peter Brook's *Measure for Measure* and the Emergent Bourgeoisie," *Comparative Drama* 18 (1984): 73.

16. How readily the model of St. Joan lends itself to religious romanticism may be judged from R. G. Hunter's perception of a "resemblance" that "can contribute to our idea of Helena" (R. G. Hunter, 115).

17. See the review by Nicholas Shrimpton in *Shakespeare Survey* 39 (1987): 203–5.

Selected Bibliography

PRIMARY WORKS: Some Significant Renaissance and Modern Editions

All's Well That Ends Well. Edited by Russell Fraser. New Cambridge Shakespeare. Cambridge: Cambridge University Press, 1985.

All's Well That Ends Well. Edited by G. K. Hunter. The New Arden Shakespeare. 3d ed. London: Methuen, 1959.

The Historie of Troylus and Cresseida. As it was acted by the Kings Maiesties seruants at the Globe [first state]. *The Famous Historie of Troylus and Cresseid. Excellently expressing the beginning of their loues, with the conceited wooing of Pandarus Prince of Licia* [second state]. London: George Eld for R. Bonian and H. Walley, 1609. (The Quarto text.) Facsimile reprint of second state available in *Shakespeare's Plays in Quarto: A Facsimile Edition of Copies Primarily from the Henry E. Huntington Library*. Edited by Michael J. B. Allen and Kenneth Muir. Berkeley: University of California Press, 1981.

Measure for Measure. Edited by Mark Eccles. A New Variorum Edition of Shakespeare. New York: Modern Language Association, 1980.

Measure for Measure. Edited by Brian Gibbons. New Cambridge Shakespeare. Cambridge: Cambridge University Press, 1991.

Measure for Measure. Edited by J. W. Lever. The New Arden Shakespeare. London: Methuen, 1965.

Measure for Measure. Edited by Ernst Leisi. An Old-Spelling and Old-Meaning Edition. New York: Hafner, 1964.

The Riverside Shakespeare. Textual editor G. Blakemore Evans. Boston: Houghton Mifflin, 1974.

Mr. William Shakespeares Comedies, Histories, & Tragedies. Published according to the True Originall Copies. London: Isaac Jaggard and Ed. Blount, 1623. (The First Folio.) Facsimile reprint available in *The Norton Facsimile: The First Folio of Shakespeare*. Prepared by Charlton Hinman. New York: Norton, 1968.

William Shakespeare: The Complete Works. Edited by Stanley Wells and Gary Taylor. The Oxford Shakespeare. One volume in modern spelling; one volume the original spelling edition. Oxford: Clarendon, 1986. (Supplemented by *William Shakespeare: A Textual Companion* [1987].)

Troilus and Cressida. Edited by Harold N. Hillebrand. Supplemental editing by T. W. Baldwin. A New Variorum Edition of Shakespeare. Philadelphia: Lippincott, 1953.

Troilus and Cressida. Edited by Kenneth Muir. The Oxford Shakespeare. Oxford: Clarendon, 1982.

Troilus and Cressida. Edited by Kenneth Palmer. The New Arden Shakespeare. London: Methuen, 1982.

Troilus and Cressida. Edited by Alice Walker. New Cambridge Shakespeare. Cambridge: Cambridge University Press, 1969.

SECONDARY WORKS

Books and Parts of Books

Adamson, Jane. Troilus and Cressida. Twayne's New Critical Introductions to Shakespeare. Boston: Twayne, 1987. Contains much engaging analysis, whose balance and limitations are both assured by the premise that "the value of human lives is . . . positively 'declared,' fully realised, in the facts of loss and death" (164).

Adelman, Janet. "'This Is and Is Not Cressid': The Characterization of Cressida." In *The (M)other Tongue: Essays in Feminist Psychoanalytic Interpretation,* edited by Shirley Nelson Garner, Claire Kahane, and Madelon Sprengnether, 119–41. Ithaca, N.Y.: Cornell University Press, 1985. An important psychoanalytic reading, proposing that Troilus's victimization of Cressida is a consequence of the neurotic ambivalence of his desire.

Alexander, Nigel. *Shakespeare:* Measure for Measure. Studies in English Literature 57. London: Arnold, 1975. A slim volume designed for students; revealing (given its date) for promoting the school of opinion that deproblematizes the play by accepting Duke as God- (and King James-) like.

Barton, Anne. *Shakespeare and the Idea of the Play.* Published originally under the name of Anne Righter. London: Chatto, 1962. Initiates metadramatic approach to Shakespeare; includes discussion of Duke in *Measure for Measure.*

Bennett, Josephine Waters. Measure for Measure *as Royal Entertainment.* New York: Columbia University Press, 1966. The most extreme "old historicist" case for the Vincentio-King James connection.

Bloom, Harold, ed. *William Shakespeare's* Measure for Measure. Modern Critical Interpretations. New York: Chelsea House, 1987. The most recent, and perhaps for this reason the narrowest in scope, of several collections of reprinted criticism devoted to the play. Bloom offers some brief introductory impressions of the work.

Boas, Frederick S. *Shakspere and His Predecessors.* 1896. Reprint. New York: Haskell House, 1968. First applies the label "Problem Plays" as "a convenient phrase from the theatre of to-day" (345).

Bradbrook, M. C. "The Balance and the Sword in *Measure for Measure.*" In *The*

Artist and Society in Shakespeare's England: The Collected Papers of Muriel Bradbook, Vol. 1, 144–54. Brighton, Sussex: Harvester; Totowa, N.J.: Barnes and Noble, 1982. Especially interesting on the relation between the Duke and his role as friar.

Bryant, J. A., Jr. *Shakespeare and the Uses of Comedy*. Lexington: University Press of Kentucky, 1986. Deals with all three plays as "anomalous" comedies, though the treatment of *Troilus and Cressida*, which stresses Troilus's destructive influence, more fully justifies this appellation than do the readings of the other plays in teleological terms of education, enlightenment, and (secular) redemption.

Bullough, Geoffrey, ed. *Narrative and Dramatic Sources of Shakespeare*. 8 vols. London: Routledge; New York: Columbia University Press, 1957–75. Selection and analysis subject to dispute, but an invaluable compilation. Volume 2 covers *Measure for Measure* and *All's Well That Ends Well*; volume 4 includes *Troilus and Cressida.*

Campbell, Oscar J. *Comicall Satyre and Shakespeare's* Troilus and Cressida. San Marino, Calif.: Huntington Library, 1938. An influential early argument for the satirical context and nature of the play.

Chambers, R. W. *The Jacobean Shakespeare and* Measure for Measure. Annual Shakespeare Lecture of the British Academy, 1937. From *Proceedings of the British Academy* vol. 23. London: Humphrey Milford, n.d. Seemingly the first, and certainly a highly influential, treatment of the play as a positive lesson in Christian moral doctrine, with the Duke as a representative of Providence; hence, a rebuttal of the widely held idea of a pessimistic Jacobean Shakespeare.

Charlton, H. B. *Shakespearian Comedy*. 1938. Reprint. London: Methuen, 1966. Defends the "dark comedies," contrary to majority critical opinion at the time, by positing their author's "intense impulse to discover the true sources of nobility in man and of joy in life" (211).

Cole, Howard. *The "All's Well" Story from Boccaccio to Shakespeare*. Urbana: University of Illinois Press, 1981. A comprehensive comparison of the various versions of the source of the play's main plot.

Dollimore, Jonathan. *Radical Tragedy: Religion, Ideology, and Power in the Drama of Shakespeare and His Contemporaries*. Chicago: University of Chicago Press, 1984. Contains a stimulating Cultural Materialist discussion of *Troilus*, focusing on the socially determined and self-contradictory nature of the play world's absolutes and on their disjunctive impact on both protagonists, especially Cressida, whose "discontinuity . . . stems not from her nature but from her position in the patriarchical [sic] order" (48).

———. "Transgression and Surveillance in *Measure for Measure*." In *Political Shakespeare: New Essays in Cultural Materialism*, edited by Jonathan Dollimore and Alan Sinfield, 72–87. Manchester: Manchester University Press,

1985. Characteristic and influential application of Cultural Materialist perspective.

Donaldson, E. Talbot. *The Swan at the Well: Shakespeare Reading Chaucer.* New Haven: Yale University Press, 1985. Contains two chapters on the relation between *Troilus and Cressida* and Chaucer's *Troilus and Criseyde.*

Empson, William. "Sense in *Measure for Measure.*" In *The Structure of Complex Words,* 270–88. 1951. Reprint. Totowa, N.J.: Rowman and Littlefield, 1979. Argues for the multiple ironic functioning of "sense" as the play's key word.

Evans, Bertrand. *Shakespeare's Comedies.* Oxford: Clarendon, 1960. Includes discussion of all three plays by way of "discrepant awareness" between audience and inhabitants of play world; approach results in focus on manipulation and dramatic layering, though with assurance of the playwright's controlling moral design (except perhaps in the case of *Troilus*).

Foakes, R. A. *Shakespeare: The Dark Comedies to the Last Plays: From Satire to Celebration.* London: Routledge, 1971. Deals with all three plays under the rubric "Shakespeare and Satirical Comedy."

Freund, Elizabeth. "'Ariachne's Broken Woof': The Rhetoric of Citation in *Troilus and Cressida.*" In *Shakespeare and the Question of Theory,* edited by Patricia Parker and Geoffrey Hartman, 19–36. New York: Methuen, 1985. Approaches the play in terms of its allusiveness.

Garber, Marjorie. *Coming of Age in Shakespeare.* London: Methuen, 1981. Deals with *All's Well* and *Measure for Measure* in terms of rites of passage and rituals of initiation, thereby producing highly teleological readings.

Geckle, George L., ed. *Twentieth Century Interpretations of* Measure for Measure. Englewood Cliffs, N.J.: Prentice-Hall, 1970. A useful compilation of reprinted articles and excerpts; Geckle provides an introductory overview of the play and its critics.

Gless, Darryl J. Measure for Measure, *the Law, and the Convent.* Princeton: Princeton University Press, 1979. Resolves the play's problems by taking the Duke as "a little image of God" (254).

Goldberg, Jonathan. *James I and the Politics of Literature: Jonson, Shakespeare, Donne, and Their Contemporaries.* Baltimore: Johns Hopkins University Press, 1983. Contains an important New Historicist treatment of *Measure for Measure.*

Greene, Gayle. "Shakespeare's Cressida: 'A Kind of Self'." In *The Woman's Part: Feminist Criticism of Shakespeare,* edited by Carolyn Ruth Swift Lenz, Gayle Greene, and Carol Thomas Neely, 133–49. Urbana: University of Illinois Press, 1980. A good example of "early" feminist criticism concerned with explaining and defending the character of Cressida.

Hawkins, Harriet. Measure for Measure. Twayne's New Critical Introductions to Shakespeare. Boston: Twayne, 1987. A useful overview of the play, its intellectual contexts, and its reception.

Hillman, Richard. *Intertextuality and Romance in Renaissance Drama: The Staging of Nostalgia.* Houndmills, Basingstoke, Hampshire: Macmillan; New York: St. Martin's, 1992. Contains a chapter approaching *Troilus and Cressida* and Chaucer's *Troilus and Criseyde* through intertextual analysis.

————. *Shakespearean Subversions: The Trickster and the Play-text.* London and New York: Routledge, 1992. Contains a chapter on the Problem Plays in terms of subversive and counter-subversive textual forces.

Honigmann, E. A. J. *Myriad-minded Shakespeare: Essays, Chiefly on the Tragedies and Problem Comedies.* Houndmills, Basingstoke, Hampshire: Macmillan; New York: St. Martin's, 1989. Contains essays on the three plays from different perspectives but displaying a common concern with genre.

Hunter, Robert Grams. *Shakespeare and the Comedy of Forgiveness.* New York: Columbia University Press, 1965. Includes chapters on *All's Well* and *Measure for Measure* as secular comedies that nevertheless follow Christian moral and spiritual patterns.

Jamieson, Michael. "The Problem Plays, 1920–1970: A Retrospective." *Shakespeare Survey* 25 (1972): 1–10; reprinted (without the subtitle) in *Aspects of Shakespeare's "Problem Plays": Articles Reprinted from* Shakespeare Survey, edited by Kenneth Muir and Stanley Wells, 126–35. Cambridge: Cambridge University Press, 1982. Chronicles changing attitudes towards the Problem Plays and concludes that they no longer deserve that name.

Kimbrough, Robert. *Shakespeare's* Troilus and Cressida *and Its Setting.* Cambridge, Mass.: Harvard University Press, 1964. Explores the play through its literary and theatrical contexts in advancing a hypothesis regarding its origin and supposed failure.

Knight, G. Wilson. "The Third Eye: An Essay on *All's Well That Ends Well.*" In *The Sovereign Flower*, 94–160. 1958. Reprint. London: Methuen, 1966. An influential essay relating *All's Well* to the Sonnets in terms of the presentation of love, though few critics influenced by it adopt its highly romantic theologizing perspective.

————. *The Wheel of Fire: Interpretations of Shakespearian Tragedy with Three New Essays.* 4th ed. 1949. Reprint. London: Methuen, 1960. Contains an influential Christianizing treatment of *Measure for Measure* (the Duke as Christ figure), as well as an analysis of *Troilus* in romantic terms of a conflict between noble Trojans and depraved Greeks.

Lascelles, Mary. *Shakespeare's* Measure for Measure. London: University of London, Athlone Press, 1953. Contains much detailed consideration of sources and analogues, as well as analysis respectful of the elusive "complexity" of a play she considers both "great" and "uneven" (164).

Lawrence, William Witherle. *Shakespeare's Problem Comedies.* Rev. ed. Penguin Shakespeare Library. Harmondsworth, Middlesex: Penguin, 1969. The pioneering study of the Problem Plays as a group (first edition 1931).

Leavis, F. R. *The Common Pursuit*. London: Chatto, 1952. Discusses *Measure for Measure* as a beneficent "controlled experiment" (170) on the part of a Providential Duke.

Levin, Richard L. "The 'King James Version' of *Measure for Measure*. In *New Readings vs. Old Plays: Recent Trends in the Reinterpretation of English Renaissance Drama*, 171–93. Chicago: University of Chicago Press, 1979. In mounting an attack on "occasionalism," skeptically reexamines the evidence that *Measure for Measure* was written to flatter King James by illustrating his ideas on kingship.

McGuire, Philip C. *Speechless Dialect: Shakespeare's Open Silences*. Berkeley: University of California Press, 1985. Includes a discussion of the implications and theatrical impact of the multiple silences, including Isabella's, at the conclusion of *Measure for Measure*.

Martin, Priscilla, ed. *Shakespeare:* Troilus and Cressida: *A Casebook*. London: Macmillan, 1976. One of the few anthologies of criticism on this play.

Miles, Rosalind. *The Problem of* Measure for Measure: *A Historical Investigation*. London: Vision, 1976. Exhaustive and generally evenhanded assessment of the play and its critics, leading to the conclusion that the work is flawed but idealistic.

Miskimin, Alice S. *The Renaissance Chaucer*. New Haven: Yale University Press, 1975. Contains a brief discussion of *Troilus and Cressida* in relation to Chaucer's poem, as well as a more extensive survey of other post-Chaucerian treatments of the legend.

Moretti, Franco. "The Great Eclipse: Tragic Form as the Deconsecration of Sovereignty." Trans. David Miller. In *Signs Taken for Wonders: Essays in the Sociology of Literary Forms*, 42–82. Trans. Susan Fischer, David Forgacs, and David Miller. Rev. ed. London: Verso, 1988. This essay, first published in Italian in 1979 and excerpted in English translation in 1982, contains a provocative treatment of *Measure for Measure*, which appears to have influenced subsequent New Historicist and Cultural Materialist readings.

Muir, Kenneth, and Stanley Wells, eds. *Aspects of Shakespeare's "Problem Plays": Articles Reprinted from* Shakespeare Survey. Cambridge: Cambridge University Press, 1982. A collection of significant articles and reviews of productions.

Mullaney, Steven. *The Place of the Stage: License, Play, and Power in Renaissance England*. Chicago: University of Chicago Press, 1988. Contains a New Historicist treatment of *Measure for Measure* with attention to the issue of subject (re)formation.

Neely, Carol Thomas. *Broken Nuptials in Shakespeare's Plays*. New Haven: Yale University Press, 1985. Contains especially useful analysis of *All's Well*, extended to *Measure for Measure*, in terms of sexual politics.

Nevo, Ruth. "Motive and Meaning in *All's Well That Ends Well.*" In *"Fanned and Winnowed Opinions": Shakespearean Essays Presented to Harold Jenkins*, edited by John W. Mahon and Thomas A. Pendleton, 26–51. London: Methuen, 1987. A teleological Freudian reading of the relation between Helena and Bertram, according to which "the text . . . inscribes their shared desire for sexual enfranchisement . . . and provides the means for its attainment" (45).

Newman, Karen. *Shakespeare's Rhetoric of Comic Characters: Dramatic Convention in Classical and Renaissance Comedy.* London: Methuen, 1985. Contains two brief but insightful chapters on *Measure for Measure.*

Novy, Marianne. *Love's Argument: Gender Relations in Shakespeare.* Chapel Hill: University of North Carolina Press, 1984. Includes discussion of *Troilus* in terms of the commodification of women and the self-centered nature of both protagonists.

Odell, George C. D. *Shakespeare from Betterton to Irving.* 2 vols. 1920. Reprint. New York: Dover, 1966. Contains much useful information on early stagings. Exemplifies early twentieth-century moral prejudice against Problem Plays.

Ornstein, Robert. *The Moral Vision of Jacobean Tragedy.* Madison: University of Wisconsin Press, 1965. Argues that the "dark comedies fall in a line of artistic thought that runs from *Hamlet* to *Lear*" (227). Offers a highly teleological reading of *Measure for Measure* ("decency and common sense have triumphed" [259]); develops in terms of paradox Knight's perception of a conflict in *Troilus* between idealism and sordid reality.

Ornstein, Robert, ed. *Discussions of Shakespeare's Problem Comedies.* Boston: Heath, 1961. Interestingly chosen excerpts and reprints from criticism dating back to Coleridge; one of the few such collections devoted to the plays as a group.

Pope, Elizabeth Marie. "The Renaissance Background of *Measure for Measure.*" *Shakespeare Survey* 2 (1949): 66–82; reprinted in *Aspects of Shakespeare's "Problem Plays": Articles Reprinted from* Shakespeare Survey, edited by Kenneth Muir and Stanley Wells, 57–73. Cambridge: Cambridge University Press, 1982. An especially influential approach through Renaissance Christian ideas, arguing that the play is actively religious and orthodox.

Price, Joseph G. *The Unfortunate Comedy: A Study of* All's Well That Ends Well *and Its Critics.* Toronto: University of Toronto Press, 1968. Particularly useful on critical and performance history.

Rose, Jacqueline. "Sexuality in the Reading of Shakespeare: *Hamlet* and *Measure for Measure.*" In *Alternative Shakespeares*, edited by John Drakakis, 95–118. London: Methuen, 1985. Critiques critical responses to Isabella in terms of attitudes towards female sexuality.

Rossiter, A. P. *Angel with Horns and Other Shakespeare Lectures*, edited by Graham

Storey. London: Longmans, 1961. Includes penetrating discussion of all three plays and of the Problem Plays as a group, based on recognition of their complexities. Essay on *All's Well* is perhaps the most productive application of the romance vs. realism dichotomy.

Rutter, Carol. With Sinead Cusack, Paola Dionisotti, Fiona Shaw, Juliet Stevenson, and Harriet Walker. *Clamorous Voices: Shakespeare's Women Today*, edited by Faith Evans. London: Women's Press, 1988. Includes discussions by contemporary actresses of their experiences in interpreting Isabella (Dionisotti and Stevenson) and Helena (Walker).

Salingar, Leo. *Shakespeare and the Traditions of Comedy*. Cambridge: Cambridge University Press, 1974. Contains perceptive remarks *passim*, especially in terms of the classical tradition and especially on *All's Well* and *Measure for Measure*, which are grouped with *The Merchant of Venice* and *Much Ado about Nothing* as "problem plays" (302).

Schanzer, Ernest. *The Problem Plays of Shakespeare: A Study of* Julius Caesar, Measure for Measure, Antony and Cleopatra. London: Routledge, 1963. Redefines Problem Play category in terms of the audience's perception of central moral issues as problematic; sees *Measure for Measure* as concerned mainly with "the nature of Justice and Good Rule" and "the choice of Isabel," though only the latter is "treated problematically" (130).

Skura, Meredith Anne. *The Literary Use of the Psychoanalytic Process*. New Haven: Yale University Press, 1981. Includes a valuable assessment of the issues involved in a psychoanalytic approach to the Duke in *Measure for Measure*.

Snyder, Richard C. "Discovering a 'Dramaturgy of Human Relationships' in Shakespearean Metadrama: *Troilus and Cressida*." In *Shakespeare and the Arts: A Collection from the Ohio Shakespeare Conference, 1981 Wright State University, Dayton, Ohio*, edited by Cecile Williamson Cary and Henry S. Limouze, 199–216. Washington, D.C.: University Press of America, 1982. One of the few approaches to the play in terms of metadrama. Limited by neglect of Troilus himself and preoccupation with "the problems in the artist/audience situation as a metaphor for the breakdown of healthy relationships in society" (201).

Soellner, Rolf. *Shakespeare's Patterns of Self-Knowledge*. Columbus: Ohio State University Press, 1972. In chapters on *Troilus and Cressida* ("Fragmenting a Divided Self") and *Measure for Measure* ("Looking into Oneself"), applies a traditional idea so as to produce insights that at times appear to anticipate those of poststructuralism.

Speaight, Robert. *Shakespeare on the Stage: An Illustrated History of Shakespearian Performance*. Boston: Little, Brown, 1973. Incorporates useful accounts of several major and obscure productions (especially European) of all three plays.

Sprague, Arthur Colby. *Shakespearian Players and Performances*. 1953. Reprint.

New York: Greenwood, 1969. Includes some worthwhile information on productions and reception of *Troilus and Cressida* and especially *Measure for Measure*; contains a chapter on William Poel's Elizabethan revivalism.

Stead, C. K., ed. *Shakespeare:* Measure for Measure: *A Casebook*. London: Macmillan, 1971. A convenient anthology of extracts and reprints with a thoughtful introduction.

Stevenson, David Lloyd. *The Achievement of Shakespeare's* Measure for Measure. Ithaca, N.Y.: Cornell University Press, 1966. Attempts to account for the play's disturbing power in terms of its ability to "release or unlock our inner world of sexual 'knowing' and our inner world of noninstitutionalized moral cognition and judgment" (5). Also makes a case for the text's historical allusiveness, especially for the relevance of the ideas of King James.

Styan, J. L. *Shakespeare in Performance*: All's Well That Ends Well. Manchester: Manchester University Press, 1984. Incorporates detailed analysis of aspects of several productions.

Tennenhouse, Leonard G. *Power on Display: The Politics of Shakespeare's Genres*. New York: Methuen, 1986. Includes discussion of *Measure for Measure* in New Historicist terms.

Thomas, Vivian. *The Moral Universe of Shakespeare's Problem Plays*. Totowa, N.J.: Barnes and Noble, 1987. In effect, a reapplication of the original concept of the Problem Plays as concerned with "the needs, passions, desires, vices and weaknesses inherent in human life within the context of attempting to change or preserve the existing social universe" (229).

Thompson, R. Ann. *Shakespeare's Chaucer*. Liverpool: University of Liverpool Press, 1978. Argues extensively for *Troilus and Cressida*'s indebtedness to Chaucer's poem.

Tillyard, E. M. W. *Shakespeare's Problem Plays*. Toronto: University of Toronto Press, 1950. Among the first major studies of the subgenre; applies New Critical aesthetic principles in assessing the response of Shakespeare's "poetic imagination" to the challenge of combining romance and realism.

Toole, William B. *Shakespeare's Problem Plays: Studies in Form and Meaning*. Studies in English Literature 19. The Hague: Mouton, 1966. Approaches the plays in terms of the pattern of Dante's *Divine Comedy*.

Van Laan, Thomas F. *Role-Playing in Shakespeare*. Toronto: University of Toronto Press, 1978. Includes discussion of the Duke in *Measure for Measure* as an internal dramatist.

Westlund, Joseph. *Shakespeare's Reparative Comedies: A Psychoanalytic View of the Middle Plays*. Chicago: University of Chicago Press, 1984. Among the six plays considered are *All's Well* and *Measure for Measure*, which are treated as playing on and ultimately disappointing an audience's idealizing impulses.

Wharton, T. F. Measure for Measure. "The Critics Debate" series. Houndmills, Basingstoke, Hampshire: Macmillan Education, 1989. A perceptive, if sometimes reductive, discussion of text and context designed for students; reflects now-prevalent skepticism regarding Duke. Well-chosen bibliography.

Wheeler, Richard P. *Shakespeare's Development and the Problem Comedies: Turn and Counter-Turn.* Berkeley: University of California Press, 1981. Offers many valuable critical insights in a heavily Freudian discussion focusing on *All's Well* and *Measure for Measure* as reflections of Shakespeare's psychological evolution. A usefully metadramatic slant on Vincentio.

Williamson, Jane. "The Duke and Isabella on the Modern Stage." In *The Triple Bond: Plays, Mainly Shakespearean, in Performance*, edited by Joseph G. Price, 149–69. University Park: Pennsylvania State University Press, 1975. An excellent analytical survey of performance practices.

Yoder, R. A. "'Sons and Daughters of the Game': An Essay on Shakespeare's *Troilus and Cressida.*" *Shakespeare Survey* 25 (1972): 11–25; reprinted in *Aspects of Shakespeare's "Problem Plays": Articles Reprinted from* Shakespeare Survey, edited by Kenneth Muir and Stanley Wells, 111–25. Cambridge: Cambridge University Press, 1982. Approaches the play as acutely relevant to American consciousness of war and corruption in the 1970s.

Zitner, Sheldon P. All's Well That Ends Well. Twayne's New Critical Introductions to Shakespeare. Boston: Twayne, 1989. To a thorough survey of basic elements adds valuable application of cultural contexts and insightful close analysis.

Articles

Asp, Carolyn. "Subjectivity, Desire and Female Friendship in *All's Well That Ends Well.*" *Literature and Psychology* 32, no. 4 (1986): 48–63. A provocative feminist psychoanalytic interpretation.

Brown, Carolyn E. "Erotic Religious Flagellation and Shakespeare's *Measure for Measure.*" *English Literary Renaissance* 16 (1986): 259–76. A psychosexual discussion, in historical context, of Isabella's attraction to martyrdom.

Charnes, Linda. "'So Unsecret to Ourselves': Notorious Identity and the Material Subject in Shakespeare's *Troilus and Cressida.*" *Shakespeare Quarterly* 40 (1989): 413–40. Focuses on the problematic of subjectivity and identity formation.

Cook, Carol. "Unbodied Figures of Desire." *Theatre Journal* 38 (1986): 34–52. Applies Luce Irigaray's theory of "hom(m)o-sexuality" to *Troilus and Cressida.*

Dawson, Anthony B. "*Measure for Measure*, New Historicism, and Theatrical Power." *Shakespeare Quarterly* 39 (1988): 328–41. A critique of the New Historicist tendency to accept the triumph of authority in the play; argues that the theatrical experience exposes the Duke's imposition of hegemony as a "hoax" (341).

Gaudet, Paul. "'As True as Troilus,' 'As False as Cressid': Tradition, Text, and the Implicated Reader." *English Studies in Canada* 16 (1990): 125–48. Focuses on the masculine construction of Cressida within the text and on the implication of audiences and readers in that process.

Geckle, George L. "Coleridge on *Measure for Measure.*" *Shakespeare Quarterly* 18 (1967): 71–73. A convenient summary and brief analysis of Coleridge's essentially moralistic objections to the play.

Hawkins, Harriet. "'The Devil's Party': Virtues and Vices in *Measure for Measure.*" *Shakespeare Survey* 31 (1978): 105–13; reprinted in *Aspects of Shakespeare's "Problem Plays": Articles Reprinted from* Shakespeare Survey, edited by Kenneth Muir and Stanley Wells, 87–95. Cambridge: Cambridge University Press, 1982. Contains an essay (also anthologized in Bloom, ed., *William Shakespeare's* Measure for Measure) offering a spirited defense, in direct rebuttal of Christianizing readings, of *Measure for Measure's* right to remain problematic.

Hodgdon, Barbara. "He Do Cressida in Different Voices." *English Literary Renaissance* 20 (1990): 254–86. A stimulating reading of the play as "consistently [turning] the act of spectatorship into a convention which interrogates, theatrically, propositions of identity and value concerning male—as well as female—bodies" (254). Applies this perspective to performance practice.

————. "The Making of Virgins and Mothers: Sexual Signs, Substitute Scenes and Doubled Presences in *All's Well That Ends Well.*" *Philological Quarterly* 66 (1987): 47–71. A feminist psychoanalytic approach that finally confirms, in its own terms, the familiar view of the play as entailing a compromise between romance and realism.

Jardine, Lisa. "Cultural Confusion and Shakespeare's Learned Heroines: 'These are old paradoxes.'" *Shakespeare Quarterly* 38 (1987): 1–18. A feminist critique dealing with *All's Well*, among other plays, in terms of its ambivalent treatment of female knowledge.

Leech, Clifford. "The Theme of Ambition in *All's Well That Ends Well.*" *ELH* 21 (1954): 17–29. One of the first attempts by a modern critic to analyze the uneasy coexistence of "ambition" and love in Helena's character, although the New Critical perspective leads to a perception of the "dramatist's failure in imagination" (29).

Leggatt, Alexander. "Substitution in *Measure for Measure.*" *Shakespeare Quarterly* 39 (1988): 342–59. A subtle tracing of the variations on the theme of substitution, with a view of the Duke and Shakespeare himself as imperfect playwrights.

Levin, Richard A. "*All's Well That Ends Well* and 'All Seems Well.'"

Shakespeare Studies 13 (1980): 131–44. Offers an extreme view of Helena as a consummate schemer.

———. "Duke Vincentio and Angelo: Would 'A Feather Turn the Scale'?" *Studies in English Literature 1500–1900* 22 (1982): 257–70. Argues that Angelo is the Duke's *semblable*, through whom the Duke vicariously pursues his sexual interests.

Lewis, Cynthia. "'Dark Deeds Darkly Answered': Duke Vincentio and Judgment in *Measure for Measure*." *Shakespeare Quarterly* 34 (1983): 271–89. Portrays the Duke as undergoing a process of self-discovery, which culminates in his "baring himself to his subjects" (288) when he declares his love for Isabella.

———. "'Derived Honesty and Achieved Goodness': Doctrines of Grace in *All's Well That Ends Well*." *Renaissance and Reformation/Renaissance et Réforme* ns 14 (1990): 147–70. As of this writing, the latest version—and an interesting one—of the approach to Helena as an embodiment of divine grace.

Mallin, Eric S. "Emulous Factions and the Collapse of Chivalry: *Troilus and Cressida*." *Representations* 29 (1990): 145–79. A wide-ranging New Historicist reading, incorporating the familiar identification of Achilles with the Earl of Essex into an analysis of misogyny and narcissism.

Parker, R. B. "War and Sex in *All's Well That Ends Well*." *Shakespeare Survey* 37 (1984): 99–113. Perhaps the most accomplished teleological reading of the play in terms of values; sees an evolution towards "wry accommodation" of the opposed "ideals" of love and war (99).

Riefer, Marcia. "'Instruments of Some More Mightier Member': The Construction of Female Power in *Measure for Measure*." *Shakespeare Quarterly* 35 (1984): 157–69. A metadramatic and feminist approach in terms of the Duke's "negation of Isabella's essentially self-defining character" (165).

Roy, Emil. "War and Manliness in Shakespeare's *Triolus and Cressida*." *Comparative Drama* 7 (1973): 107–20. A reductive pre-Lacanian psychoanalytic reading, which concludes that the "play seems uniquely designed for our time and no other" (119).

Schleiner, Louise. "Providential Improvisation in *Measure for Measure*." *PMLA* 97 (1982): 227–36. An especially optimistic variation on the Duke-as-Providence theme, arguing that the effect is "comically, to point up that he is not God but a ruler attempting *imitatio dei* in his government, with partly successful and sometimes humorous results" (235).

Scott, Margaret. "'Our City's Institutions': Some Further Reflections on the Marriage Contracts in *Measure for Measure*." *ELH* 49 (1982): 790–804. Brings to bear the historical status of marriage law in Catholic Vienna.

Sohlich, Wolfgang. "Prolegomenon for a Theory of Dramatic Reception: Peter Brook's *Measure for Measure* and the Emergent Bourgeoisie." *Comparative Drama* 18 (1984): 54–81. Finds that Brook's 1979 Paris production (of a

French translation), though self-consciously feminist in its treatment of Isabella, panders to the bourgeoisie and "equivocates on the subject of power" (77).

Wentersdorf, Karl P. "The Marriage Contracts in *Measure for Measure*." *Shakespeare Survey* 32 (1979): 129–44. A balanced review of this vexed question, although the conclusion denying any "dramatic flaw" (144) leaves the audience out of account.

Index

The Author

Richard Hillman is Associate Professor of English at York University, Toronto. He has published numerous articles on Medieval and Renaissance literature, especially Shakespearean drama, and is the author of two books: *Shakespearean Subversions: The Trickster and the Play-text* (London and New York: Routledge, 1992) and *Intertextuality and Romance in Renaissance Drama: The Staging of Nostalgia* (Houndmills, Basingstoke, Hampshire: Macmillan; New York: St. Martin's, 1992).